Counseling
and
Therapy
Skills

Counseling and Therapy Skills

David G. Martin
University of Manitoba

WAVELAND

PRESS, INC.

Prospect Heights, Illinois

For information about this book, write or call:
Waveland Press, Inc.
P.O. Box 400
Prospect Heights, Illinois 60070
(708) 634-0081

To my own little therapy group:
Nona, Melissa, Kristen, Mark,
Kathy, Laura, and Joel

PREFACE

The goal of this book is to communicate more than an academic understanding of the principles of therapy: to give the reader skills that can actually be applied in the counseling setting. Beginning therapists approach the frightening task of counseling or therapy uneasily and usually with only some common-sense notions of how to be helpful to a person in emotional trouble. These common-sense notions seem to fall into one of two categories: on the one hand, therapists often have some idea that empathy is a passive sort of pleasant listening skill, or, on the other hand, they try to fill the role of expert advice giver and interpreter. There is a third alternative that therapists in training welcome as valid and useful and within their ability to do, once they understand it. Evocative empathy is a skill that draws from a long tradition of theory, therapeutic practice, and research evidence. After 15 years of teaching these skills, I now think I know how to show how to be ahead of the client in a helpful way that brings to life the client's deep experiences without taking over control of therapy—that permits the client to be the problem solver but gives the therapist a truly helpful and active role.

The book is designed for the beginning counselor or therapist, either in courses dealing with skill development or in practicum settings. These courses and practica are found in clinical psychology programs and in education departments that stress educational psychology or counseling. I believe the how-to-do-it message of the book will appeal to trainees. It is also likely that other programs that involve counseling skills, such as nursing and social work, will also use the book. Since the presentation is at a beginning level, virtually any of the helping professions would find it useful.

The first section of the book describes the fundamental skills, and the second section is aimed at developing the reader's skills through a number of devices that engage him or her in actual practice exercises. The written format is painfully limited for communicating the practice of therapeutic communication, but there is some value in exercises of a workbook nature in which the trainee reads client responses and then writes possible therapist responses. Accordingly, transcripts of therapy sessions in Chapter 8 provide client statements for the trainee to respond to. In addition, these transcripts provide an opportunity to "observe" other therapists doing therapy. The reader is urged to practice the skills in role playing with one or two others, and I give advice about how to do this on the basis of my experience with role playing in my classes. In addition, and unique to this book, is a cassette tape that includes excerpts from five sessions illustrating skillful therapy, with written comments by the therapists involved.

The third section of the book rounds out the treatment of what the beginning therapist needs to know. It is more formal in that it discusses issues and offers practical advice about beginning sessions, settings for therapy, ethical issues, different formats for therapy, and other such topics. These topics are often found at the beginning of books on therapy, but I think that this practice sets the mood of a book in the direction of formality and pedantic understanding of concepts, rather than toward the excitement and flow of what one actually does as a therapist. I prefer this more structured material at the end, so that the book starts out at a full run with the material that means the most to the reader.

Although the emphasis of the book is on developing skills, a fourth section also deals with the research evidence that this approach to therapy actually works and with a theoretical understanding of the nature of neurosis that gives the therapist a foundation for understanding why it works. These explanations draw most heavily from a cognitive approach to general learning theory. Thus, this book grows out of the integration of what are clearly the two most influential streams of thought in counseling and therapy in academic settings in North America. Starting with Carl Rogers's seminal work, which has grown and developed into a general approach to "helping skills," the teaching of empathic skills has become recognized as essential in nearly all approaches to counseling and therapy. The essential truth that is often missed, however, is that truly accurate empathy goes far beyond simple reflection and is active, arousing, and evocative. It is this essential truth that this book tries to convey. The second tradition, learning theory, has usually found expression through behavior modification, but recent trends have placed greater emphasis on cognitive factors. This book argues that a perfectly respectable learning theorist can understand that both cognition and emotion are important parts of behavior and that they are both deeply involved in counseling and therapy. It is not a contradiction in terms to be an empathic learning theorist.

As a general comment, the main differences between this book and other similar ones are the heavy emphasis here on presenting material that the reader can use—can translate into behavior—and the clear message that therapy demands active involvement, that empathy must be evocative, and that the therapist must work at the leading edge of the client's experiencing. Thus, my presentation is more personal and less academic. My students have often found that the material in other books is "testable" in the sense that they can write exam questions on the material but that the pedantic structure leaves them with only a vague understanding of what to do; and, I have found, they often are left with the common misunderstanding that empathy is relatively passive.

I would like to thank the reviewers of this book for their many helpful suggestions: Richard L. Bednar of the University of Kentucky, Sharon E. Kahn of the University of British Columbia, Jane O'Hern of Boston University, and Bill K. Richardson of North Texas State University.

Finally, the work and struggle of producing a book have been made easier by having a good publisher. Claire Verduin has been supportive for many years, and Rephah Berg edited the manuscript skillfully. I especially want to thank Joan Marsh for caringly and enthusiastically shepherding the manuscript through to its finished form.

David G. Martin

CONTENTS

PART ONE
Developing Basic Skills

1 The Third Alternative—Evocative Empathy 3

Lead or Follow? 5
Levels of Empathy 6
Evocative Empathy and Interpretation 6
Empathy Is Not Sympathy 8
This Is Hard Work 9
Rating the "Core Conditions" 12
Rating Empathic Behavior 12
A Theoretical Preview 16

2 Learning to Hear 17

Basic Listening Skills 18
Hearing the Implicit Message 20
Where Is the Leading Edge? 24
You Hear Selectively 26
Listening to Silence 29

3 Finding the Words 31

Bring It to Life 32
Starting Out 34
Structuring and Focusing 36
Skillful Tentativeness 39
Unique Language 43
When You Miss 50

4 **Confronting Experience** 52

Combining Cognitive and Emotional 53
Therapist as Chicken—Intellectualizing Is Easy 58
Confrontation 59
Defensiveness and Resistance 63

5 **The Basic Principle—The Client Is the Problem Solver** 69

Solving Problems, Getting Strong 70
The Client's Job 72
Trusting Your Client—A Bit of Theory 78
Using Questions 79
The Content of Therapy 82
Influencing the Process 87
Setting Goals 89

6 **Relationship Issues** 92

Respect and Prizing 93
Sharing Your Experiencing 97
Genuineness 99
Immediacy—Dealing with Your Relationship 101
Relationship Weakeners 107
Dependency and Attachment 110
Values and Expectancy Effects 116
Sex Roles and Therapy 117

PART TWO
Putting It Into Practice

7 **Getting Started** 120

Written Exercises 120
Role Playing 121
The Value of Tape Work 122

8 **Observing Others** 126

Observing Bob Lee 126
Observing David Martin 143
Observing Bill Coulson 153
Observing Joan Strachan 161
Observing Morgan Henderson 169

PART THREE
Beyond the Basic Skills

9 Direct Interventions 176

Behavior Modification 176
Combining Approaches 180
Direct Environmental Interventions 182

10 Assessment 186

What Treatment for Whom? 187
Assessment within Therapy 191

11 Ethical Issues 194

In Whose Best Interest? 194
Role Conflicts 196
Confidentiality 198
Therapist Competence 200

12 Beginning and Ending 202

Arrangements 202
The Initial Interview 206
Termination 208

13 Other Formats—Building on the Foundation 212

Responding to Several People at Once 212
Groups 213
Couples and Families 216

PART FOUR
Theory and Evidence

14 Why Theory and Evidence? 222

The Seat of Your Pants off the Top of Your Head Isn't
Enough 222
The Key Question—Why Can You Trust the Client? 224
Humanistic Theory 226
An Empathic Learning Theorist? 227

Contents

Psychoanalytic Contributions   229
Information Processing and Cognitive Theory   230
Being Eclectic   232

15 The Nature of Anxiety-Based Problems   233

Principles of Fear   233
Conflict and Anxiety   236
Repression and Cognitive Distortions   241
Maladaptive Behavior ("Symptom") Development   246
Problems in Living   251

16 A Theoretical Understanding of Therapy   253

Trusting Your Client   253
Relieving Conflicts—In Theory   254
Relieving Conflicts—In Practice   256
Breaking Old Schemes   257
The Effects of Therapy   257
The Consequences of Ineffective Therapy   260

17   Research Evidence   265

Client Perceptions of the Core Conditions   266
Raters' Perceptions of the Core Conditions   268
Can the Skills Be Taught?   269
For Better or Worse—Some Do Damage   270

Bibliography   273
Name Index   281
Subject Index   284

PART ONE

Developing Basic Skills

CHAPTER ONE

The Third Alternative—Evocative Empathy

It has been my experience that beginning therapists feel they have only two options in responding to their clients. Some see "empathy" as some kind of warm and supportive reflection of what the client has just said, and others think they need to gather evidence and give advice, reassurance, and clever interpretations. Neither of these approaches works very well, but they seem to be the only ones that life prepares us for. There is a third alternative, a skill that will not be easy to learn and that will feel awkward at first, but one you need to master if you want to be a good counselor or therapist. The most important goal of this book is to get you started toward this mastery. There seems to be no really clear label for this skill, but I think Laura Rice's (1974) "evocative empathy" comes closest. To say it plainly, this skill is the fundamental skill for doing therapy. There will be many other things you will have to do, and there will be many times when evocative empathy is not appropriate, but for any of the other things to work, you must first make your client feel deeply understood.

I am about to give you a formal definition of *empathy* that will sound pretty sterile and cold, but I will spend a couple of hundred pages warming up our definition. Empathy is "communicated understanding of the other person's intended message." Every word counts in this definition. It is not enough to understand what the person said; you must hear what he or she *meant* to say, the intended message. It is not enough to understand, even deeply; you must communicate that understanding somehow. It is absolutely essential that the other person feel understood—that the understanding be perceived (Barrett-Lennard, 1962, 1981; Gurman, 1977). It's not clear from the formal definition, but the part of the intended message that will be critical is the emotional part of the message; therapy is both an intellectual and an emotional process, and it is the feelings that your client (and maybe you and I) are going to have the most trouble dealing with. You will be listening for what your client is trying to say, and one way you will be doing this is to hear the feelings *implicit* in his or her message.

The business of therapy often involves some pretty painful stuff, and it is easier to talk in cognitive terms. A client might say, "It's not fair when less qualified people at work are given promotions." At one level, this is an entirely accurate statement of fact about simple justice. Obviously, however, it is a very feelingful message— implicitly. Your job as the therapist is to bring the feelings to life in a way that leaves your client with the sense that you really under- stood what was meant. You might say, "I guess you're feeling cheated by that." Let me go through my thinking as the therapist here. There are two steps I went through. First, I had to understand what was meant, and so I was naming to myself several possibilities, such as anger, hurt, and feeling cheated, and I tried to get a sense of which of these possible feelings the person wanted me to hear. Second, I had to find the words to let him know that I understood.

I could have been "behind" him with a simple reflection like "There's no justice in a situation like that," and although this response wouldn't do any damage, it wouldn't be much help either, because it does nothing with the client's *reactions*. It is easier to talk about things outside ourselves in objective ways, and this includes the way we talk about feelings. You might have been tempted to word your response as "That kind of situation can certainly arouse feel- ings of being cheated." This is more effective than "There's no justice in a situation like that" but less effective than "I guess you're feeling cheated by that." The difference may be subtle, but it is crucial. In one case we are talking about feelings as things, objectively, as they can be aroused. In the other, we are naming a particular person's particular reaction in the here and now. We are bringing an expe- rience to life.

You might be thinking that my response to my client was pretty tame, since there are lots of other feelings that could be present, consciously or unconsciously, and besides, how do we know that he is not distorting the justice of the situation? Perhaps we should confront him with this or at least get some more information from him about whether the people promoted really were less qualified. You will have to trust me on this for now, but I guarantee you that the fastest way to get to the client's truth, and to get there in a way that will help the client, is by helping him face the leading edge of what he is trying to say but can't quite say. The critical guideline is the phrase "the intended message." Maybe my client does feel more than cheated. Maybe he feels furious or hopeless or vengeful, but I have to be able to sense what he is trying to say right now and help him articulate that.

LEAD OR FOLLOW?

Sometimes therapy approaches can be described as "leading" or "following" styles, but this distinction is inappropriate for understanding the nature of evocative empathy. In one sense you are following your client, because it is not your job to determine the content or topic of what is talked about. You are not urging certain issues to the front; you are listening with focused intensity for where your client is trying to go. But in another sense, you are leading, since, to be most effective, you stay that one step ahead by dealing with what your client has only implied.

I hope it is becoming clear that there is a critical region where therapy takes place. If you lead too far, you will get off the track, take over the direction of therapy, threaten your client into needing his defenses against you, and probably start giving lousy advice. If you just repeat your client's words (or, worse, are behind him and deaden the process), he might as well be talking to his dog, who probably will do him more good just by being nonjudgmental. I'm being too harsh, of course, because sometimes you will have to give advice and offer opinions, and sometimes being right with your client will be just the right thing to do. My concern is, though, that these are the things you will do most of the time, when effective therapy requires that you concentrate on making the implicit explicit.

A question that often arises here is whether the therapist has to wait for the client to say something before dealing with it, and isn't that inefficient? This question grows out of a misunderstanding of evocative empathy as passive. If you waited for your client to say everything explicitly, it would be inefficient and probably quite frustrating for both of you. If, however, you have "good ears" and can hear what the client is hinting at, you will seldom be repeating the client's words. In one sense, you will be leading, but in another you will not, because the ideas you articulate will be ones your client really was thinking and will recognize as such. One goal of your response is that your clients think "Oh, right, exactly . . . That's just what I meant." They don't always say this out loud, of course, but it is rewarding feedback to get. It lets you know that you're working well.

LEVELS OF EMPATHY

Some writers have used terms like *additive responses* (Hammond, Hepworth, & Smith, 1978) and *advanced accurate empathy* (Egan, 1982) to describe approximately what I am talking about. Usually, however, these responses are prescribed only for later in therapy, when a strong relationship has been established. Some (Carkhuff, 1969) caution that too much empathy early in therapy can create so much anxiety for the client that therapy is hampered. If you understand what I am saying, however, you will see that therapy doesn't progress in stages, with different kinds of understanding appropriate for different stages; it progresses along a continuum. Your guideline to this continuum is in the phrase "the intended message."

Of course, later in therapy the therapist can go a lot further and say much more emotionally poignant things—because the client intends for the therapist to hear so much more then. The principle is still the same as it was early in the process; you articulate what the other person meant to be communicating. Early in the relationship, the other person will be cautiously building trust in you, not intending that you see or hear everything. But you still can go beyond the actual words spoken without threatening your client. Nearly every statement has some implicit meanings in its message. Whether you know the person well or have just met, your most effective response, the response that will make the other person feel most deeply understood, will be to put into words what she *meant*.

This means that you will sound quite different later in therapy, since the client will have given you so much more to work with. An outside observer might describe you as more passive earlier in therapy and almost interpretive later in therapy, but relative to what the client was trying to say, you will be doing about the same things.

EVOCATIVE EMPATHY AND INTERPRETATION

There are some strong resemblances between evocative reflections and what psychoanalytic therapists refer to as moderate interpretations or interpretations at the preconscious level. They are not the same thing, however, and it is important that you understand why. The intentions of the therapist are different, and consequently the process for the client is different.

An interpretation is given from the therapist's frame of reference to point out to the client relationships and insights that the more perceptive therapist understands better than the client. The therapist is the source. The empathic therapist, in contrast, sees the client as the source, sees the client as the problem solver. Of course, the empathic therapist has to do some internal "interpreting" in the sense that hearing the implicit message requires drawing inferences, making connections, and seeing subtle relationships. This ability to hear with the "third ear" (Reik, 1948) is one of the two basic skills you must learn. (The other is finding the words to express your understanding.) The empathic therapist's *intent*, however, is not to cleverly guide the client toward the truth but to bring the client's experiencing to life, so the client will deal with it and find his or her own truth—will accurately know his or her own experience.

Some of these differences are pointed out strikingly by Karl Menninger, a famous analytically oriented therapist. He says: "It is helpful to some young analysts to have it put thus: One tells a patient what the patient *almost* sees for himself and one tells him in such a way that the patient—not the analyst—takes the 'credit' for the discovery" (1958, p. 134). In some ways, Menninger's description of the timing of interpretations is remarkably similar to the process I have been describing, and I suspect that his therapy was effective and sounded very much like that of effective empathic therapists. The sharpest difference, of course, lies between Menninger's view of the therapist's role as the expert who really brings out the truth and the view that the client is capable of finding the truth with a specific kind of help from the therapist; the client truly does deserve the credit for the discovery.

Rice (1974) says it well:

Evocative reflection is *not* the same as an interpretation. Although a "good" interpretation and a "good" evocative response may sound very similar, the aim of the reflection is different; attempts to demonstrate their similarity only serve to blur a worthwhile distinction .... The aim of an interpretation is to go beyond the client's statement, to point out patterns and connections, and to offer to the client new ways of viewing his experience. The aim of an evocative reflection is to open up the experience and provide the client with a process whereby he can form successively more accurate constructions of his own experience [p. 290].[1]

It seems likely that if interpretive and empathic therapists really did sound just alike and differed only in their intentions, it would make little difference to clients or to the process of therapy. Clients' perceptions of their therapists as empathic, caring, and honest are among the best predictors of successful therapy (Gurman, 1977). Intentions, however, get reflected in behavior. Differences in wording, inflection, and content responded to do appear between interpretive and empathic therapists, and these do affect therapy.

EMPATHY IS NOT SYMPATHY

It is common to confuse empathy with a lot of other things, such as personal warmth, caring for another person, agreeing with the other person, and sympathy. These qualities may appear with empathy, but they are definitely not the same as empathy. I can be empathic with a person whose presence I can barely stand, who disagrees with me, and for whom I feel no sympathy. It would be difficult, but it could be done, because empathy just says: I understand what you are trying to say and how you feel, and I would articulate it this way. The purpose of empathy is to help the other person face her experience—to face what she feels and thinks but can't quite look at clearly. In doing this, I am not saying that I see it the same way or that I agree with it. I am also not saying that I care for or respect the other person, just as a result of being empathic, although respect and dependable acceptance are crucial parts of therapy. We will talk about these relationship issues later; for now, I want it clear that empathy and acceptance are different things even though they usually go together.

Most important, empathy is not sympathy. Sympathy implies pity; empathy implies trust. I am saying to my client that she is strong enough to solve problems, that I will not condescend pityingly, and that our work together is not just handholding.

[1]From "The Evocative Function of the Therapist," by L. N. Rice. In D. A. Wexler and L. N. Rice (Eds.), *Innovations in Client-Centered Therapy.* Copyright © 1974 by John Wiley & Sons, Inc. This and all other quotations from this source are reprinted by permission of John Wiley & Sons, Inc.

THIS IS HARD WORK

Good therapy is an active process that demands concentration, feeling, and quick thinking. Probably the most common misunderstanding of empathy is that it is supposed to be passive. This misunderstanding is so pervasive that I almost hesitate to mention the enormous debt that empathy-oriented therapy owes to Carl Rogers. It has been my experience that people instantly associate his name with passivity, although that is clearly not what he meant his approach to imply. As long ago as 1942, he said:

> Often the client has attitudes which are implied in what he says or which the counselor through shrewd observation judges him to have. Recognition of such attitudes which have not yet appeared in the client's conversation may, if the attitudes are not too deeply repressed, hasten the progress of therapy [1942, p. 173].

He probably would be more comfortable with this more recent wording of the same thought.

> [Empathy] involves being sensitive, moment to moment, to the changing felt meanings which flow in this other person, to the fear or rage or tenderness or confusion or whatever, that he/she is experiencing. It means temporarily living in his/her life, moving about in it delicately without making judgments, sensing meanings of which he/she is scarcely aware, but not trying to uncover feelings of which the person is totally unaware, since this would be too threatening [1975, p. 4].

He gives a common-sense test for when empathy is accurately sensitive.

> If the therapist has communicated a superficial understanding of the client's expression, the client's inner response and perhaps verbal response will be "Of course. That's what I just said." Clearly, this has not done much to advance self-exploration. When the therapist has communicated an effectively empathic response, the client's reaction is likely to be "That's exactly right! I didn't suppose anyone could understand what I really meant. Now I wish to tell you some more." When the therapist is exceptionally effective and has caught the subtle meanings on the edge of the client's awareness, the client's reaction is likely to be first a pause, then a gradual appreciation: "Yes, I think you're right! I had never thought of it in just that way before, but that *is* what I've been feeling and experiencing. And now I see some more" [Rogers, 1980, p. 2155].

There is an old and not very amusing joke about Rogers that illustrates this misunderstanding. Maybe I shouldn't tell it, but better you should hear it from me than from some kid on the street who will have it all wrong. The client says "I feel so depressed," and Rogers replies "Your feeling is unhappiness."

"I am going to end it all."

"You feel like committing suicide."

The client goes over to sit on the ledge of an open window and says "This is it. I'm going to jump."

"You feel like jumping right now."

The client jumps, and Rogers leans out the window and says "Plop."

Rogers was asked about this joke, and as the interviewer (Hall, 1967) started to tell it, he replied (with, I would guess, barely muffled annoyance) "I *know* the story. My answer, for once and for all time, is that I would not have let him jump out the window" (p. 66). He has been "more than a little horrified at the interpretation of my approach which has sometimes crept into the teaching and training of counselors. . . . a wooden technique of pseudo-understanding in which the counselor reflects back what the client has just said" (Rogers, 1962, p. 420).

One interchange between client and therapist actually sounded like this:

> **Client:** All you ever do is repeat back what I just said.
>
> **Therapist:** You feel that all I ever do is repeat your words to you.
>
> **C:** There! You're doing it right now.
>
> **T:** You feel that I am doing it right at this moment.

This painfully awful exchange continued for several more lines, but I can't stand it anymore. The therapist had read a little about "reflection," figured it was easy to do, and set out to do good. You, however, would have been listening for the implicit message in what the client said and would have responded with something like "I think you mean I can be pretty frustrating, that I just leave you to wallow around in this stuff, which is pretty hard to deal with. I guess my passivity annoys you a lot." Actually, you likely wouldn't be in this fix, since your evocative responding would not have been "saying back what I just said," but you will face similar situations when clients will find you frustrating or annoying. It will be difficult to hear the attack on you because of your own feelings of being threatened, but you should listen for the implied meaning and put it into words.

A common feeling among new therapists is that they are redundant, that their clients really would do just as well talking to a nice cocker spaniel. The temptation is to start "doing more to the client" to feel that the therapist has a useful and powerful role to fill. This almost inevitably means offering interpretations, advice, confrontations, questions, homework assignments, and rational analyses. Then the therapist feels useful. When these don't work the therapist might drop back to passive reflections, until the frustration of uselessness sets in again. I can promise you two things. First, you probably don't yet know how to give evocative empathy (unless you are a very rare beginning therapist), and so you are not in a position to say it doesn't work and is frustratingly passive. Second, as you become better at it, you will find your contribution to the process rewarding and active and plenty difficult enough to satisfy your need to be "doing something."

It used to bother me when a client would say, at the end of therapy, "I feel good that I was able to do this myself. You didn't really solve my problems for me." Of course this is the perfect way for the client to feel, and my being bothered was just from my own need for recognition of the fact that I thought I had been working pretty hard. One goal of therapy is the client's independence, however, and it really did please me when one client said "I did this myself. You never did anything but repeat back what I said, but you said it a little stronger." Perfect. He perceived what I said as really his message, just said in a little different way that made its impact stronger.

As a therapist, you will be an expert on a process, not on the nature and content of a particular person's problems.

One last thought about therapy being a demanding enterprise: some therapists do damage. I will discuss this at length in later chapters, but it is important that you know that therapy can be helpful or it can leave the client worse off than she or he would have been without therapy. This sobering thought should lead you to work hard at becoming as good as you can, to be as open as you can to the sometimes threatening process of growth you face in becoming an effective helper.

RATING THE "CORE CONDITIONS"

I have focused on evocative empathy in this chapter, partly because it is fundamental and partly because it is the most "teachable" of the fundamental things a therapist must offer his or her clients. I will be talking about many other aspects of being a therapist throughout the book, and a brief summary of part of what lies ahead will probably be helpful. A number of writers have built on Rogers' early work to outline the "core conditions" essential to good therapy (Carkhuff & Berenson, 1967, 1977; Truax & Carkhuff, 1967; Rogers, Gendlin, Kiesler, & Truax, 1967; Egan, 1982; Hammond, Hepworth, & Smith, 1978; Patterson, 1974). Another purpose of this summary section is to introduce you to the rating scales that have been designed to operationalize the therapist behaviors that communicate the core conditions.

The core "helper dimensions" are accurate empathy, respect for the client, genuineness, and concreteness. The core "helpee dimensions"—the client's jobs—are exploration, understanding, and action (Carkhuff & Berenson, 1967, 1977).

I have already discussed empathy to some extent. Briefly, *respect* is reflected in the dependable acceptance the therapist gives the client—a nonjudgmental openness to let the client think, feel and say whatever he is experiencing without losing the sense that the therapist accepts him as a person with worth. *Genuineness* is difficult to define but generally means that the therapist is not phony and relating within a role. Many writers go beyond this definition to talk about "authenticity" and "openness," topics I will discuss in Chapter 6. *Concreteness* refers to the therapist's responding in ways that are specific to the particular client, using words that uniquely bring that client's experience to life, rather than making generalized statements.

Each of these dimensions describes therapist behavior that can be described operationally, and rating scales have been developed to permit quantified judgments of therapist behavior within the session. These scales were developed for research purposes, but they are also widely used for training, since they specify behaviors, rather than using only abstract descriptions. Because the empathy scale is especially useful for our purposes, we will look at it now.

RATING EMPATHIC BEHAVIOR

Several empathy scales have been developed and validated (Truax & Carkhuff, 1967; Rogers, Gendlin, Kiesler, & Truax, 1967), but I will draw most heavily from Carkhuff's (1969) five-point scale, which reduces some of the ambiguity of previous scales and is designed to be applicable to all human relations. The scale is based on observable behaviors, so that raters listening to tape recordings can reliably judge the degree of empathy being communicated, and this behavioral focus should also be helpful to you as you try to learn the skill. In Chapter 17 we will learn some of the complexities and limitations of using these scales in research. We will also discover (in Chapters 6 and 17) that clients' perceptions of these qualities in their therapists are more strongly related to successful therapy than are ratings done by observers using these scales (Barrett-Lennard, 1962, 1981; Gurman, 1977). My only purpose now is to give you some idea of the skills you will be trying to learn.

Levels 1 and 2 describe nonempathic behavior, and so I will discuss them later. Briefly, a "1" is a response from the therapist's frame of reference that ignores the client's message, and a "2" is an attempt to understand that responds to the client's message but in a way that lessens its impact. Level 3 is what I would call a response right at or slightly behind where the client is working: the therapist responds only to the explicitly stated content and feeling of the client's response.

> *Level 3.* The expressions of the first person (therapist) in response to the expressed feelings of the second person(s) (client) are essentially *interchangeable* with those of the second person in that they express essentially the same affect and meaning [Carkhuff, 1969, p. 316].[2]

This level of responding is often called the "minimally facilitative" level. The therapist is responding to the surface expressions only and either does not hear or ignores feelings implicit in the client's response. This kind of response is not bad, it is just minimally facilitative. It can express the therapist's interest in a nonthreatening way and set the stage for later exploration and is often the most appropriate response to make. The therapist who always responds at this level, however, will have disappointing results.

> *Level 4.* The responses of the first person add noticeably to the expressions of the second person(s) in such a way as to express feelings a level deeper than the second person was able to express himself [p. 316].

Here the therapist is adding at least something new from what was implicit in the client's intended message. The therapist must have

---

[2]From *Helping and Human Relations*, Vol. II, by Robert R. Carkhuff. Copyright © 1969 by Holt, Rinehart and Winston. Reprinted by permission of Holt, Rinehart and Winston, CBS College Publishing.

been able to hear what the client was *trying* to say. The client might have said, for example, "When I left home, my mother didn't even say goodbye." A Level 3 response to the explicit content might have been "Not even a goodbye—at a time when goodbyes were called for." The more deeply empathic therapist would have responded to the whole message, hearing nonverbal clues to what the client meant, clues we can't hear or see on paper. "Sounds like you were standing there waiting . . . for a goodbye that would mean she cared and then felt pretty empty when not even that came."

> *Level 5.* The first person's responses add significantly to the feeling and meaning of the expressions of the second person(s) in such a way as to (1) accurately express feelings below what the person himself was able to express or (2) in the event of ongoing deep self-exploration on the second person's part, to be fully with him in his deepest moments (p. 317).

The differences between Levels 4 and 5 are largely differences in the degree to which the therapist has added to the client's message; a "5" brings the message to vivid life, restating it with precision, deep feeling, and the unique nuances that are part of the client's experience. It is critical that Level 5 responses must still be responses to the client's intended communication if they are to be defined as empathic. Going beyond what the client can recognize as part of the message is going into interpretations. Accurate Level 5 responses may be the most therapeutic, but they require considerable finesse at hearing the client accurately, and they are not common, even in the best therapy.

When the therapist goes beyond the intended message, he or she begins to respond from his or her own preconceived notions and enters what I would call interpretations and Level 1 on the empathy scale. This includes introducing new material, pointing out inconsistencies, contradicting the client, and suggesting explanations that the client hasn't suggested. Occasionally, each of these approaches might be helpful, but only rarely. I will argue repeatedly that these are the easy things for us intellectually oriented therapists to do, but they are not the most helpful.

> *Level 1.* The verbal and behavioral expressions of the first person either *do not attend* to or *detract significantly* from the verbal and behavioral expressions of the second person(s) in that they communicate significantly less of the second person's feelings than the second person has

communicated himself . . . . The first person may be bored or uninterested or simply operating from a preconceived frame of reference which totally excludes that of the other person(s) [p. 315].

A Level 1 response simply shows no empathic intent on the therapist's part. A Level 2 response, in contrast, is an attempt to be empathic but one that detracts from or distorts what the client communicates.

> *Level 2.* While the first person responds to the expressed feelings of the second person(s), he does so in such a way that *subtracts noticeable affect from the communications* of the second person. The first person may communicate some awareness of obvious surface feelings of the second person but his communications drain off a level of the affect and distort the level of meaning. The first person may communicate his own ideas of what may be going on but these are not congruent with the expressions of the second person [p. 315].

Level 2 responses will slip into your therapy at times when you don't expect them. Your client might say "For the first time in my life, I'm feeling good about myself . . . liking myself." You respond "So you see real progress in the direction you're going." Your response is not inaccurate, but it is dampening. Your client was expressing feelings, and you responded with a cognitive generalization.

At the risk of making our discussions mechanistic, we can refer to therapist responses as "3s" or "just less than a 3," because it can be a useful shorthand if we all understand the complexity of what the shorthand means. (This can get silly, though, with references to "threeish" therapists and "that's a 3.65.")

To close this section, Carkhuff and Berenson (1977) report a disconcerting study that should motivate you to work hard at developing your skills. It is not likely that these skills are a natural part of your behavior right now.

The modal (most common) level of functioning in interpersonal skills among general and professional populations was assessed. The general public and college freshmen scored at 1.5, nurses and teachers at 1.7, guidance counselors at 1.9, graduate students in psychology at 2.1, trained subprofessional and subdoctoral helpers at 2.7, and functioning professionals with advanced training in the skills at 4.0. If level 3 really is "minimally facilitative," we're in a little trouble.

A THEORETICAL PREVIEW

My main goal in writing this book is to help you learn skills, but being able to explain how therapy works in theoretical terms is also important. In the last four chapters, I will switch from practice to theory. A number of readers have commented that they are surprised in reading the theoretical chapters to find that my theoretical orientation is quite eclectic. I don't like being put in a category, but it would be useful for you to know that my eclecticism draws most heavily from a cognitive approach to learning theory, with elements of information processing and some emphasis on unconscious processes such as repression.

CHAPTER TWO

Learning to Hear

Responding effectively requires two abilities; you must be able to hear well, and then you must be quick enough to articulate what you have heard. The third thing that must happen is that your client perceive your understanding (Barrett-Lennard, 1981). These are both difficult skills, and sometimes people who do one well have trouble with the other. Most people, however, have to work hard at both until experience and practice make them come easily and naturally.

I can't decide which one beginning therapists have the more trouble with. Often, when role-playing therapy or listening to a tape of a session, I have stopped to ask the struggling new therapist to sit and think for a minute what the client was feeling when he or she said the last response. Usually, the therapist can name, fairly accurately, some of the client's feelings but then says "I knew that, but I couldn't find the words to say it right." So you may feel the most awkwardness and frustration at the task of learning to articulate. With practice (and only with practice, by the way), though, you will get better at this; articulating responses is a trainable skill.

Learning to hear the implicit message, however, may be easier only at the beginning, when it seems reasonably easy to name some general feelings such as anger, fear, and happiness. Your job is going to be to hear subtle nuances and the complexities of unique experiences. A psychiatrist I know says he can spot the new psychiatric residents who will be able to do therapy because they have a natural empathy that he doesn't think the others will be able to learn. I don't think the issue is quite this discouraging, but developing this sensitivity to the experience of others probably will take more time and experience than your other therapeutic skills. I can remember listening to a tape of one of the therapists who trained me and thinking "Where did he get that? She didn't say that," when he responded to a client. The client answered something like "Exactly," and I knew I had a long way to go.

17

BASIC LISTENING SKILLS

I have started this book at a full run, discussing evocative empathy in all its complexity. It is likely, however, that you have to start at a simpler level, and much of what you will do in therapy probably will be and should be at a simpler level. You will be using basic listening skills.

Attending

The first requirement for listening is that you pay attention to the other person. This may seem obvious, but many social interchanges are marked by a detached passivity in which the "listener" is just waiting for the other person to stop talking in order to get his or her next speech into the conversation. Attending is marked by a focused intensity. The listener's posture says "I am interested. I am listening." Eye contact is frequent, and the therapist is probably leaning a bit toward the client in an open and relaxed manner. Don't take this physical description too seriously, though. If you are thinking about the angle of your torso to the chair and your rate of eye-blinks, you won't be attending, no matter how good you look. Be focused and interested and really trying to hear, and your body will take care of itself.

Even your voice tonal quality will be communicating your attending. If you are listening hard, your voice will come out more solid, and if you're not, there will be an empty, just-here-doing-my-job quality to it. Again, though, you cannot fake this quality; it will be there if you are attending.

I have been critical of passivity in the therapist, and rightly so, but I think that in the process I have underestimated the power of focused attending. It is a rare thing in most human relationships to be listened to, and it can make a person feel valued and can free that person to explore new thoughts. The first client I ever saw said, at the end of fairly successful therapy, "I never knew it could be so much help just to have somebody listen to me." I was lucky, of course, to start out with such a good client, and this "compliment" really meant I wasn't all that hot as a therapist, but he was right in that focused listening can be helpful.

Acknowledgment Responses

Your goal is to make the client feel understood, and one way to do this, as she explores and thinks and feels, is to use short responses that simply say "I am with you, keep going." Phrases like "I see . . . I understand that . . . OK . . . Uh huh" can serve this function, and so can one- or two-word offerings that complete a sentence or are synonyms for something the client just said. Acknowledgment responses can include nods of the head and gestures and are what Phillips, Lockhart, and Moreland (1969) call "minimal encourages to talk." Acknowledgment responses say "I understand," but they don't prove it. The proof of understanding comes from articulated responses.

Maintenance Responses

Probably the most frequent therapist response is the "reciprocal response" (Hammond, Hepworth, & Smith, 1978) or the "maintenance response" (Rice, 1974). These are "Level 3" responses from Carkhuff's rating scale; they are essentially interchangeable with what the client has said, both in feeling and in content. Sometimes maintenance responses are nearly exact repeats of what the client said, but those often sound so trite that the therapist usually paraphrases the client's message. One woman tried to apply some of these skills in her home relationships (generally a good idea, since they are the foundation of all relationships) until her teenage daughter finally said, "Mother, what's wrong with you? Have you gone nuts? All you've been doing this last week is repeating everything I say."

The goal of a reciprocal response is to make the other person feel understood, and a good paraphrase is often the best way to do this. Hammond, Hepworth, and Smith say that reciprocal responses should be thought of as the therapist's "baseline" response and that "additive" responses (evocative empathy) should be done carefully and generally later in therapy. I agree that later in therapy the therapist will be using more complete and evocative language; an outside observer might say the therapist was being more "additive." *Relative to the client*, however, the therapist is working similarly in both instances. The goal is the same for the early as for the later responses— to articulate the intended message. It's difficult to do, but you need to be able to sense what it is that the client wants you to hear, what she is *trying to say*. Early in therapy, this will often be just about what she has said explicitly, and a fancy response with lots of emotions and imagery could be beyond what was intended.

In Chapter 1 I said that these "Level 3" responses are usually called "minimally facilitative" responses. This phrase seems derogatory unless we pay attention to the "facilitative." Very few people interact at a "3" level, and as we will discouragedly discover in Chapter 17, research indicates that very few therapists operate at even this level. Reciprocal responses *are* facilitative. They hold up to the client what he has just said and help the client face the thoughts involved. Clients often will surprise you by denying that what you responded was what they said at all, even though you felt you were just repeating it back. Hearing another person say what we just said often makes us look at our statement from a different perspective.

Thus, paraphrasing what your client has said can be helpful, and even if this were all you ever did, you probably would have some success as a therapist. The problem is that it is slower than therapy needs to be. You certainly need to develop the ability to give your client reciprocal maintenance responses; in fact, this is probably the level at which you will start working. Then we can work on fine-tuning you, helping you learn to make the implicit explicit.

HEARING THE IMPLICIT MESSAGE

Learning to hear what another person has said is difficult. Hearing what the person was trying to say—what was meant—is more difficult.

First Look for Reactions

If the client says "People today just don't care about each other," you might paraphrase this as "It's sort of a sign of the times how indifferent people are to each other." Not bad, but you haven't dealt with the *implicit reactions*. Stop reading for a minute and name the feelings intended by the client to be implicit in the comment.

You might have said "I guess it saddens you to see all that indifference," and I think the client would have had the internal reaction that we are aiming for. He would have recognized that as what he meant, and you would have taken him a step forward, because the statement was not only a cognitive observation; you named the feelings implied in it. That is your job.

We could have gone further with our response, of course. In our cleverness we might figure that actually the client is talking about loneliness and feeling not cared about, and ultimately we might be right. If we go beyond what the client intended, however, we will slow therapy down by threatening him with our expertness and with his own thoughts that are frightening enough that he needs to defend against them. The difficult trick is to be ahead of the client as far as we can get without going beyond what he will recognize as part of the intended message, as part of current experiencing.

Clear-cut examples are difficult to think of, and I am aware that this last example could be misleading. I can easily imagine a client I knew well saying "People today just don't care about each other" and meaning far more than "This indifference between people saddens me." I might well draw on things the client has said in the past and respond "And that's what gets to you so much . . . you reach out and ask to be cared about, and all you get is coldness back." Whether this response will be effective depends on what the client was trying to say and what he assumed I already knew. If he is assuming I know this past information, I have gone well beyond the client's factual statement, but I have not given an interpretation; I brought the implied experience to life.

Rice says: "The first principle for evocative responding is that the therapist should listen for and respond to reactions, either explicit or implicit" (1974, p. 303). This is your first guideline for learning to hear. Read some of the client statements in Chapter 8 and, without looking at the therapist's response, name the feelings implicit in the statements. Listen to the tape that comes with this book or other tapes of therapy and stop the recorder after a client statement so you can practice naming reactions—feelings—explicit and implicit. Try for a moment to suppress your own need for intellectual understanding of the causes of the client's behavior; stop trying to put some overall "sensible" structure on things; just practice knowing what another person is saying about his or her reactions in the present moment.

The Big Issue versus the Last 12 Words

One common error among beginning therapists is to lose sight of what the client means by focusing on the last few words, as though it were illegal to go beyond what was just said in making a "reflection." It is necessary to hear the whole message, which includes the words actually said, the tone of voice, the posture, and the assumed shared knowledge of what was said before. Often, for example, a client will bring up an issue and then go into an elaborate illustration of it with the telling of an incident. The therapist is steadily following the story, responding to it, and articulating experiences within it, all the while having mentally "red-flagged" the issue that brought the story up in the first place. The therapist is thinking "What does all this mean to this person?"

Your client might start out talking about feelings of discouragement and then drift through a story about his best friend's father's depression over a business failure. You will be listening for the point of the story, red-flagging the entry to the story so you can return to it. Then, not getting lost in details, you might say "I see . . . what got you started on all this a few minutes ago was wondering whether all this studying is going to help you find anything meaningful in life. And then this story about your friend's father sort of illustrates how much life can be wasted. It's like you're asking, 'Am I going to waste my life?' " This response recognizes all of what the client was saying, but it stays on track by focusing on the main point of his message and by focusing on his reactions.

Nonverbal Communication

When I talked about attending, it was clear that much of your interest and caring will be expressed by the way you sit, where you are looking, and the tone of your voice. Similarly, much of the client's intended message will be expressed nonverbally, in subtle shadings of facial expression, in voice quality, in position and posture, and in small behaviors. Again, there is an important line between what are nonverbal parts of the intended message and what are things the therapist might be able to interpret from nonverbal cues that are not part of the message.

A client could say "She left without saying goodbye" in a tone of voice that communicated anger, indifference, hurt, pleasure, revenge, or any combination of these and other feelings. The words will be the same; the message will be entirely different in each case. Your client might say this with an angry voice and downcast eyes, and you might respond "It's all a jumble of hurt and anger, isn't it?" You haven't said anything about anybody leaving without saying goodbye; it can be assumed that you heard that factual part of the message, because you went beyond it so accurately. You were able to go beyond it because you accurately read the voice tone and downcast eyes as part of what you were meant to hear.

What if your client grimly says "When she left, she didn't even say goodbye, and I could not care less," but you pick up nonverbal cues that say there's a lot of caring going on? This is tricky. If you say "Your words tell me one thing, that you don't care, and your clenched jaw tells me another, that you do care," you might be quite right and very clever, but the majority of times that you respond like this, you will slow your client down by being far enough ahead to threaten her. Actually, this technique of pointing out discrepancies will help occasionally, but the problem will be that you will remember the few times it worked and not notice the many times it slowed therapy down. There is an alternative, and it is not just passive acceptance of the verbal statement. Your job is to find some way to get as far ahead of the client as you can without losing what the client will recognize as part of the message. You might have said "I guess you think about her leaving without even so much as the decency to say goodbye and feel 'Well, the hell with her,'" getting into your voice a strong hint of the feeling the client was expressing. This response does not intellectually point out discrepancies to the client; it does something far more powerful by holding up and bringing to life all of what the client has said. She has to recognize your response as a version of what she just said, and now there it is, in full color, and it has to be dealt with. You have used the nonverbal cues to hear the whole message and helped your client face it, without taking over as the expert showing the client the "truth."

Here and Now Can Include the Past

It should be obvious by now that this style of therapy is very much oriented toward present experiencing. The phrase *here and now* is most commonly used to describe this focus, and it captures the spirit of how therapy works. It is, however, often misunderstood to mean that we can deal only with issues in the historical present and leave the past for more psychoanalytically-oriented therapists. This belief is based on a misunderstanding of both the empathic approach and more psychoanalytic approaches, which often do deal with the past but also stress things like the reexperiencing of old hurts through "corrective emotional experiences" in therapy (Alexander, 1948).

I'll have to convince you later of the validity of this next statement, but for now go along with me: your client will try to talk about the things he needs to talk about, and so you will not have to expertly direct the topic of conversation.[1] This may mean you will talk about issues in the present or in the past; that's not the point. What matters is *reactions* in the here and now. It happens very often that events

---

[1] I will be making this assertion throughout the book. Because it is essential to this whole approach to therapy, I will spend a lot of time substantiating it in Part 4. These first chapters will flow better for you if you at least tentatively accept the statement. If you are skeptical, you might want to read Part 4 first.

from the past still have an enormous impact on a person, and it is this impact that is the focus of therapy. A memory from childhood can bring tears or pleasure in the present. If your client said "Whenever I used to bring home something I made in school, my father would say 'I don't want that junk around here,' " you might respond "It sounds like, being back there in your mind, you can still feel the wanting-to-cry feeling of his not wanting something you were trying to please him with." You are helping your client live that experience over again, which will give him a chance to deal with the experience in a way he wouldn't have otherwise. The memory hurts and will normally be avoided, but if it means things that still affect your client, the memory has to be dealt with.

Contrast what you have just done, bringing to life in the here and now the impact of a past experience, with what your response might have been. Many therapists would have heard the client's comment and made a causal connection, which probably is logically correct but which won't help the client reprocess an old experience. Such a therapist might have said "So it makes sense why you don't think much of your own abilities now, with that kind of upbringing." Again, this is not a destructive response; it's just not as helpful as one that is experience-oriented.

WHERE IS THE LEADING EDGE?

The Third Ear

Theodore Reik (1948) called a book *Listening with the Third Ear*, because he was trying to describe a process in which the therapist uses his or her own internal experiencing to hear meanings beyond the words the client uses. It seems that a few people are "naturals" at this kind of deep understanding; I remember one therapist in training who couldn't understand why I was so pleased at the quality of therapy she was doing with her first client, since this was the way she talked with her friends. Most of us, however, are not "naturals," but this does not mean we are doomed to lives of doing mediocre therapy. You can develop your "third ear," your ability to draw inferences that accurately reflect the meaning in another person's words.

My first piece of advice will frustrate you: get lots of experience. I think there is no quick way to develop your ability to hear; it will grow as you do therapy, sharing in the experience of more and more people and getting more and more feedback on when you have heard accurately and when you have not. Experience by itself is obviously not the issue, though, since everybody gains experience with others with increasing age; I'm sure you know some empathically dense people who have been talking with others for many years. What I am trying to do is to make absolutely clear what you are aiming for in the interactions that will help you hear better. The experience you seek is that of trying to see things through another person's eyes, of sensing what that person is experiencing, and then putting your understanding into words that the other person will recognize as his or her view. Then you should humbly listen for feedback, and when you are wrong, try again, correcting your distortions and becoming sensitive to your own blind spots.

The second approach is more quickly available, although not as powerful. Chapters 7 and 8 and the tape that comes with this book include exercises in which you are to read or listen to a client's comments and then put into words your understanding of the implicit message. The book and tape will give you some feedback on your accuracy, but it would be more helpful if you could find a few friends to share in this exercise, each independently responding to the exercises and then discussing together your differences in perception. It may bother you how much disagreement there is among you about the meaning of some of the responses, and I would hope this humbles you a bit. Cockiness over your brilliance of understanding will detract more from your therapy than almost anything else. Get feedback.

The important thing is to go beyond your own limited experience and share in others' experience. If you enjoy good fiction, I hereby assign you to read lots of it, or experience good drama, or talk with your friends a lot.

How Far Is Too Far?

It may be a little intimidating to be told that there is a critical region, just ahead but not too far ahead of the client, where therapy takes place most efficiently. Most beginning therapists are better off to err a bit on the side of caution until their ability to hear the leading edge of the implicit message develops. The consequences of being too far ahead of the client (and often too far ahead in the wrong direction) are more serious than the slowness that comes from working right with the client. (Of course, working behind the client can be just as destructive as working too far ahead, since the client can give up in frustration.) The rule of thumb, as you know, is that the leading edge is the message that includes everything that the client intended as "signs." This includes verbal and nonverbal cues, as well as all the material that the client has "put on the table" and assumes you know from previous discussions. Thus, a very short response can be filled with meaning. It can be a strange experience to listen to a conversation between people who have known each other intimately for several years. What sound to us like grunts and one-word comments can be to them a full and mutually empathic sharing; they have a huge pool of common experience that their words and grunts refer to. Similarly, as therapy progresses, the leading edge includes this common experience as assumed in what is said.

You can often tell after the fact when you have gone beyond the intended message, since the other person rejects what you have said or falls silent and withdraws or suddenly changes the topic. These experiences are feedback to you as you develop your ability to hear without going too far, an ability that you need because you want to know ahead of time how far is too far. Probably the most helpful guideline I can give you is to tell you to think how the person is going to react to what you are about to say. Will the person feel "Yes, that's it exactly. That's what I was trying to say"? Occasionally, a client will "self-overdose," saying things which are horribly frightening and which she or he can't handle without running from therapy or building strong defenses that will slow therapy down. Part of the therapist's job is also to hear the next intended message, which is likely to be something that means "This is too much . . . I have to back off," and so the therapist might say, "Things are going too fast . . . it's time to slow down, I guess." Even though the client did say the first things, they were beyond what she or he intended the therapist to hear. Usually, however, your sense of how much the client means for you to hear will help you define the leading edge of the message. *Your goal is to get as far ahead of the client as you can but have the client recognize what you say as part of what she or he meant.*

YOU HEAR SELECTIVELY

So far I have been talking as though there will always be only one message in what the client says, and your job is to hear it. This is oversimplified, of course, since a client will say many things, sometimes in only a few words. "I see myself as an independent person who likes to be alone. I can accomplish more that way. My wife is different . . . so was my mother, come to think of it." What are you going to respond to—the importance of his aloneness and the good feeling that gives him, the implied incongruence between him and his wife, the just-noticed similarity between his wife and his mother, the newly implied incongruence between him and his mother, or his need and desire to accomplish? You really can't respond to it all without going into a very long speech, and so the first thing you must do is admit to yourself that you will respond selectively. Clearly, your selectivity will have an enormous influence on the course of therapy, and it is therefore incumbent on you to be aware of how you are being selective. There is a clear danger that you will subtly lead the client in your direction, rather than give him the opportunity to solve his unique problems.

Personal Needs and Theories

In Chapter 6 I will discuss the therapist's own distortions and blind spots. For the issue of selectivity, it is important to recognize that you filter everything you hear and that you have theories of human behavior to which you have some personal commitment. The striking lesson of the literature on self-fulfilling prophecies (Rosenthal & Rubin, 1978) is that not only do we distort our perceptions because we tend to see what we expect to see, we influence others to fulfill our expectations by subtly reinforcing them when they behave as we expect them to—ironically, even when we believe we don't want them to behave this way.

It is not easy to know what to do about this problem, because the solution to it lies in the therapist's self-awareness—not an easy topic to do much about in a book like this. Personal therapy can help (be sure you get an evocatively empathic therapist for yourself), as can sharing your therapy with another therapist/friend or two. You will probably have some kind of practicum experience, in which a supervisor will likely monitor you quite closely and perhaps listen to tapes of your therapy. Your need for this kind of outside feedback will not stop with the end of your training, however, and each therapist should seek out a similar arrangement for continuing feedback.

Limits of Your Experience

You might be wondering whether it is necessary that you have had the same experience as the client in order to be able to understand it. The answer is no and yes. Obviously, you can't possibly have experienced all the same things as all your clients or even, for that matter, one of your clients. It is impossible for one person to really know what it is like to be another person. As in Carson McCullers's (1940) poignant novel, our hearts are all lonely hunters. We try to come close to understanding, and that isn't everything, but it is worth a lot. The more thoroughly you have lived, however, the easier it will be to sense similarities between your experience and your client's and to feel, with an "as if" quality, feelings that your client has. They do not then become your feelings, but you are more able to express your understanding of them.

The breadth of your own experience will come partly from your vicarious experiencing of clients' lives. The more therapy you do, the more you will have to draw from to understand your current clients.

All this speaks to the problem of selectivity because you will respond selectively not only because of your own needs and theories but also because you will understand some things better than others. Your reaction to this should be to try to broaden your experience through sensitive living of your own life and seeking out vicarious sharing with others.

Selective, Not Manipulative

All I have said so far about therapist selectivity has implied that it is destructive and results from distortions and limited experience, but since selectivity is inevitable, there has to be a best way to approach it. Likely you do have notions about whether it is more important to deal with issues of independence or issues of commitment to relationships, notions that may grow out of a quite consciously held theory of human behavior. If you are aware of these notions, they might guide your selectivity as a therapist. The danger is that you will try to fit all your clients into a mold that makes sense to you but is not what is best for the client. For some people, independence at the expense of intimacy is better, and for others the opposite is true. Your solutions might be all right for you, but a lot of humility about what the Good Life is like is called for in a therapist.

A good friend of mine calls this style of therapy "sneaky interpretation." I'm pretty sure he's kidding, but there is a disturbing possibility that the remarkable power of evocative empathy can be used manipulatively, to lead the client where you want in an insidious way. At least an interpretation is up front where it can be seen and possibly rejected. If, however, you respond to your client with what is really your analysis or emphasis but couch the response in language that says "Here is what I think you're saying—I'm not trying to lay anything on you," you are being sneaky.

Poignancy

So how can you be honestly selective? Your goal is to capture, from all the complexity of what the client says, what is most important to her. You can trust that the person will try to talk about the important issues; your job is to hear this attempt—to hear what is most important.

Your first guideline is to listen for implicit and explicit reactions. A second one that Rice (1974) discusses is *poignancy*. She says it well:

> The criterion of poignancy, or liveness, seems to be the therapist's best guide. How then is poignancy recognized? How can we recognize that the client is moving into an "unfinished" experience? . . . The most obvious sign is that the client feels something inconsistent or discomforting in the situation. In other cases, a kind of intensity comes through in the voice. On the other hand, the feeling may not be especially intense, but the client may feel that he somehow can't quite assimilate the experience [p. 304].

Another way to say this is that you listen for the part of the message that seems invested with the most feeling, with the most sense of "there's something in this that I know is important and sort of understand but can't get into words."

LISTENING TO SILENCE

Finally, in this chapter on learning to listen, I need to deal with silence. Silences are a lot harder on beginning therapists than they are on clients. One of my fellow students in graduate school wanted to shut off the tape recorder during silences even when we were role-playing, so as not to "waste tape." The tape wasn't being wasted, of course, but there was something so nerve-racking about all that unfilled time that he had to do something to stop the process. You will be tempted to fill silences at all costs, and likely you will start asking questions to get the client talking. There is a place for questions (see Chapter 5), but it is no accident that beginning therapists ask more questions than experienced ones do (Ornston, Cicchetti,

Levine, & Fierman, 1968). For one thing, experienced therapists can live through silences and even see them as constructive; for another, well-done evocative empathy makes it easy for the client to talk without being prompted by questions.

The question before us now, however, is how to listen to silences. Sometimes the client is using the silence to think or explore or assimilate something, and your need to keep the chatter going will stop these processes. Sometimes the client is suffering and embarrassed at not being able to think of anything to say, and the most empathic response you could make would be something like "It's hard to get things into words, huh?" or "I guess you've hit a dead end" or "I can tell it's hard to get going. I suppose it could be just not knowing where to start or going blank or something like that." In the first case, when the client was using the silence, your best response was to respect the silence and wait for the client to break it. In the second case, you were "listening" to mostly nonverbal cues and letting your client know you understood.

CHAPTER THREE

Finding the Words

There are two steps in responding: first you must hear the message, and then you must find the words to articulate what was intended. Most people are not used to responding with words that focus on what the other person said. We tend to ask questions, offer opinions, and make speeches. As an effective therapist, however, your job is to help your client face what he has just said. You might say that that seems silly in a way, since if the person just said it, there is no need to face it. The fact is, though, that the person often isn't feeling the full impact of what he is trying to say, especially when the material is difficult.

First, you will find it remarkable at times when you think you have just about repeated back the other person's words and the other person will say "Is that what I said? I guess it is, but it sure sounds different to hear you say it." Even more striking are instances when the other person says "No, that's not what I mean at all." Of course, some of these will be times that you have missed the message, but sometimes you truly will have only repeated back a "Level 3" response. The words have more impact when they come reflected back, since we seem to be able to emit words but avoid their impact.

The second way you are helping your client face what she has said is by being ahead of her, articulating what has been *implied*. We avoid what hurts, both in overt behavior and in our thinking, so that even when your client is talking about feelings, you might hear "I know there is risk in my involvement with him." You respond "Part of you is scared that if you care too much, you could really get hurt." Your response didn't really mean anything your client hadn't said, but by articulating the implied feelings, you are helping her face and experience a truth she couldn't quite stand to look at directly.

I will talk about how all this works in Chapter 15, but for now it is useful to know that your client is in trouble partly because she fears her own thoughts and feelings. Fearing them, she avoids them as much as possible, still being bothered by them but not able to do something wise about them because she is avoiding thinking and experiencing accurately. The only way to get rid of a fear is to face the thing you fear, feel the fear (in small doses), and have nothing bad happen. You are helping your client face feared thoughts and feelings—in small doses. How do you know what "size" these doses should be? By staying at the leading edge of what the client implies.

In the pages ahead, you will be told to "bring the client's experience to life" and to add "structure and focus" with your response. To give you some structure to hold onto right now, there are two general formulas that will help you find the words with which to respond. The general form of your response will be "It sounds like you feel _____ because of _____ ." You name reactions and the causes of those reactions. When possible, you can go on to say "I guess what you want is _____ ." This response goes on to focus on goals, on action, and on moving forward. Please don't cling to these formulas any longer than you have to, though; they are so simple that they are simplistic.

BRING IT TO LIFE

Your job is to find the words that will exactly capture your client's meaning and evoke (arouse, stimulate) the feelings your client is moving toward. You are to bring to life what is only being talked *about*. The word *evoke* means "to bring forth," and that is what you do when you bring the client's experiences to life. You do not *provoke* a response, since that would put you in control as the person who is deciding which experiences are to be felt. The client is the source of the experience, and your job is to *evoke* or facilitate the thoughts and experiences that come from the client—by bringing them vividly to life.

Painting the Picture

An image that some therapists find helpful is that of taking the raw material the client has laid on the table in bits and pieces and putting it all together as a whole scene—using it to paint a vivid picture and holding the picture up before the client, where he has to look at it. The therapist says with his or her actions, "Look, this is what you've said. We have to look at it in all its complexity and confusingness. Look." The therapist is not offering solutions or even suggesting which topics should be dealt with next but is just saying "Look at all of what you are saying." Then the client has to deal with it, has to take the next step in exploring.

State All Sides of the Message

Part of "painting the picture" is painting the whole picture. Many therapists seem to think that only one thing can be true at a time and have difficulty acknowledging contradictory parts of their clients' experience. It is quite clearly our nature to have contradictory experiences, no matter how much that offends our need for logical order. Conflict is fundamental to human functioning and, as we will see later, underlies most human emotional problems. To deny conflict in our responding dooms us to incomplete understanding. A common helpful remark in therapy is something like "You really feel both ways, don't you? It's like you want it more than anything but can't stand the thought of having it." And that's the truth for the client right now; further work and exploring and understanding might show a way out of the conflict, but not if some simple-minded therapist says "Well, which is it? Do you want it or don't you?" I am not saying that every message contains conflict; I am saying that when you respond, you should listen for and put into words all the sides of the issue that the client is trying to deal with.

Several paragraphs ago, I mentioned your client who said "I know there is risk in my involvement with him." The response I suggested was "Part of you is scared that if you care too much, you could really get hurt," but my response missed an important part of the message. Actually, I hinted at the other part of the message by saying "Part of you," but I hear this client's voice plaintively emphasizing the word *know*, and a better response being "Part of you is scared that if you care too much, you could really get hurt, and the other part is saying 'But I want him, and I do care.' "

Using the First Person

In the last response, I used a powerful tool of language for bringing the experience to life. Using the first person singular when articulating the client's own message makes it clear that the therapist is focusing on the client's experience and permits a more personally stated form of the response. There is a risk of being misunderstood when you do this, and a therapist who does it all the time can sound silly, but used sensitively, the *I* can help.

STARTING OUT

I think that finding the words to respond empathically looks a lot easier when you're reading about it than it really is. When you try to do it, I would anticipate a kind of blocking that may surprise you. When I teach these skills in groups, I often have the participants role-play different situations, with one of them as the talker and one as the empathic listener. To force the issue, I at first *prohibit* the listener's use of questions, advice, and suggestions. It is amazing how tongue-tied these rules leave people. These are the foundations of most social interchanges; we keep our conversations going by asking questions and telling people things. Life does not prepare us very well to be empathic (and I suspect this is one reason so few do well in relationships, but that's another book), and so we sit there at a loss.

Awkwardness

Unless you are a rare person, empathic responding will not feel smooth and natural at first. A useful analogy, though, is to think of playing tennis for ten years, having evolved your own choppy forehand with no follow-through. This stroke serves you quite well and, along with your amazing reflexes, lets you maintain a respectable standing among your friends. Now, however, you have stopped improving and seek professional help. As the pro teaches you a better stroke, it feels terrible and awkward, and, worst of all, your arrogant friends have started to beat you. Only by forcing a change in style and *practicing* will you become comfortable with a follow-through and eventually be a much better player. The temptation, however, is overwhelming to give in to the awkwardness and go back to chopping.

One reason I will talk about role playing in Chapter 7 is that it gives you a chance to practice your new awkward empathy in a relatively low-threat situation. Only with practice will it become natural and start to feel "right." You will be rattled by silences that will seem ten times as long as they are, and you will feel that you're looking foolish parroting back words. It will be tempting to start asking questions to fill in the time and get the other person talking, but it will be worth the effort to make yourself formulate your responses in the declarative form rather than the interrogative. This is not to say that questions are bad; they are often the most effective thing to use. The problem is that they are usually not as powerful as empathic responses, but they are what most of us use most of the time. You need practice with declarative empathic statements, and so I am advising you to force yourself to do this practice.

Another advantage of starting out with role-playing is that early attempts at developing these skills usually involve a lot of "Level 3" responding—that is, repeating back pretty much what the other person said. It is difficult to learn to find the words that stay just ahead of the other person, and when the skill is developing, it is easy to feel redundant or silly about repeating the other person's words. In role playing or with a friend who knows what you are doing, this initial clumsiness won't matter so much or be so threatening.

Real-Time Responding

Another problem that beginning therapists often report is that they could come up with terrific responses if we could just build in a 15-second delay during which time stopped for the client so the therapist could think. The cure for this problem is also practice. If your opponent's returns could be slowed to about one-third speed, your new forehand would be wonderful, but there just doesn't seem to be enough time for the backstroke before the ball gets there. Six months from now, of course, you will hardly be able to believe that the backstroke was ever a problem, since it seems to happen without your even thinking about it. It will just be natural. What's "natural" is what you've done so many times that it's overlearned.

You will get faster, but for now it would be useful to use a tape recorder in several ways. First, you can record your role playing, or if you are already engaged in doing therapy, you certainly should record your sessions. With the tape and a supervisor or colleague, stop the session immediately after some client response, and take all the time you want to formulate a good response. Discuss different possible responses and then listen to what the therapist actually said. Second, the tape that accompanies this book has several excerpts of therapy sessions (see Chapter 8). You can stop the tape after some client responses so that you can respond to the tape as though you were the therapist and then hear what the original therapist actually said. Of course, the actual therapist response is not the only one or even the best possible one that could have been given, but these tapes generally represent effective therapy, and it would be worthwhile to analyze what the therapists on the tape are doing. Chapter 8 also includes the therapists' discussion of what they see themselves doing. Third, the process of supervision is an essential part of your training. Most people dislike hearing themselves on tape (Sackeim & Gur, 1978), partly because nearly all of us misperceive ourselves to some extent, and the tape confronts us with ourselves. Your supervisor or colleague adds to this self-confrontation just by being there and articulating his or her own responses to your work, and a supervisor or colleague can also comment and give you feedback on what you could have done.

The Inevitable Pause

Joseph Schubert (1977) has pointed out that there has to be *some* pause between the end of the client's response and the beginning of the therapist's because the therapist has to have some time to formulate a response. If the therapist is formulating a response while the client is still talking, she or he has to be forcing closure on the client's message and must miss some of the message. Schubert (as does Bourbonnais, 1980) presents some evidence that more experienced therapists demonstrate this momentary pause more than beginners. If, however, you sit there silently counting "One hippopotamus, two hippopotamus" in order to get the correct pause in before you respond, you have probably missed some of the finer points of our discussion.

STRUCTURING AND FOCUSING

Therapy is both a cognitive and an emotional process. There is a risk of overemphasizing one and losing the integration of both aspects of experience, and I suspect that the impression I have created so far is that only the emotional matters. In this section, and in Chapter 5, I will dispel this impression as I discuss the cognitive, or intellectual, parts of therapy. I should explain that so much attention is being paid to the feeling part of therapy because my experience has been that most beginning therapists, perhaps even most people in our culture, are oriented toward the intellectual and the rational at the expense of the emotional and intuitive. The two must be integrated.

One way that you will help your client face what he or she is saying is to add sensible structure to it—not that you offer a logical analysis, but that you draw diffuseness together. Your client says "A lot of the time it seems like people are . . . I don't know . . . really mean . . . no, not mean . . . they're loving, I guess . . . at least some

. . . like some I know are." You might respond "I'm not sure I got all that, but let me try. It sounds confusing . . . trying to know how you feel about the way people are toward you. The ones that matter to you seem to be loving, you guess, but at the same time that doesn't seem quite the whole truth because they seem mean in some ways too. Is that close to what you mean?"

We have to be careful not to impose meaning that the client didn't intend, and that is always a danger of working ahead of the person's explicit words, but let's assume for this time that the therapist's response was accurate. What is interesting right now is that it took the jumbled expressions of the client and stated them in a way that made sense, that was structured. The client still recognizes it as what he meant but now has a chance to look at it in a much clearer form, which means that he must confront what he said in a way that wouldn't have happened if the therapist hadn't been there to add the clarity.

Focus Rather Than Elaborate

Another misunderstanding that often arises is that therapists think they should talk a lot, believing that in order to bring the client's experience to life they have to use lots of words and add elaborate verbal constructions. Your job is to hear the *essence* of the message and bring that to life. I talked in the last chapter about using "poignancy" as a guideline to what part of the message to respond to, and it can serve us here too. The client may be using lots of words and saying several things at once, but your job is to hear the central point. In fact, it is sometimes useful to be thinking, as you listen, what *is* the point here, as the client sees it? You are listening for the "big issue" rather than the last 12 words. Then your words sharpen that issue by focusing and illuminating it, rather than going into a complex elaboration of your own. The client is supposed to be doing the work here, in an active and ongoing process. You are supposed to facilitate this process in the client, and if we have to stop and listen to your clever speeches, the client will lose the momentum of the exploring process.

Client Rambling

Clients ramble for many reasons. Sometimes rambling is a defense against fear of engaging in real contact with the therapist; sometimes it is a well-established defense against facing painful thoughts and feelings; sometimes it is just a casual verbal wandering that results from not feeling very much at all at the moment; sometimes it results from a habitually wordy style of talking; there are dozens of possibilities. Therapeutic growth results from exploration and self-confrontation, neither of which is likely during rambling, and one purpose of having the therapist in the room is to focus the process. The therapist facilitates exploration and self-confrontation by frequently articulating the intended message.

When the client rambles, the therapist is still doing the same thing, bringing focus to the process, but it can be more difficult to bring structure to what can seem like a swamp of details. One thing the therapist is doing is scrambling to keep the big issue marked with a red flag and to understand the details in the perspective of what the person is trying to get to among all the words. You might say "OK, let me stop you for a minute to see if I've got what you're saying right so far. I think you mean that this story about how your aunt and uncle sold their house sort of illustrates what you were talking about before—that you wish there were something permanent—that you'd feel safer. Is that the point?"

Here you keep making it clear that you have empathic intent. Your behavior is not saying, "Here's what all this means." It is saying "We are engaged in an intense exploration process in which I will try very hard to help you explore all this, through your eyes." However, you are not just a passive follower. Your words add structure and focus.

Summarizing

Another kind of structure you can bring to the process results from summarizing responses. Again, of course, your job is not to add new material; it is to take what's on the table and pull it together, in an exploring, let's-see-if-I-understand-this-so-far way. In the process, you will probably be drawing in contradictory feelings and observations and will be presenting together aspects of the whole issue that may not have entered the discussion together. The summarizing response is not formulated to draw these new relationships for the client or to confront him or her with contradictions that had better be resolved right now; rather, it is a way of painting a larger picture than usual. The function it can serve is to present the client with a larger panorama to deal with, and if the connections are there to be made or the contradictions to be resolved, the client can do it. You help him or her look at the issue in a more complete way. Then the client can do the work.

Summarizing responses can be especially helpful when both you and the client seem to have hit a brick wall. You might say "It's hard to know where to go from here? . . . Here's where I see us having got so far . . ." (and then you draw together what's been said so far and bring it to life).

Frequency of Responding

In trying to decide how frequently to respond, we need to look at two effects we can have on the process of therapy. On one hand, the therapist needs to respond frequently because his or her function is partly to be the vehicle for self-confrontation by the client. Frequent responding keeps therapy going by giving feedback, by making the client feel understood, by preventing aimless circling, and by making mutual exploring the overall focus of therapy. All of these effects demand active participation by the therapist. A passive listener will leave the client to do all the exploring. As noted in Chapter 2, passive listening can be a powerful influence, and many clients will eventually solve problems with it. But it is slow and frequently ineffective because it doesn't help the client break circles of avoidance behavior and it doesn't help the client hear what he or she is implying. On the other hand, if the therapist responds too frequently, he or she can dominate the process, not letting the client do the work. The client is the problem solver, and the benefits of therapy are stronger and generalize more if the client goes through the steps of problem solving. Clearly, then, it is possible to respond too frequently.

In general, the answer to the question of how often to respond is "Fairly frequently." Your role in therapy is an active one but not a dominant one. To guide yourself, be sensitive to whether you are letting the client work on issues, whether the client's self-exploring talk is increasing over the course of sessions, and whether you find yourself interrupting the client a lot. These are observations that usually require feedback through tape listening and having someone else listen to you doing therapy.

SKILLFUL TENTATIVENESS

You may have noticed that many of the examples of dialogue in this book include phrases like "I guess you mean . . . ," "I'm not sure this is right, but . . . ," "I think I hear you. . . ." Each of these introduces a tentativeness that communicates that the client is the *source of* information about his or her own experience—that says to the client: "I am a fellow explorer going with you through this, but you are the final authority. I have things to add and things to share, but I offer them to you to use, rather than insist that I am right and am giving you the truth." This tentativeness is not permissive weakness; the therapist is quite insistent on staying with the process and confronting experience, but he or she is not insistent on one particular version of the "true content" of the client's life problems.

One function of this tentativeness is to give the client freedom to reject what the therapist says and to take some direction other than the one seen by the therapist. Many written examples of therapy seem to start out "You feel . . . ." This can be an excellent way to start a response—usually when it is pretty obvious what the client has said. In this situation, the client clearly knows that you mean to put into words what he just tried to say. When you are working ahead of the client, however, starting out with "You feel . . ." can sound as if you are telling the client what he is feeling, and the further ahead I am, the more I like to use skillful tentativeness, starting out with something like "I guess you feel . . . ." Here there can be no doubt that I am not trying to take over the process and explain things but rather want to understand. Of course, this also eases matters when you have heard the client incorrectly. If our job is mutual exploring, and I miss the point, there is no great loss; I drop back a step and try again.

Empathic Intent

As your client learns that even when you are ahead, even when you miss the point, even when the material is painful, your intent is consistently that of facilitating his or her thinking and feeling, an expectation of trust builds. If your intentions are perceived as empathic, the need for defenses against you lessens. The thoughts and feelings and things in the person's life become the sources of threat, not you. You are taking away the need for defenses in the therapy process itself. One way you do this is with skillful tentativeness.

Empathic Guesses

Once trust in your empathic intent is established, you have the foundation for making empathic guesses. These are just one way to be working ahead of the client when you are not very clear about what the implicit message is. You might start out with "This is partly a shot in the dark, and tell me if I'm off base, but when you say 'I don't know if marriage is for me,' it sounds like there's some of that old fear of confrontation eating at you." Here I am using a lot of material the client has told me in the past, but I really don't know whether this is what he's saying right now. I think it might be, so I check it out. If our relationship is based on a mood of mutual exploration, he will tell me if I'm off. If I'm hearing correctly, we'll take a big step forward together.

The obvious danger is that empathic guesses can be used to disguise sneaky interpretations. Maybe it's my little theory that his reluctance to marry has a lot to do with his fear of anger, and I'm getting impatient with his not getting around to confirming my theory. Even if he is not implying this, I could make a sneaky interpretation by making it look as though I were being empathic with "If I hear you correctly, what you're trying to say is that one thing that holds you back from marriage is that anger frightens you." It would be more honest of me just to say what my theory is. It wouldn't do much good if he's not ready for it, but at least he could deal with it as what it is—my interpretation. By dishonestly couching it in words that make it look like empathy, I make it a lot harder to deal with openly. I may even have a better chance of bringing him around to agree with me, but my experience has been that many clients recognize a sneaky interpretation as just that. How do I know this, you ask, if I haven't done some sneaky interpreting and been caught at it? Good question.

Done honestly with a client who trusts your empathic intent, empathic guesses can be a helpful occasional tool. Done dishonestly, they can undermine trust, insidiously lead the client toward incorrect beliefs and solutions (when you're wrong, which will be fairly often), and subtly lead the client toward correct beliefs and solutions (when you're right). Even this last benefit, however, is won at the price of the client's dependence on your wisdom rather than his or her own growing independence.

Lead-In Phrases

Much of the skillful tentativeness I am discussing is communicated in the first few words of the therapist's responses—in the "lead-in." This may seem a bit "techniquey," but many people have found it very useful to have a list of potential lead-in phrases. Hammond, Hepworth, and Smith (1978) present an excellent list, pointing out that it is too easy to fall into the habit of using a few favorite phrases that can come to sound artificial with overuse. In graduate school, I remember "You seem to feel . . ." as a big favorite that became so habitual with so many of us that it was silly: "You seem to feel that factor analysis would be the best approach to these data." Keep in mind that you are trying to convey skillfully tentative empathic intent, and then say what feels right.

As I told you earlier, one of the most useful lead-ins is "It sounds like . . . ." When I was writing this book, one trainee said he couldn't wait for the book to come out; I had to give him a list of lead-ins right away. After we had spent one session discussing evocative empathy he started saying "It sounds like . . . " so often that one client asked him whether he was learning a new technique. To help you with a variety of possible lead-ins, here is Hammond, Hepworth, and Smith's list.[1]

Empathic Response Leads

Kind of feeling . . .
Sort of saying . . .
As I get it, you felt that . . .
I'm picking up that you . . .
Sort of a feeling that . . .
If I'm hearing you correctly . . .
To me it's almost like you are saying, "I . . .
Sort of hear you saying that maybe you . . .
Kind of made (makes) you feel . . .
The thing you feel most right now is sort of like . . .
So you feel . . .
What I hear you saying is . . .
So, as you see it . . .
As I get it, you're saying . . .
What I guess I'm hearing is . . .
I'm not sure I'm with you, but . . .
I somehow sense that maybe you feel . . .
You feel . . .
I really hear you saying that . . .
I wonder if you're expressing a concern that . . .
It sounds as if you're indicating you . . .
I wonder if you're saying . . .
You place a high value on . . .

[1]From *Improving Therapeutic Communication*, by D. C. Hammond, D. H. Hepworth and V. G. Smith. Copyright © 1978 by Jossey-Bass, Inc., Publishers. Reprinted by permission.

It seems to you . . .
Like right now . . .
You often feel . . .
You feel, perhaps . . .
You appear to be feeling . . .
It appears to you . . .
As I hear it, you . . .
So, from where you sit . . .
Your feeling now is that . . .
I read you as . . .
Sometimes you . . .
You must have felt . . .
I sense that you're feeling . . .
Very much feeling . . .
Your message seems to be, "I . . . "
You appear . . .
Listening to you it seems as if . . .
I gather . . .
So your world is a place where you . . .
You communicate (convey) a sense of . . .

Study this list, so that if you never use one of these lead-ins exactly, you will understand how they convey empathic intent.

UNIQUE LANGUAGE

The easiest kind of therapy to master is "five phrase therapy." All you have to do is memorize the following five phrases and intersperse them judiciously in what your client says: (1) "That seems to bother you." (2) "I guess you're pulled two ways about all that." (3) "I can't help wondering how much all this means to you." (4) "Under that anger I think I hear some hurt." (5) "Under that hurt I think I hear some anger."

There. This information alone is worth the price of the whole book.

Actually, these phrases are not too bad as therapist responses, and you will hear yourself using them at times. One beginning therapist I know really did use Phrase 1 just about whenever he couldn't think what to say, and he reported that it usually worked quite well. The problem with the five phrases is that they are not exact, not specific to the experience of the client and therefore only weakly able to bring the client's experience to life.

Suppose a client said "She has a particular nasal tone of voice that she comes at me with when I feel weak, and it is most unpleasant." Notice that your client has made entirely factual statements about things outside himself. There are no reactions; he says "It is most unpleasant" rather than "I hate it." Clearly, there are a lot of feelings implied here, but the client has trouble approaching them directly. Your job is to hear what is implied and to help your client experience it. Compare the impact of your saying "That seems to bother you" with that of "When she starts that condescending whine, you seem to feel like getting away and hitting back, all at the same time." The second response has several advantages. It clearly brings the feelings to life more vividly. You are trying to help your client confront his experience—to actually feel the impact of the incidents he only described. By naming the feelings and reactions, by painting the picture vividly, you are far more likely to arouse the emotions that your client is trying to get to and to face. You have used language that is specific and concrete, that captures the precise nuance of what the client was trying to say. Your job is to name the feelings he has only implied and to name them in ways that make him confront the experience he has hinted at. The second response does all this. Another way that the second response is more helpful is that it names not only the reaction but also the cause of the reaction very specifically. I can't convey the therapist's tone of voice on this page, but I picture the words "condescending whine" being said with a hint of the tone that upsets the client so, and then the words "getting away" being said more softly, with perhaps a slightly firmer tone to "hitting back." The uniqueness of the therapist's response lies in the pregnant words used and in nonverbal voice qualities.

I want to be careful that the last few lines not lead you to be conscious of "acting" with your voice quality. Working at having the "right" voice quality would almost certainly make you sound false. What I am trying to imply is that if you are interested, intensely listening, and trying to move within what the client is experiencing, then your voice will speak quite naturally with both words and tone.

Concreteness

Truax and Carkhuff (1967) proposed the term *concreteness* to refer to avoidance of vague and abstract in favor of the specific and personal. Therapists frequently classify and categorize what clients say, trying to draw broad generalizations. This seems to come from approaching therapy as an intellectual process in which correctly identifying the causes of the client's problems will somehow cure those problems. This intellectualized approach is bad enough, but when it is coupled with attempts to place the client into categories that fit some personality theory, meaningful emotional change for this particular client with this particular set of problems becomes less likely.

When the client says, with reddening eyes, "I'm just no good . . . people would be better off without me around, damn it," a disturbing number of therapists would say "Anger, especially anger at oneself, is often an important part of depression." Finally, the therapist thinks, here's something I read about—aggression turned inward—now we're getting somewhere. But this generalized abstraction (which may be true in many cases, for all we know), with its finality, cuts off the client's exploration, as though the problem were solved; it moves the client away from current experiencing toward intellectualizing; it does not give the therapist a chance to get accurate feedback on whether he or she has heard the client correctly; and it teaches the client, by example, to deal in abstractions.

Conversely, an evocatively empathic therapist would have said something like "You can hardly stand how you're feeling about yourself right now . . . like you're a burden on others . . . it's a sadness and anger at yourself all at once, I guess."

Rice (1974) offers three words that capture the richness of the unique language required better than *concreteness* does. She says that the evocative response is *particular*, *subjective*, and *connotative*.

Particularity

The opposite of drawing generalizations and pointing out similarities among the client's experiences, the particular response focuses vividly on current experiences. Rather than draw relationships, as many therapists are fond of doing, the evocatively empathic therapist facilitates experiencing. "After a client has grasped an experience freshly in this way, he may begin to explore similarities and patterns, and get very excited about the new avenues that are opened up. However, the generalization follows rather than leads to a new experience" (Rice, 1974, p. 307).

Subjectivity

Subjective refers to the individual's internal processes and reactions, as opposed to *objective*, which refers to external, unprejudiced, detached perspectives. I have frequently noted the need to focus on reactions—to pay most attention to how the person feels in response to situations, rather than talk about the situations or even about the person's feelings.

> Rather than the usual condensed feeling words like "anxious" or "guilty" one might pick up a sense of the client feeling "stretched tight" or of feeling "dubious and slimy." Or, rather than putting a facile label on the situation being described, the therapist might make an exploratory response—"When he said that and you resigned—I'd like to get the flavor of that. Can you tell me more about what it is like?" [Rice, 1974, p. 308]

Connotativeness

One student said that the most pleasant assignment she had been given all year was when I suggested that reading good fiction could be an important way to develop a precision of language for doing therapy. Powerful prose and poetry differ from common language in some way that makes them arouse us to experience things in fresh, new ways. They use the same old words that you and I do, but fresh, vivid metaphors make us see what the novelist sees; rhythm and sound make us feel what the poet feels; sensory images carry a richness of associations that make us know what it would be like to smell or touch or hurt in certain ways.

A client might be talking about feeling confused, isolated, and rejected, and you respond "It sounds like being little and lost in a big store and feeling sick when people think it's all so funny." Or to another client, "You reach out and say 'please' and he cuts you, like he's slicing at you with a razor." Or "I guess you try not to think about all this, but it haunts you . . . always somewhere behind something ready to grab your stomach with cold hands."

Each of these examples assumes that you have accurately understood the intended message, of course.

Concise and Vivid—Not Necessarily Long

It is a lot to ask that you be particular, subjective, and connotative in the few seconds you have to respond, but it is important to remember that you do have only a few seconds. Some trainees interpret "particular," "subjective," and especially "connotative" to mean "elaborate, flowery, and dramatic." The most important principle is that your response accurately capture your client's experiencing, and this is more likely to happen if you respond concisely and vividly. Lots of words that finally get around to the issue are not nearly as effective as a few powerful ones. Your connotative language will use voice quality to heighten the power of the words, but here again, you must be sure not to "overact" and go beyond what the client will recognize as his or her experience.

Successive Approximations

It is probably obvious by now that therapy occurs in steps. The client is approaching thoughts and feelings, many of which are threatening, as closely as possible and then backing off when the discomfort starts. When you take each step with the person and "take the curse off" the threatening thoughts by talking about them openly and without discomfort of your own or rejection or judgment of the client, you help make that step less threatening. Now the person is able to go on to other material that used to be too threatening even to approach. The person is trying to get to "the truth," to accurately know his or her own experiencing. Likely we never know ourselves completely accurately, but the closer we can get, the more wisely and well we can live. You and the client are making ever more accurate explorations of what is true for the person, and you do this by successive approximations. You try to understand, and you are never completely accurate, but you get feedback and try again and explore a newly-found path and try again. Since each approximation of "the truth" is bound to be inaccurate in some way, it is held only tentatively, as a more accurate one is searched for. An implicit rule of your relationship is that nothing gets written in stone; you and the client can change your mind next week without having to defend yourselves because the mood of therapy is one of mutual search.

After observing me doing therapy, a trainee recently pointed out one way I use successive approximations, although I was not aware I did it. The example she pointed out was something like "I guess that makes you annoyed . . . angry, even." She said I seemed to start out with a less strong word and "read" the client's reaction to it as I was talking. This nonverbal feedback gave clues about whether stronger words would still be within the intended message—whether the client would recognize them as part of what he or she meant to say. The trainee articulated a useful way to get as far ahead of the client as possible without taking over direction.

A Vocabulary of Shadings

To capture accurately the complex nuances of meaning in what a particular person feels requires a large vocabulary of "feeling words." You can hardly articulate many successive approximations if your repertoire of hostile words is *mad, irritated*, and *angry*. I have often said something like "That seems to make you angry" and had the client emphatically reject my statement and back off a bit, clearly threatened. A few moments later, though, we might quite comfortably be using the word *annoyed*. Perhaps I was right that what the client was experiencing was anger, but I clearly had gone beyond the intended message with a clumsily too-heavy word. My guess is that, shortly, this client and I will be talking about anger, but we will have to approach it through more finely-shaded gradations of meaning. You also have to be sensitive to what particular words mean to particular clients. With one client I remember, the word *anger* meant violent screaming and physical abuse, and it took me some time to figure out why some of my responses were so threatening.

In the last paragraph, I put *feeling words* in quotation marks because the job of developing a vocabulary of finely shaded meanings goes beyond what are traditionally thought of as "feeling words." Hostile words, for example, can include *miffed, irked, impatient, annoyed, irritated, resentful, bitter* and *furious*, but they also can include *gagging on screams, twitching*, and *stretched tight*, depending on the person doing the feeling. Each of these words has a different meaning (which is why they all exist, obviously), and clearly you need to have the most complete vocabulary you can.

The following paragraphs offer a sample of common feeling words and their shadings taken from a thesaurus and dictionary of synonyms. (Hammond, Hepworth, and Smith, 1978, present a similar list.) All this list does, though, is give you a start toward developing a usable vocabulary. It would be a good exercise to work up your own list, including regional terms or faddish terms for various feelings. Study this list, and then choose one word and try to think of as many shadings of meaning as you can to that one word. Imagine a client in front of you describing the feeling.

Unhappy words can include *dejected, low, sad, depressed, down, lost, blue, melancholy, brood, dreary, flat, joyless, downhearted, somber, gloomy, dreadful, dismal, empty, grim, desolate, hopeless, mourning, desperate, blah, glum, disappointed, aching, anguish, grieving, rotten, barren, awful, teary*, and *terrible*. Study this list or listen to lots of sad country songs.

Affection words: *love, friendly, caring, like, fond of, respect, admire, trust, close, adore, devoted, regard, tenderness, attachment, yearning, longing, infatuated, fellowship, attraction, favor, prize, hold dear, fall for, passionate, pitch woo* (pitch woo?), *revere, cherish,* and *idolize.*

Guilt words: *blame, regret, shame, embarrassed, at fault, reprehensible, wrong, remorseful, crummy, rotten, humiliated, unforgivable, mortified, ashamed,* and *disgraceful.*

Anger words: *resentment, irritation, rage, fury, annoyance, provoked, infuriated, inflamed, displeasure, animosity, wrath, indignation, exasperation, pique, huff, miff, sore, bitter, temper, hate, fume, dander, ferment, tiff, passion* (sometimes), *sullen, morose, bristle, bridle, sulk, pout, frown, chafe, seethe, boil, rage, offend, rile, aggravate, rankle, worked up, cross, burning, pissed off, outraged, ticked off, hateful, vengeful,* and *mad.* There sure are a lot of these words.

Fear words: *timid, diffident, anxious, worried, apprehensive, misgiving, doubt, qualm, hesitant, fright, terror, horror, dismay, panic, consternation, scared, nervous, restless, trepidation, quivering, shaking, trembling, intimidated, cold sweat, dread, despondent, creeps, shivers, jitters, cower, afraid, tremulous, vulnerable, butterflies, jumpy, worried, uneasy,* and *unsure.*

Confused words: *bewildered, puzzled, flustered, overwhelmed, mixed up, muddled, perplexed, tumult, chaos, jumbled, uncertain, undecided, ambivalent, drifting, baffled, trapped, in a quandary, tangled, scrambled, unraveled, disjointed, swamped, drowning,* and *frustrated.*

Happy words: *contented, joyous, ecstatic, glad, cheerful, glee, optimistic, hopeful, alive, lively, merry, exhilarated, jovial, satisfied, comfortable, animated, inspired, elated, encouraged, heartened, refreshed, genial, light, buoyant, bright, saucy, jolly, playful, exultant, pleased, gratified, zest, bliss, thrilled, tickled, sensational, terrific, euphoric, enthusiastic, glowing, neat, good,* and *fine.* Actually, there are a lot of these too.

Hurt words: *neglected, put down, rejected, demeaned, scorned, used, criticized, belittled, shot down, cast off, discarded, let down, disappointed, devastated, humiliated, betrayed, harmed, embarrassed, dumped on, ripped off, disillusioned, disparaged, maligned, laughed at,* and *exploited.*

Strength words: *responsible, confident, adequate, powerful, certain, sure, efficient, important, competent, effective, superior, cope,* potent, able, lucid, adaptable, forceful, effectual, incisive, influential, growing, moving forward, and alive.

This, quite obviously, is only a start. I have left out dozens of good words, and so you should make your own long list, in addition to reading all that good fiction. An important thing to note is that many of these words, although they carry useful nuances of meaning, are not common words, and particular clients may not know their meaning. If you are to communicate understanding, you obviously must match your words to your client. If you are being skillfully tentative, you will be getting regular feedback on your accuracy, and this will give you a chance to check out whether your words are the right ones for this person.

WHEN YOU MISS

These last chapters have set you a difficult task—not impossible, but difficult. You must hear well and you must articulate accurately and quickly. To top it all off, you will inevitably be wrong at times and must be ready to deal with these errors. The risk is that you will become defensive and worry about "losing face" when you miss, but this risk is greatly diminished if your goal really is to understand rather than to look like an expert. Your skillful tentativeness, for all the good things it does for the client, also covers you when you misunderstand. Because you make it easy for the client to disagree with you, you make it easy for yourself to say "I missed on that one . . . say some more and let me try to understand it again."

In this case, missing means misunderstanding the intended message. When you say something that the client rejects or backs away from, you may have been quite right in some ultimate sense, but it won't do therapy any good to try to establish the accuracy of your opinion. It's not the truth that sets the client free nearly so much as it is the process of finding the truth. I had one client who told me about a dream in which he was forcing an ice cream cone down a woman's throat. I didn't have to be too clever or even very Freudian to see symbolism in this, and I gave in to the temptation to be clever, saying "I wonder if there is some sexual and aggressive meaning to your dream." The client thought I was way off base and told me so, and I reluctantly backed off. About six weeks later, he said "Do you remember that dream I had about the ice cream cone? I think I see something in it . . . I think it had a lot to do with how I see women and how anger and sex are mixed up together for me." I'll never know whether my comment delayed or speeded up his figuring this out (I suspect it slowed things down), but he saw it when he was ready. I am quite sure that if I had pursued the issue and convinced him of the accuracy of my interpretation, I could have made him agree with me intellectually but actually prevented his emotional growth by making him defend himself against me and against the feelings surrounding sex and aggression.

One last word of reassurance for when you miss: you can make a lot of mistakes and miss a lot of things, but the client will repeatedly try to return to the issues that matter most. If you are consistently off, the client will give up on you, but you can trust the client to continually approach the things she needs to deal with, as closely as she can stand to. Chapters 15 and 16 will discuss why you can trust the client in this way.

CHAPTER FOUR

Confronting Experience

One student described this approach to therapy as "continuously confronting the client. Each thing the therapist says is a little confrontation, even though it is said gently." He was right, and there are useful things to learn from what he said, as long as we are clear about what the word *confrontation* means. Most people seem to use *confrontation* to mean that the therapist is pointing out discrepancies in the client's thinking and presenting alternative views that the client hasn't seen or can't see for himself or herself. These things are presented in a challenging way. In contrast, the confrontation that occurs in evocatively empathic therapy is done by being a step ahead of clients and facing them with the meaning of what they said. In a sense, it is self-confrontation, done in the "spirit of accurate empathy" (Egan, 1982). The therapist, however, is not passive either. He or she confronts the client with the implied part of what the client says and thus makes the client confront his or her experiences. Patterson recognizes this when he says "It is possible that confrontation should not be considered as a separate condition or dimension of psychotherapy. . . . The recognition and communication of discrepancies in the client's verbalizations and behaviors does seem to be an aspect of empathy" (1974, p. 77).

As has been true so often before in our discussion, much depends on the therapist's intent. An empathic confrontation does not communicate "Here, let me point out to you things you should have seen but haven't"; it communicates "You seem to feel many different ways all at the same time; let me put it all into words so we can look at it together." The therapist can help the client confront his or her own experience with a comment like "As I hear you, you feel both ways—you think bosses are unfair, and you worry that you don't perceive other people, bosses included, accurately. It's hard to know what's true."

COMBINING COGNITIVE AND EMOTIONAL

One of the most important lessons in this book is that effective therapy (effective living, for that matter) requires an integration of cognitive and emotional functioning. Some therapy approaches, most notably Ellis's (1962), assume that cognitions determine emotions, while other, "experiential" approaches focus on unstructured feelings, "letting it all hang out." There is good reason to believe, however, that emotional reactions and preferences can be established independently of cognitive activity (Zajonc, 1980, 1981; Chapters 14 and 15 of this book), and it is clear that some degree of rationality is required to survive and live an effective life. I suspect that some of the "pure experience" approaches to therapy developed as a reaction against the powerfully intellectualized nature of more traditional therapy, and it is my impression too that much of the therapy practiced by professionals educated in our university systems tends toward "pure cognition." There is, in fact, a growing trend toward cognitive approaches, which have many strengths but which also seem to teach that cognition controls all, including emotional responses. Cognitive and emotional functioning are closely intertwined, but they can and do operate independently too. Fears, for example, are the result of conditioning experiences, and although "expectations" and "preferences" and other cognitions become involved in them, a well established principle of conditioning is that *the only way to get rid of a fear is to feel it.* In other words, changing emotions requires emotional experiencing. Sometimes talking gets rid of fears but not because one can reason away the fear; rather, in the process of the talking, some of the fear is aroused and has a chance to extinguish.

Therapy is both a rational process and a "corrective emotional experience" (Alexander, 1948). When helping the client confront himself or herself emotionally, the therapist provides the client with an opportunity to feel fears and other emotions in a safe setting and to solve problems. Material that used to be too emotionally threatening to be clearly thought becomes available to think with—to find new solutions that permit more effective living outside of therapy.

Conclusions versus Experiences

As I will say many times, many therapists tend toward cognitive solutions. This could reflect a North American cultural bias (Messer & Winokur, 1980) toward a belief in rationality and the pioneering spirit that believes there is a workable solution to every problem if we just lay out the steps and follow them. It certainly reflects the fact that to become a professional in our educational system, you must use intellectual prowess nearly exclusively. In therapeutic style, this seems to result in therapists who are constantly searching for *conclusions*. Conclusions and insights are important, let me repeat, but the therapist's job is to set up the conditions within which the client can come to the conclusions, and this is done by facilitating experiencing.

Shaping toward Experiencing

A therapist I know once said to me "I just don't have the patience to shape clients the way you do." He meant this as a criticism and politely worded advice that therapy goes a lot faster if the therapist controls the process more and tells the client more from the therapist's point of view. I am quite sure that this particular therapist did not understand the nature of evocative empathy and saw it as relatively passive, and I am quite sure that the apparent speed of his more directive approach was an illusion, an observation I will discuss more in Chapter 16. What really interested me, though, was his use of the word *shape*. He was using it, of course, in the operant-conditioning sense of reinforcing small steps, or successive approximations of the final desired behavior. It would detract from therapy to be sitting there thinking in terms of delivering reinforcers for successive approximations, but in a sense that is what is happening when you see through the client's eyes and help him or her confront experiences.

One common way to move clients toward dealing with feelings is to ask "How did you feel about that?" In this case, you might get to feelings, but they will be ones you drew out of the client, and, more important, your question implies that you did not hear whatever feelings were implicit in the client's message. By asking the question, you lose the facilitative effects of an empathic response. In contrast, you could articulate the reactions implied in what the client said, and now the client is emitting the feelings, rather than having them elicited by you. Most important, she has been rewarded for making the approach to feelings that she did, however subtle and incomplete that may have been. By responding in an empathic and accepting way to that part of the message, you are rewarding experiencing behavior—in a sense, "shaping" toward more complete experiencing.

While we're talking in these learning terms, consider for a moment the effect of your behavior in terms of modeling or imitation. When you use experience-oriented words, made more meaningful and poignant by nonverbal parts of your response, you are teaching by example that therapy is a process of exploration and experiencing. In contrast, when you ask questions, even questions like "How do you feel?," to some extent you are teaching by example that an intellectual approach is called for. This is especially true when the therapist consistently engages in rational analysis of feelings, searching for the "correct conclusions." Such a therapist resembles the parent who says "If you hit your sister one more time, I'm gonna hit you," teaching one lesson with the words and, unawares, the opposite lesson more powerfully with behavior.

Preventing Avoidance Gently

One reason your client is in trouble is that he fears[1] his or her own thoughts, memories, feelings, and impulses—internal processes of which he is only partly aware. The only way to get rid of a fear is to feel it, but we all avoid the things we fear, and this is one reason fears are so persistent. For your client, the feared thoughts and feelings are usually avoided too quickly to be dealt with, and so they can still cause bad feelings but never be faced directly. This also means that the client can't solve life problems wisely because some of the "truth" is too painful to look at.

You gently prevent the avoidance of these thoughts in a step-by-step way by articulating the implicit message. You put into words what the client *is trying to say and can't quite say* and thus help him face what he would normally have avoided. He faces the mildly painful thoughts in the safe surroundings of your relationship, nothing bad happens, and the fear dissipates (extinguishes, actually), so that the client feels fear reduction.

Look at the powerful thing you have done. The client made some response *that came from him,* felt some fear, and then felt relief. Fear reduction is one of the most powerful reinforcers of human behavior, and what you have done is to help your client feel fear reduction immediately after an act of self-confrontation. If this happens hundreds of times in therapy, as it should, your client will become more and more self-confrontative, more open to his own experience.

[1]The word *fear* is used very broadly here and includes many aversive emotions, such as guilt, shame, and anxiety.

Facing Fear, Facing Joy

There is good reason that I focus so much on the role of fear in discussing therapy, but we must remember that one of our goals is an openness to *all* experiences—an openness that is necessary to live a full, complete life. As the therapist listens, he or she is not just trying to hear pain but is listening for *poignancy*, for the central part of whatever experience the client is moving toward. Often that will include pain, but sometimes it will be a mixture of pain and joy; sometimes it will be only joy or affection; sometimes it will be peaceful; sometimes it will be chaotic or angry. Your job is to facilitate experiencing, not to determine which experiences are the appropriate ones.

Reprocessing Experience

The last few paragraphs have used learning principles to explain how self-confrontation helps the client. The language of information processing theory can give a different perspective on the same process.[2] There is good reason to think (Ornstein, 1977) that each person's perception of reality is a "construction," a perceived version of reality that is not accurate but is limited by selective perception and by the distortions imposed by "schemes" (Rice, 1974) that we develop. These "schemes" are like templates that we fit reality to; they are what we expect to perceive, and we tend to perceive what we expect to perceive. Bruner (1962) reports an experiment in which people saw playing cards flashed quickly and were told to name each card. Occasionally an "anomalous" card, such as a red six of spades, was flashed, and many subjects reported it as a six of hearts. They "saw" what they expected to see. Similarly, the "schemes" within which we perceive life are limited and prematurely close off our processing of experience. An evocative empathy response prevents this closing off and forces continued processing of the experience by "putting the person back into the situation" in a vivid way.

Experiential Focusing

Gendlin (1962, 1969, 1974, 1978) has emphasized as strongly as anyone that emotional growth requires both cognitive and experiential involvement. He argues that "direct experiencing is 'implic-

---

[2] See Chapters 14, 15, and 16 for a more complete integration of the theoretical issues involved.

itly' rich in meanings, but is never equatable to words or concepts" (1974, p. 227).[3] He thus makes it clear that we have a complex challenge in therapy: our tool is language, but much of what matters most cannot be adequately expressed in language. It can be felt, but the *felt sense* is a physical process that is only inadequately expressible in concepts. Gendlin has developed a method called *focusing* to help the therapist and client engage in a process that deals with direct experiencing. When the client directly experiences his or her felt sense, there is a noticeable sensation of resolution or falling-into-place that Gendlin calls a *felt shift*. Afterward, this felt shift might well be followed by better conceptual or intellectual understanding, but an enormous amount has happened at the experiential level that simply cannot be expressed.

Focusing involves an explicit procedure for paying attention to what's going on inside the person's body. Gendlin (1978) argues that anyone can learn to focus and that most therapists simply do not facilitate the process; in fact, they often hamper the client's experiencing process. In therapy, "if clients do not, of their own accord, engage in this every few minutes, I try to bring it about. I ask people to stop talking and to sense inwardly into themselves. Let it form and let it tell you what it is" (1974, p. 228).

Gendlin's writings seem to give the therapist a role as somewhat more directive of the process than what I have been recommending, and so it is important for me to clarify this issue. In practice, Gendlin strongly argues that whatever else a therapist does, she or he must constantly return to the "baseline" of empathic responding. "Only in this way can the therapist stay constantly in touch with what is occurring in the person, and thus know and help make good use of whatever beneficial results other therapeutic procedures may have" (1974, p.216). He makes the "very serious charge . . . that most therapists leave their patients inwardly alone. . . . One does not know what is happening for the person just now. Thus, one is blind. [Empathy] is not just one of many ways, but a precondition for the other ways" (p. 217). Even when he is instructing the client to focus, the spirit of what he does quite clearly is designed to leave the control of the therapy process in the client's hands. My impression is that the only real difference between us in how we do therapy is

---

[3]From "Client-Centered and Experiential Psychotherapy," by E. T. Gendlin. In D. A. Wexler and L. N. Rice (Eds.), *Innovations in Client-Centered Therapy.* Copyright © 1974 by John Wiley & Sons, Inc. This and all other quotations from this source are reprinted by permission of John Wiley & Sons, Inc.

that I think evocative empathy, done well, facilitates the same experiential focusing for the client as does Gendlin's more explicitly guided focusing process.

THERAPIST AS CHICKEN—
INTELLECTUALIZING IS EASY

One therapist in training was having trouble staying focused on emotional issues with his clients, and as we discussed how difficult therapy was, he suddenly realized that a lot of his difficulty came from his fear of dealing with feelings. He said he liked to offer explanations and make interpretations and look for causes and categorize things because that was what he knew how to do, and it kept him from getting too involved with the client. Meaningful as this insight was to him, however, it did not suddenly make it easy to plunge into evocative responding; understanding an emotional reaction is not enough by itself to change that reaction, for us as well as for our clients. You have heard this somewhere before, but the only way to get rid of a fear is to feel it, and only through practice and getting feedback and facing your own fears of feelings will you become comfortable with experience-oriented therapy.

The MUM Effect

We have a strong tendency to avoid giving bad news to others, the MUM effect (Tesser & Rosen, 1972). Partly, we fear negative reactions from the other person; partly, it makes us feel bad to feel like the cause of painful feelings in the other person. Egan (1982) has said that the MUM effect often keeps counselors and therapists from using confrontation, and if every evocatively empathic response is a self-confrontation, there will be many times when you will be making your clients face painful things. I remember vividly the first time a client started weeping in therapy. I was scared that maybe this process didn't really work, and what was I going to do if she couldn't stop, and what if I was making her *worse* somehow by making her feel so bad. Now I do trust the process (which may be small comfort to you when your clients start weeping), and many of my clients cry at some point in therapy—and not because I'm mean. Many therapists have said that this is one of the hardest things about doing therapy; it takes time and experience and personal strength to be able to go through intense emotional pain with another person who matters to you.

The "Maybe It's Because" Game

The favorite refuge of cowardly therapists is to look for causes of problems in the past, and clients are only too happy to go along with the game. A common stereotype of therapy is that the client suddenly has a blinding flash of insight in which it all comes clear that his inability to deal with authority figures stems from the time his father beat him with a studded belt because he kissed his mother too often. I'm being a bit flip, but the stereotype is distressingly common. In fact, most clients make their progress and find their insights in small steps over a period of time. They often are surprised to find themselves much better as they look back on old problems that now seem so remote it is as though some other person had the problem. "I don't see how it could have been from therapy," they say, "because I didn't really have any big insights." The changes have come from incremental emotional and cognitive experiences, not from smashing insights.

Remarkable "aha" experiences of sudden insight do occur in therapy sometimes, and they probably stand out in our memories because of their power. The misleading part is if they lead us to think that it was the new knowledge that was the whole source of therapeutic gain. It is not the truth alone that frees the client but also the process of finding the truth. The client's problem has been that the truth was too painful to look at, and so the feelings must change, through gradual exposure to the thoughts and feelings, to permit the insight to occur. Sometimes the insight brings emotional growth; sometimes the emotional growth brings insight. Both cognitive and emotional processes are essential parts of therapy, and the therapist's search for causes is usually a way to avoid the emotional part of the process.

CONFRONTATION

All of this chapter has been an attempt to redefine the word *confrontation*. Its usual meaning carries an aggressive, shake-'em-up-good connotation that implies that the therapist is the expert who has to guide the client toward the truth.

Abuses of Confrontation

Things that some therapists say in describing their behavior with particular clients include "What he needed was a good swift boot in the rear to get off that self-pitying stuff" and "I told him it was time to shit or get off the pot" and "I pointed out to her that for all her talk about wanting to make friends, the way she treated them was designed to drive friends away." To use the language of learning principles, these comments reflect a punitive approach to therapy. Evocatively empathic therapy uses confrontative responses in a way that rewards (with fear reduction) problem solving by the client. Traditional confrontations are attempts to punish the failure to problem-solve. Put this way, the long-term effects of the two approaches become clearer. Punishment is popular because it *seems* to work quickly, since the other person shows rapid behavior change *if the punisher holds sufficient coercive power.* Long term change is unlikely, however, for several reasons. Punishment only teaches what not to do; it does not reinforce the more desired behavior. Punishment only suppresses the punished behavior; it does not weaken the behavior, since the only way to do that is through extinction. Punishment causes a lot of unintended aversive effects, such as punishing the child for being in school or the client for being in therapy, in addition to punishing the targeted behavior. Punishment often requires the continued presence of the punisher's coercive power (Martin, 1976).

Evocatively empathic therapy, in contrast, is based on principles of reward, of positive reinforcement. "People do what they are reinforced for doing" is a powerful truth. In contrast to the effects of punishment, positive approaches specifically establish desirable behavior, making the undesirable behavior unnecessary. Positive approaches reward interaction with the parent or teacher or friend or therapist, in addition to rewarding particular behaviors. Positive approaches establish the independence of the other person.

In a way, I have been too harsh with the people who made the comments at the beginning of this section. I can share their frustration at passive acceptance of the client's evasive behavior, contradictory verbalizations and actions, and whining. But a direct attack on these things will only bring, at best, a temporary compliance and, at worst, a building of new and stronger defenses against the therapist. I think some of this frustration grows out of a lack of familiarity with a workable alternative. Passive approaches seem so futile.

In the Spirit of Accurate Empathy
The alternative they seek is an active, confrontative-of-experience let's-explore-all-the-edges way of facing the client with what he or she has said. It is critical that this be done in the spirit of empathy.

The therapist's intention is to make it clear that the client is the source of new knowledge, and the therapist's role is to keep the client working at the edges of his or her thinking and feeling. Cameron (1963) says it nicely:

> The good therapist does not of course coerce his patient to move too rapidly into sensitive areas. As French has often expressed it, the good therapist, like the good gardener, waits until he recognizes something which is struggling to emerge and then makes it easier for it to emerge. He never tries to drag anything up from the unconscious or deep preconscious into awareness [p. 769].

Cameron speaks from a psychoanalytic viewpoint, but the attitude of the good therapist could hardly be better described.

Contradictions and Distortions

The traditional confrontation says "Aha, I've caught you in a contradiction," while the empathic confrontation says "I can understand your confusion when you feel both X and Y at the same time." Both responses focus on the contradiction, but the second one does not *judge* it. The second response just says "We have to look at this to see where we're going next."

Similarly with distortions. Only if distortions are based on a *lack of information* can you talk a person out of them. In most cases, distortions will be based on the inability to use information that, objectively, is just as available to the client as it is to you, and persuasion is probably worse than nothing because the client will have to defend the distortion or, worse, give you a "Yes, doctor" response and quietly withdraw. I remember a client whose problem clearly involved a sexual incident for which the police had threatened him with legal action. Early in therapy, the client said "Well, I'm sure that sex doesn't have anything to do with all this." I nearly choked, since he had talked so much about the incident. My response was "So the way you see it, sex isn't a central part of this . . . it looks now like the important part is worrying about losing control and doing something you don't even know you're doing." Notice that I haven't agreed with him or disagreed with him—my version of the truth is not an important part of our process together. I am sure that a direct confrontation would have stopped him dead, although I probably could have done better than I did by including in my response some reference to the incident, while still acknowledging that it was not central to him. This particular client was in therapy for a relatively long time, but it is interesting that near the end of therapy he said "It's pretty obvious that all of this I've been through has centered around sex."

The fastest way to really get to the truth is to make the truth bearable.

Arguing with Clients

One bind that you automatically avoid by adopting an empathic mutual-exploration stance is that of arguing with your clients in order to save your own face or pride. I hope no therapist would have an out-and-out argument with a client, but it is not uncommon for therapists to engage in subtle arguments, with what we might politely call "firm persuasion." If you have a pet theory or interpretation or piece of advice that the client rejects, you are in a position where you must either back down, in the sense of losing out, or argue the client into backing down and accepting what you say. As with most direct attacks, this forces the client to defend against you and what you say and is almost always counterproductive. If you win the argument, you will have intellectual compliance but you cannot have emotional change, as that comes from the client's experiencing. If you win the argument and are wrong, you will have led the client down, at best, a blind alley and, at worst, a destructive course. Unless you are irrationally arrogant, you must admit that at least some of what you would tell a client has to be wrong. What are the consequences when you impose such advice on a client?

You are an expert on the process of therapy but not on the content of this particular client's therapy. You keep the client working in a particular way but not on any particular content that you determine. Thus, you are never wrong; you may hear incorrectly, but if you do, you simply say so and try again. There is no need to argue.

The State of the Relationship

Earlier I referred to confrontation done in the spirit of accurate empathy and to confrontation being a part of evocative empathy. In the first chapter I also talked about different intensities of interaction at different stages of therapy. Both these observations are related to how "confrontative" the therapist can be and still be facilitative.

To repeat the fundamental principle, the therapist responds to the message that the client intends to be saying. Later in therapy, the client will trust the therapist to be nonjudgmental, to respect the client, to be honest, and to be willing to be tentative and nonauthoritarian to a much greater extent than she will trust these things early in therapy. Thus, the client will be trying to say more later in therapy, and the therapist will have much more freedom to respond to implicit material without threatening the client. I will devote Chapter 6 to the incredibly complex issues of the therapeutic relationship, but for now it is important to name those aspects of the relationship that make the confrontativeness of evocative empathy effective. A number of writers talk about those who "are entitled to confront" (Carkhuff & Berenson, 1977; Berenson & Mitchell, 1974). The entitlement to confront must be earned through the development of a good relationship.

Expertness versus Empathic Intent

A lot of your style as a therapist will have to do with how you picture your role. If it is important to you to be an expert, and one of your motives for being a therapist is to have direct control over others, you will have a lot of discomfort with this approach to therapy. In the direct sense, you must give up control and operate in an egalitarian way. Obviously, however, if all I have discussed is true, you will have an enormous influence, but as a facilitator, not a controller. This is not the place to examine your motives for being a therapist (although you should do that somewhere), but the need to be an expert is an important issue in understanding the place of confrontation in your therapy.

Advantages of Self-Confrontation

To summarize, then, your job is to help the client confront the implications of what she is saying. In doing this, you reward self-exploration, you help make frightening thoughts and feelings less frightening, you help the client become a strong problem solver, you reward her for talking to you, you help her open up to emotional sensitivity in general, and you facilitate the solving of immediate problems.

DEFENSIVENESS AND RESISTANCE

Some people come to therapy in great pain, while others come with life difficulties but little felt emotion. Therapy will usually go faster for the first than for the second group because they are more strongly motivated to change and because they are more sharply feeling whatever it is that is bothering them. The well-defended client, in contrast, has worked out ways of avoiding emotional pain and will have difficulty giving up those defenses. Briefly (more on this in Chapter 15), he has, consciously and unconsciously, developed avoidance behaviors that include partly inhibiting frightening thoughts and feelings. The therapy process asks that he give up these defenses and face pain, as a first step toward a better solution to life. This is a lot to ask and is the main reason therapy with highly defended people takes longer.

Mistrustful Clients

One subtle kind of resistance comes from a general mistrust of others. This doesn't have to be an obvious suspiciousness. It can be a fearful holding back; it can be a frustrated inability to think of anything to say—an inability that puzzles and confuses the client; it can be verbal diarrhea that never stops to let the therapist get close to anything. Intimacy of any kind inevitably involves vulnerability to the other person, who gains the power to hurt you to the extent that you reveal your weaknesses to him or her. Most human emotional problems have a lot to do with previous relationships in one way or another, and so it is no surprise that clients have trouble trusting their therapists enough to make themselves vulnerable. Trust must be earned through dependable acceptance, through respect, through being nonjudgmental, through not hurting the other person, and through dependable understanding. These things take time to develop, and to the extent that trust is a problem, therapy demands patience.

Deeply mistrustful, strongly suspicious clients are very difficult to work with, and it is especially important to be sensitive to the limits of the intended message. You can sometimes make "empathic guesses" with clients who trust you, but it is important to "stay close" to the message with very untrusting clients.

Intellectualizing

I have been pretty hard on therapists who intellectualize a lot, arguing that they don't do very good therapy. One reason they don't is that their style feeds right into one of the most effective of the defenses against feelings. If feelings are hard to handle, as they are for many (probably most) people who seek therapy, there is great relief in dealing with everything at a cognitive level. You can even talk *about* feelings and analyze them to death without letting yourself know you are actually avoiding feelings. Surely, the person thinks, if I talk about feelings all the time and even join discussion groups where we discuss the nature of emotion, I'm a feeling person. Rational analysis does serve us well in controlling many aspects of life, and so we read books about positive thinking and try to talk ourselves out of and into different feelings.

The insidious thing about intellectualization by the client is that it can so easily draw the therapist into a similar style. Like the therapist mentioned earlier, we're comfortable with ideas and rational analysis. You survived the educational system this long not by being emotionally sensitive but by being an organized thinker. In Chapter 17 we will look at some evidence that indicates that graduate school can make people worse therapists than when they started, primarily because of the stress on intellectualization.

To repeat, though, we are not going to abandon reason for "pure feeling"; we are going to try to integrate the two. When the client says "There is an aspect of our marriage that fits the general notion of increasing isolation in the middle stages of a relationship," you will know that he has made an important emotional statement, but in intellectual terms. A direct attack might be to say "You are talking about your marriage in intellectual terms. How do you feel about it?" Here you are trying to get him to the feelings, an excellent goal, but you have not acknowledged that he was *trying* to talk about feelings. He might say, in response to your question, "Well, the isolation is the hardest part." This is sort of a feeling response, but he is still talking about feelings rather than experiencing them. You might have said "So you're pretty lonely for the way she used to love you." It's the same meaning as his statement but worded in a subtly different way that makes all the difference.

Taking Away the Need for Defenses

Therapy with well-defended clients can be frustratingly slow. Most writers on therapy agree that there is no fast way to do such therapy, although there is disagreement about what is the fastest of the slow approaches to use. The therapist's frustration often leads to a desire to attack the client's defenses directly, and some therapists recommend this technique for defensive clients (Reich, 1949; Ellis, 1962; Carkhuff & Berenson, 1967). Defensiveness, however, has developed for such clients through the process of anxiety reduction and has, in this sense, been "successful." To the extent that such defenses are anxiety-reducing, they have been strongly established and can be given up only with considerable pain. Truax and Carkhuff (1967) say that the research literature suggests a poor prognosis for very defensive clients, regardless of the approach used.

The client will not give up the defenses as long as the need for them exists. We must somehow take away the need for the defenses, admitting to ourselves that this is going to take a long time.

The dilemma a therapist faces is how to respond empathically to the client whose verbalizations seem primarily defensive. The therapist might fear that empathic and accepting responses to defensive verbalizations will reinforce the client's defenses. To some extent this is possible. However, by confronting and attacking the defenses, the therapist is punishing the client's few self-exploratory responses and establishing himself or herself as a source of aversive feelings. The therapist's job can be described as taking away the client's need for defenses within the therapy hour by not being an anxiety arouser himself or herself and by offering understanding and acceptance without punishing the client for being defensive. It is unlikely that any client's verbalizations are entirely defensive. The client will be trying to approach troubling feelings and then backing off. It is the therapist's job to hear these attempts and to articulate them in a nonthreatening way.

I am saying all this more strongly than I did some years ago (Martin, 1972) because I am now more convinced that defensive clients can benefit from therapy, but the therapist must enter such therapy with the knowledge that a commitment of time and effort is required. There are limits to what therapy can do, and there are limits on what you can do; this is one of the times when it is important to know what those limits are.

A Different View of Confrontation

Carkhuff and Berenson (1967) call defensive clients "low-level functioning" clients and argue that therapy with these clients "must be on the therapist's terms" (p. 182). Direct guidance of the discussion, active intervention, and confrontation are recommended, and Carkhuff and Berenson offer some evidence (Pierce & Drasgow, 1969) that confrontation facilitates client self-exploration when it is offered by a therapist functioning at high levels of empathy, genuineness, and respect for the client. Pierce and Drasgow used these notions to study one-hour therapy sessions with three hospitalized veterans being treated for war injuries. During the session, each "client" received 20 minutes of therapist responses described as "classical nondirective reflection"; 20 minutes of "conflict attention," which was defined as "going beyond reflection . . . by confronting the client with what he has not said between the lines, or what he has implied apart from the utilized content, or with any of the various implications of what he has said at deeper levels of meaning." If whatever we add amounts to focusing on a conflict, then we have "conflict attention," (p. 341); and finally, 20 minutes during which both reflection and conflict attention were withheld. Client self-exploration was greatest during the segment of conflict attention, next greatest following reflection, and least during the period of withholding. None of this is very surprising, since "conflict attention" sounds very similar to evocative empathy, as I have been discussing it. I suspect that much of the disagreement over the use of confrontation is semantic. If "conflict attention" is what is meant by *confrontation*, then there is no problem with this disagreement.

Carkhuff and Berenson's approach to confrontation, however, clearly goes beyond evocative empathy when they are dealing with "low-level functioning" clients. Their descriptions and examples suggest a direct attack on the client's defenses, with therapist interventions such as "Right now shut up Stan!—and you listen to me (reaches over and shakes the client by the shoulders and shouts) Damn! You think too much—listen!" (p. 183). This approach is clearly inconsistent with evocative empathy, mainly because the therapist has taken over the process and is using a punitive approach. It is possible that this incident would increase the client's attention to therapy, perhaps making him try harder to listen, and maybe even giving him some feeling that the therapist was really interested and cared about him. These gains, however, are won at a price that need not be paid. Such attacks face the client with either defending against the therapist, perhaps by having a "flight into health" and suddenly getting "well," or dependently conforming to the therapist's admonitions.

Carkhuff and Berenson might argue that evocative empathy would be much slower, but I would answer that comparisons of speed are completely misleading because the two approaches end up with very different results.

Assuming Good Intentions

There is something about these last few sections that is troublesome. I have been talking about "very defensive clients" as though they were a diagnostic group that is somehow different from other clients.

Like nearly all human problems, defensiveness is on a continuum. We are all defensive to some degree, for the same reasons that "very defensive" people are, and we all have difficulty giving up our defenses, in the very same way that "very defensive" people do. The principles are all the same; what I want to do is to alert you to the difficult issues that defensiveness brings, not to start you looking for a category of clients that are "very defensive" and should be either avoided or treated differently.

The effective therapist (maybe even the effective person) assumes good intentions on the client's part. At the very least, it is clear that every client is trying to live the best life he or she can. Sometimes clients (and the rest of us too) do things that are destructive to themselves and others, but there are reasons for such behaviors. The effective therapist believes in the importance of personal responsibility but has little use for the concept of blame in under-standing human behavior. Seen this way, defensiveness loses some of its power to frustrate the therapist, whose job it is to facilitate the client's good intentions—the client's attempts to live the best life he or she can. If distortions block good living, it is our job to help take away the need for the distortions.

CHAPTER FIVE

The Basic Principle—
The Client Is the
Problem Solver

The fundamental philosophical basis of this approach to therapy is that the client is responsible for his own life and that he is capable of solving his own problems, with a special kind of help from the therapist.[1] This principle has a lot of implications for the therapist's role—implications that are not always obvious to therapists, implications that I will explore in this chapter.

I will also stress that therapy and counseling are very much problem-solving processes. I have been pretty hard on intellectualizing clients and therapists, and for good reason, but I must now repeat that therapy is neither a process of "pure reason" nor one of "pure feeling." Some approaches to therapy argue that cognitions determine emotions (Ellis, 1962), while others stress encountering current experiencing and prohibit talking *about* feelings (Perls, 1970). Cognitions do affect feelings to some extent, and feelings do distort cognitions to some extent. However, there is good reason to think that thinking and feeling can operate independently of each other (Zajonc, 1980, 1981), and it seems clear that both are important—that effective therapy *integrates* them. The client is trying to solve real-life problems, and the therapist helps with this by helping the client face thoughts and feelings that are too painful for the client to face alone. Both thinking and feeling become clearer and lead to more effective living.

---

[1]This statement of principle refers to the treatment of anxiety-based disorders. Later chapters will discuss modifications of approach required for some antisocial behavior and some severe thought disorders.

SOLVING PROBLEMS, GETTING STRONG

All approaches to therapy are aimed at solving the client's problems, and nearly all say that one of their goals is increased independence and personal responsibility on the client's part. But there is a strange paradox here if the therapist is the primary problem solver. In a way, the therapist is saying "You be independent because I am telling you to." If the client does the problem solving, he or she gains *two* benefits, and in the long run, the second benefit may be the more important. The person's current life problems get solved, *and* the person has gone through the process of problem solving—of facing internal experiences and successfully and independently thinking his or her way through. Like my client who said "I did this myself! You never did anything but say back to me what I just said, only you said it a little stronger," your clients will leave therapy stronger. Your goal as a therapist is never to be needed again.

The way you accomplish this goal is by creating the conditions in which the client can think independently. You say, sometimes explicitly but usually through your behavior, "You must solve your problems yourself. I can't do that for you, but I know how to help you solve your problems. What I have to offer is a powerful process in which I help you explore and think, and together we will find your solutions. In a sense, I don't know where we need to go together, but I know how to get there."

When I started doing therapy, I used to say only the first part of this statement, "You must solve your problems yourself. I can't do that for you," until I realized that this sounded weak and frightening to my clients, who must have wondered exactly why they were talking to me. Many clients come to therapy looking for advice and solutions to be provided by the therapist, and just to say I wouldn't be giving advice, without saying what I *would* do, probably sounded as if I didn't have a clue about what I was doing. The therapist's confidence in therapy is a powerful curative factor, and so you need to say what you can do as well as what you cannot.

When a client asks how therapy works, I often say "Your job is to explore whatever is on your mind. It doesn't all have to fit together before you say it—just explore. And my job is to help you do that exploring. My experience has been that three things will happen as we do that exploring. You will discover things about yourself and your life that you didn't know before; as we talk, your feelings will change; and you will figure out new solutions." It is worth our while to look at these events and how they come about when we make the client the primary problem solver—processes that are made clearest by talking in learning terms for a minute.

Deconditioning Feared Thoughts

Anxiety constricts behavior, both internally and externally, so that the anxious person takes in less of what is happening in the environment and thinks and feels fewer of the processes that are happening internally. Anxiety can be fears of things in the environment but more powerfully and painfully results from fears of one's own thoughts and feelings (see Chapter 15). The only way to get rid of a fear is to feel it, in small doses, and not have bad consequences follow. Fear must be faced to be beaten, and what therapy does is to help the client face painful thoughts and feelings, making them less painful. The person comes to think and feel more accurately and fully, both knowing himself or herself more accurately and seeing solutions and information in the environment more clearly. Thus the discoveries of "things you didn't know about yourself" and "new solutions."

Thus, also, "the feelings change as we talk," because a lot of the internal pain the client brought to therapy will fade away as thoughts and feelings that used to be frightening lose their ability to frighten through exposure (because of extinction and the counterconditioning effect of facing them in the context of an accepting relationship).

Reinforcing Thinking

A directive, advice-giving therapist could give a client some of the benefits mentioned in the last section if the therapist were exceedingly brilliant about what thoughts and feelings were frightening the client. He or she would directly expose the client to those thoughts and feelings, and extinction would take place. The therapist would *elicit* the appropriate responses. Even assuming, however, that he or she was always right about what the appropriate responses were (no therapist ever is), he or she is depriving the client of the process of independent problem solving. In a paradoxical irony, the therapist can make the client dependent on outside problem-solving help by doing the problem solving.

In evocatively empathic therapy, the client *emits* the appropriate responses—thinking and facing internal experiencing—and then the therapist responds in a way that helps the client face what she has approached. Think for a minute what is being reinforced. The client takes a step forward, trying to face something, trying to explore something. If she were alone, she would have felt some threatening emotions, retreated from the pain, and felt some relief; unfortunately, she will have been reinforced for the retreat and avoidance. With the evocatively empathic therapist, however, the client makes the attempt to explore and approach, feels some threatening emotions, but doesn't retreat, because the therapist puts the difficult material into words and the two of them face it together. Now the threatening emotions also diminish but not because of retreat; rather, facing them "takes the curse off them" (that is, extinction and counterconditioning take place). What has been reinforced is the approach, the attempt to face experience and to explore it. This process happens thousands of times in good therapy, and so the client is being reinforced thousands of times for independent thinking.

There are other ways that the person is rewarded for problem solving too, of course. Exploring pleasant emotions is obviously rewarding, and simply the thrill of succeeding at solving something challenging figures in too; therapy doesn't deal only with painful emotions and thoughts.

But the absolutely critical difference between evocatively empathic therapy and therapy directed by the therapist is that the client goes through the problem-solving process. It is not just the truth that makes the client free and strong; it is going through the process of finding that truth.

THE CLIENT'S JOB

Earlier I suggested telling the client that his or her job was to "explore whatever is on your mind." This wording seems to make the most sense to clients, but the client's work can be more fully described as including self-exploration, self-understanding, and developing action programs (Carkhuff & Berenson, 1967, 1977; Egan, 1982). Egan divides therapy into three overlapping stages and says that each of these is the primary client task for each of the stages. It makes sense that the three tasks follow in the order listed, since understanding would grow out of exploration, and appropriate action would depend on first understanding the problem, but therapy is probably more usefully seen as a continuous process rather than occurring in stages. Clearly there will be proportionally more self-exploration early in therapy and proportionally more taking action later, but both are important in every session. Clients often talk about trying solutions and changing behavior in the first few sessions, and continuing to explore experiencing is important in the last session. Come to think of it, there never is a "last session" to good therapy. The client and therapist stop meeting, of course, but the whole point of therapy was to start a continuous process of effective living, which will always involve self-exploration, new self-understanding, and taking action.

Exploration

Most clients come to therapy implicitly saying "I'm in trouble and I don't know why." When we first ask the person what the problem is, we will get an answer that will reflect the client's current understanding, but it will inevitably be incomplete and inaccurate in many ways. If he really knew what the problem was, he probably wouldn't need to be in therapy. So therapy is largely a shared search. The client's first job is self-exploration, without a need to make sense out of everything before it is said—with a need to feel around the edges of whatever comes to mind. In some ways this resembles the analyst's rule of free association, although the therapist obviously has a more active role in evocatively empathic therapy.

The client is doing a lot of self-disclosing, both to the therapist and to himself. He is saying new things and things that have never been put into words before. A gratifying statement that you will hear from clients, especially early in therapy, is "I've never told anybody this before. I'm amazed I was able to tell you." So self-exploration is difficult for the client because he is having to look at new demons in the fog *and* trust you to be able to accept and handle not only the awful things he could never share before but also the unknown ones that might suddenly emerge.

One goal of the exploration is discovery of "things you didn't know about yourself"—discovery that leads to new understanding.

Understanding

Dollard and Miller (1950) used the term *neurotic stupidity* to describe the unwise way that a person with anxiety-based problems often approaches life problems. Foolish, self-defeating behavior seems to follow from distorted beliefs about others and about himself or herself. As we will see in Chapter 15, this is largely because so much of the information needed for problem solving and living well is distorted or even not used by the person at all—not because the information isn't available to be seen and used, but because the person is unable to use it. You already know that this is partly the result of anxiety; internal processes such as thoughts and feelings are so threatening that they are avoided one way or another, and this avoidance behavior becomes habitual and persistent, since it works so well to reduce the intense discomfort of anxiety.

New understanding in therapy results partly from the discoveries made during self-exploration. Thoughts and feelings that were too threatening to be looked at lose their power to frighten, and the client says "How stupid! Of course that's part of the problem: I'm afraid that if I stand up to him, he'll leave me, but if I really look at it, I know he won't." So a discovery has been made, and now the person has more information with which to think—more information with which to develop more complete understanding. She knows herself better, intellectually and emotionally, and can come up with wiser, more accurate solutions. For this client, the very thought that "he'll leave me" was so threatening that she couldn't think it in anywhere near complete form without becoming so scared that she stopped thinking. All she knew was that she couldn't stand up to him.

So, you are thinking, she had an insight. *Insight* is a widely used word that seems to capture one popular stereotype of what therapy is. In fact, London (1964) separated therapies into "insight therapies" and "action therapies." He probably would call evocatively empathic therapy an "insight" approach, although I hope it is clear to you by now that this reflects a superficial understanding of evocative empathy. The popular stereotype is that all that is necessary is talking and understanding, and every now and then the client will have a dramatic insight that will cause progress to happen in therapy. Generally, *insight* has been used to describe the process of seeing new knowledge or gaining new understanding in a relatively sudden way and with relatively strong emotion. These "aha" flashes are dramatic and important but, probably because of their intensity, have attracted attention disproportionate to their frequency in therapy. Most growth and progress in therapy is quite gradual, with step-by-step increases in understanding, but the experience of insight is often associated with moments of therapeutic growth, and this leads many people to think that the insight *causes* the growth. They then try to provide their clients with directly given new knowledge as a therapeutic technique. The problem that nearly all therapists have faced then is the difficult-to-explain fact that this clever new knowledge almost never brings the hoped-for flash of new understanding.

The insight often comes as the old painful knowledge becomes less painful—the therapeutic growth and emotional experiencing may cause the "insight," not the other way around. An emotional release occasionally accompanies the sudden realization of a new understanding as anxiety reduction takes place.

Thus, the natural aftermath of exploration is understanding, as the client clears away the fog by facing it and grappling with it. New ideas start coming; new solutions to old problems become apparent; the person feels a new strength and knows himself or herself better.

Taking Action—Talk Is Not Enough

But talk is not enough. Another part of the stereotype of therapy is that it is a cerebral exercise sometimes described as "navel-gazing," in which the client and therapist wallow around in words and feelings and self-understanding for their own sakes. Above all else, however, therapy should be a problem-solving process. Although some therapists may encourage navel-gazing, the stereotype is wrong or at least incomplete. Our goal is to do therapy that helps clients both think better and live better.

The client comes to therapy with serious problems in living and wants new solutions to problems—wants to live differently. Facile advice will do no good, and neither will teaching, if the person has an anxiety-based problem. The problem is not the unavailability of better solutions but the person's inability to use what's available. The goals of therapy are to help the person become more able to think and feel and find new solutions more successfully—in his or her life outside therapy. New understanding needs to be structured and operationalized and applied in the client's life.

Egan (1982) calls the final stage of therapy "action programs." Effective action will follow accurate understanding, but an emphasis on action and new solutions should be mixed in throughout therapy.[2]

Before we lose sight of evocative empathy, let me say that this action-oriented emphasis grows out of the client's attempts to solve problems. The client will try to approach what she needs to deal with and will get as close as she can stand to and then will back off. These approaches will include the experiencing and emotions we talked about so much in the first several chapters, and they will

---

[2]Egan does say that some problems will yield solutions with only the skills of his first two stages, self-exploration and dynamic self-understanding, and so he doesn't insist that all action programs be deferred until late in therapy.

also include attempts to solve problems. If you are evocatively empathic, you will hear and respond to all of this.

Your client might say "I always sit near the door in any classroom, so I can leave if the situation arises that I really have to." Again, this can be seen as a purely factual statement devoid of feeling and of any attempt to solve problems, but to see it this way would be to hear none of the *intended message*. You could both bring the experiencing to life and respond to an implicit attempt to solve problems by saying "so one way you try to handle that sudden trapped panic in class is by clearing the way to run. It sounds like you really think about all this a lot—about how much you want to find some way to manage and to make things different." All of this was implied by the client, although he said it obscurely. Your response recognized both feelings and attempts at problem solving.

Another client might say "I can't seem to make friends. Nothing works . . . if you smile . . .or listen . . .or try to be interesting . . . all that sucking up to people that's supposed to be so charming . . . they just put you down anyway." Most people would respond to this person with some advice about how to win friends and influence people—advice the person has heard a dozen times already—or would pick up the hostility in her voice and point out that she probably drives people away, advice that, of course, will drive this person away. The evocatively empathic therapist will hear a lot of implicit feeling in this remark and will also hear some implicit goals and some implicit attempts at problem solving. Does all that seem unlikely to be in this one comment? How about responding "It's frustrating to reach out—even irritating, it sounds like—wanting people to like you but feeling like you have to sort of crawl to please them . . . and then even that doesn't work and you feel shunned . . . What *will* work!?"? (This last "What *will* work!?" is said in a tone of voice that clearly means the therapist is speaking as though he or she were the client.)

Many therapists are terribly "task-oriented"; they want specific goals with specific solutions, and they want them right now, so that advice about possible solutions rolls easily off their tongues with "You could try joining a group where you'll meet people who share your interests, or how about starting to jog at the Y?" Only advice columnists can solve human problems this easily; the rest of us are stuck with tedious methods like building therapeutic relationships and exploring and facilitating the client's own problem solving. Likely you are thinking that it would at least be useful to suggest alternatives for the client to think about. But the most common client response you will get then is "Yeah, I thought about that, but . . . ." Offering suggestions this way will be useful only if there is information available to you that is not available to the client. Ask yourself whether the "suggestions" you are offering are things that are not available to the client to think of. Does she know about the "Y" or that you can meet people jogging or taking dancing lessons? Obviously, in most cases, the problem is not a lack of information; it is an inability to use the information available.

Getting Bogged Down

One student who read a draft of this book said that one of the most useful things to him was advice on how to go from talking and understanding to action. He would feel his therapy bog down, get uneasy, and "frantically start designing action programs for the client." Students do seem to have trouble seeing the talking-to-action transition; part of the problem seems to be that "action programs" seem as if they have to be very structured and identifiable as programs (often with some way to keep score, such as on charts). Your clients are constantly in an action program; every waking minute they are doing something that affects their lives. They will frequently be talking about how they live those lives day to day; this talk is about the real action that they are taking to live—far more than a "program" would be.

As practical advice, refer back to our second "formula response" in Chapter 3. When you say "I guess what you want is _____," you focus on goals and action. The point is not that you should use this particular wording all the time. (You don't want a client to ask whether you're learning a new technique.) Understand the principle behind this formula. Clients are nearly always implying something they want or want to change; be sure to respond to these hints. Your job is to facilitate the *client's* problem solving, and you do this most powerfully by hearing and acknowledging the client's experiencing and attempts at problem solving. If you ask rhetorical questions ("How about trying . . . ?") or make suggestions, you are focusing on the solutions to the current problems, but you are ignoring and thus failing to reinforce the attempts that the client is making. You are helping solve a particular problem (assuming you give good advice, which will be true only part of the time), but you are not working toward the second major benefit of therapy—the client's own independent strength as a thinker and problem solver.

Acceptance

There is a danger in describing "the client's job." We can come to think of exploration, understanding, and action as some kind of prescription that the client *must* go through. My experience has been that we therapists are especially likely to push the client toward overt action. An extremely important and common experience in successful therapy is that the client comes to a sense of *acceptance*—acceptance of self, of others, of circumstances, of the wisdom of not taking overt action sometimes. The client is discovering all kinds of experiences that were only vaguely known, and part of this discovery may bring the insight that nothing new needs to be done, now that the client feels differently.

We need to trust the process. The client will do the problem solving. If that means making internal changes, then we do a serious disservice by urging toward some particular solution, such as taking overt action.

TRUSTING YOUR CLIENT—A BIT OF THEORY

We need to look briefly at an important theoretical question here if we are going to be comfortable with the amount of control that this approach to therapy gives the client. How can you trust your client to talk about the things he or she needs to talk about? Many people would say "It's all very well to be empathic and warm, and every therapist should provide these things—they are necessary but surely not sufficient for therapy to take place. The client is confused and troubled and can't think clearly, while the therapist is the expert who knows a great deal more about effective living than the client and knows a great deal more about the nature of anxiety-based problems."

First, this comment reflects a serious misunderstanding of the process of evocative empathy; it reflects the common misunderstanding of empathy as passive. More important for this discussion, however, it confuses the therapist's greater knowledge of the process of therapy and the nature of anxiety-based problems in general with expertness about *this particular client's problems*. Only the client can really know his or her own problems, although the therapist can know the process to deal with those problems. The client is confused and is distorting things, but two general principles make it clear that he or she can be trusted to solve problems, given the process of therapy: First, any person with average or above-average intelligence has the capacity to solve human problems—the problem is distortions. (I will tentatively limit this statement to people with anxiety-based problems and discuss special difficulties with psychopathic and psychotic problems, in Chapters 10 and 16.) Second, it is the nature of anxiety-based problems that the person is constantly approaching the sources of anxiety and backing off in the face of the emotional pain. Detailed discussion of this is included in Chapters 14, 15, and 16, but trust me for now. Your client *will try* to deal with the things he or she needs to deal with. If you hear these attempts and respond to them, you will help break the vicious circle of suffering and avoidance.

USING QUESTIONS

I have been pretty harsh about therapists who ask a lot of questions, pointing out how inexperienced therapists ask more than experienced therapists and how questions fail to acknowledge the client's message, implying that the client hasn't done things right. Questions, however, are sometimes appropriate and helpful.

Questions Are Easy

The use of questions is clearly a big issue for beginning therapists. When I prohibit the use of questions by the person role-playing the therapist in training sessions, an almost universal reaction is that he feels helpless to keep the discussion going in the "therapy." We depend on questions to get responses from other people, to fill in awkward silences, to gather information, and to solve problems. Questions are easy to depend on because they demand a response, and so we use them a lot. Sometimes, however, they don't facilitate the other person's own processes as much as an evocatively empathic response. An evocatively empathic response also virtually demands a response when it takes what the other person almost said and puts it right back in front of him. In fact, trainees often accuse me of asking questions when I am role-playing the therapist, but when we listen back to what was actually said, the response is clearly a statement of understanding. "But," they then say, "it sure *felt* like a question." It felt like a question because an evocative response *evokes* a reaction.

Empathic Questions

Most questions are attempts to elicit information from the other person, but there is a kind of question that serves the purpose of skillful tentativeness and conveys empathy. Clearly this is what the therapist intends with "Are you saying that you don't care but you want to care?" Other examples of empathic questions will be less clear in print because their accuracy will depend on their context, the tone of voice, and the therapist's intent. Asking "Are you scared right now?" could be a marvelous response in which the therapist is clearly with the client, or it could be straight off the wall.

An empathic question is often the best way to word a response when you are working quite far ahead of the client and think you understand but aren't sure. You make it clear that you are groping and exploring *with* the client and that control of therapy is still in his or her hands.

The trouble is that the form of empathic questions is also an easy way to do sneaky interpretations. In fact, a very common manipulative trick in discussions is to preface a statement of personal opinion with "Don't you think that . . .?" In form, this preface implies that the speaker isn't expressing a position but rather putting into words the other person's position. Watch your friends and point this out to them when they do it. I'm sure they'll really appreciate your charm and helpfulness.

Perry Mason Therapy

In one training clinic, therapists were required to write up a detailed report on their clients after the fourth interview, and this requirement changed the process of therapy from facilitating problem solving by the client to information gathering and diagnosis by the therapist, who *had* to have a lot of very specific information in a very short time. Learning to write such reports is probably important, but as a goal they distort the process of therapy. In this situation it was possible to have the therapists just ignore the requirement for detailed facts, do therapy, and then set aside a specific time after the fourth interview just to gather information from the client. The point is that this report writing exaggerated a tendency that already exists in most beginning therapists—the tendency to gather information and facts. Presumably, the expert therapist simply needs enough such facts to formulate an accurate appraisal of the problem, and this will lead to effective solutions. This tendency, like our intellectualization, almost certainly comes from a lifetime of solving problems academically by gathering facts. I know you're sick of hearing this, but it is not the truth that matters nearly so much as the process of the client's finding the truth.

In Perry Mason therapy, the therapist sets out looking for the evidence, asking lots of questions. This question asking, especially in the first interview, creates a powerful "set" for the client. The client is learning how to do therapy and how therapy works by the example set by the therapist in this early encounter; it is not reasonable of the therapist to expect to ask a lot of questions and then have the client suddenly start self-exploration.

Genuine, Reality, Chatty, and Manipulative

Schubert (1977) describes four kinds of questions therapists ask and argues that only one of them is really facilitative. "Genuine questions" ask for the client's personal view of an event or experience and can be answered only by the client. A therapist might ask "How do you feel when you fail at something?" Schubert then would insist that the therapist respond to the answer with intent listening and empathic responding. "Reality questions" ask for information that anyone could provide—that do not depend on the client's personal frame of reference. "Chatty questions" ask for therapeutically-irrelevant small talk. These two are neither very helpful nor very hurtful of therapy. "Manipulative questions," however, are like the sneaky interpretation questions discussed earlier—their goal is to win a point. The questioner is not interested in the answer but in getting the other person to admit she is wrong or inadequate.

This is a useful way to categorize questions if we add "empathic questions" (which may really be questions only in grammatical form). Genuine questions can be very helpful in therapy because they communicate a desire to understand without taking control. They are asked within the atmosphere of mutual exploration and often permit the therapist to formulate a response when there is little material to respond to. They leave the direction of therapy in the client's hands and are asked tentatively. The risk is that the therapist will disguise manipulative questions as genuine questions, carefully selecting questions to lead the client in some particular direction, but this risk also exists for sneaky interpretaions disguised as evocative empathy.

I do ask a fair number of genuine questions in therapy, but given a choice, I use a similarly worded evocatively empathic response if I can think of one. Rather than ask "How do you feel when you fail?," you could say "I guess part of what you feel when you fail is fear of something, but it sounds like there's more to it, too." This response shows that you understood some and gives the client "credit" for an attempt to talk about feelings, and it also leaves the door wide open for further exploration—accomplishing what the question would accomplish and more.

THE CONTENT OF THERAPY

Many books on therapy, especially psychoanalytic books, discuss a great deal about the content of therapy—what particular emotional issues are dealt with—and have little to say about specific techniques—the process of therapy. This book has focused nearly exclusively on the process and neglected the content, even though content is extremely important. This neglect has been partly intentional, because it is my conviction that each client's conflicts and problems are extremely complicated and unique to him or her, and the therapist's job is to understand this uniqueness with great precision.

Uniqueness and Commonalities

There clearly are commonalities among human needs and problems; behavior does seem to be lawful; and a knowledge of human psychology and psychopathology can help you be a better therapist. But it can also make you a worse therapist. Think back to our discussion of the need for concreteness, for particularity and subjectivity. This particular client's growth comes out of experiencing the unique felt nuances of his or her own life. We do a disservice when we try to generalize the client's process to fit some principle like "Depression is aggression turned inward" or "People catastrophize disapproval from others."

There is truth in these general principles (and hundreds of others), and understanding them can help the therapist hear implicit messages earlier than she or he would have heard them without the theoretical knowledge. The more you know about human behavior, the better your chance of developing a "third ear." The other edge of this sword, though, is that you might cling to the few hundred principles you know and hear *only* within their framework. Depression isn't always aggression turned inward. Being hurt by rejection isn't always the result of catastrophizing. We all perceive reality imperfectly, and there is reason to think that you will hear what you expect to hear. Even worse, you will tend to draw out from others what you expect to hear. If you are not victim to these distortions, you are the first person in history to be so perceptive; the rest of us have to admit to them and try to hold our understanding of the nature of life tentatively.

Directive in Process, Not Content

One unfortunate word that was used to describe empathy-oriented therapy in the 1940s was *nondirective*. It was meant to distinguish this approach from therapy in which the therapist guided the client through particular emotional and developmental issues and was clearly the superior expert. *Nondirective*, however, sounds pretty wimpy and led to a lot of misunderstanding. Evocatively empathic therapy is clearly quite directive about the general process of therapy, but it leaves in the client's hands the discovery of the specific content of his or her problems.

I Have Never Had a Client Who Didn't Surprise Me

All the therapists I have talked with about this (including myself) have said that they are constantly formulating "little theories" about their particular client, even when they are trying to listen and stay with the person and stay as flexible and tuned in and open as possible. Just like your knowledge of principles of behavior, these "little theories" can both help and hinder you as a therapist. It seems inevitable that you will be thinking about the implications of what your client is saying, as you listen and respond, and your own personal intuitions and understandings can serve you well *if* they tune you in to hear better. You might hear a theme developing and see a number of possible implications and future directions ahead of where your client is; when your client tries to go toward these things, you will be ready to hear the attempt to go with him or her sooner than you would have been otherwise.

There are at least two ways these "little theories" can do damage, however. First, even if you are as brilliant as your mother says you are and accurately know what direction your client needs to go in, responding ahead of the intended message will threaten the client and slow therapy down. Second, a lot of the time you will not only be ahead of the client, you will be going in the wrong direction. Again, you will be vulnerable to confirming your notions through selective listening and self-fulfilling prophecies, and this may be an especially serious problem if you feel a commitment to the ideas you develop about the client. They become "my insights" and evidence of expert cleverness, and it will be threatening to you to have to hear contradictory evidence from the client.

When the client starts therapy, he or she reports certain things as the problem, but it seldom turns out that those things were the "real" problem. The client isn't lying, of course, but neither of you knows ahead of time what the "real" problem is. The beauty of evocatively empathic therapy is that you, as the therapist, aren't required to know the truth for this particular client ahead of time. You know the process for finding the truth. Hard as I try not to, I sometimes succumb to the temptation to formulate my "little theories" about clients, especially ones that look as if they fit some category I've read about, but this clearly grows out of my own need for structure, because every category we have for human behavior is only a crude approximation of any one individual. Every time I start to get committed to one of these formulations, I get startled when the client goes some completely unexpected place. One client seemed quite clearly to me to be having trouble leaving home because her mother had her in a complex guilt conflict over dependency, and in my mind this became "the problem." I heard evidence for it everywhere in what the client said and was amazed when she cried for the first time in therapy when her older *sister* left home. I hadn't been entirely wrong; she had tried to talk about her mother, but I had been so intent and become so narrow in my expectations that I could now look back over weeks of therapy in which she had been trying to talk about her sister and see that I, in my cleverness, had not heard her.

The best protection against this kind of distortion is probably to formulate lots of "little theories"—to think ahead, which seems to be inevitable, but constantly to realize that there are dozens of possible directions to go in and implications to see and to listen for as many of them as possible. I really have never had a client who didn't surprise me.

You and I Are Not That Smart

I hope that you are self-actualized and living a meaningful, full life in which you never do self-defeating things, and your relationships are filled with mutual understanding and unconditional acceptance. A bit more realistically, I hope that things are all right for you and that the solutions you have for your life are working pretty well, even though sometimes you can feel pretty bad. It's hard enough trying to live one life well and to see through your own distortions and to find workable solutions for yourself. It really is overwhelmingly unlikely that your solutions are what is best for another person. What I am getting at is that giving advice and solving other people's problems doesn't work—not just because the other person resists but also because nobody is smart enough to do such an incredibly complicated thing for another person. The advice giver will inevitably give destructive advice as well as helpful advice. Because only the other person can fully know his or her own experience, only he or she can ever have all the necessary information to find wise solutions.

The beauty of evocatively empathic therapy is that you don't have to be an expert about your client's life. You only have to be an expert about a process.

Personality Theories

A lot of your training has probably included the study of different theories of personality—study that has no doubt made you a better person or at least taught you a lot of new terms. There are dozens of such theories, and many of them offer brilliant and helpful insights into human functioning. Each of them makes some sweeping claims about the fundamental nature of humans, however, and many of them flatly contradict each other. They obviously can't all be right, and it is likely that none of them is right in any kind of a complete way. It's a cliché to say that psychology is an infant science dealing with incredibly complex matters, but it's true, and this truth must humble the therapist.

You probably know what I am about to say, because I've said it twice before in this chapter, but personality theories can both help and hinder you as a therapist. Their valid insights can help you hear implicit messages sooner than you would have if you knew nothing about "idealized self-images" or "oedipal conflicts" or "the child talking to the adult within you." Study personality theories carefully. But the danger is that you will become so committed to a theory that you will try to fit everybody into it. Our theories are crude; our categories are crude; nobody really fits any theory exactly. Historically, schools of personality theory have been very much like religions, with a guru who has disciples and followers who attack the followers of other gurus as clearly wrong and probably even infantile. The schools are even named after the guru, so that you know what I mean when I say something like "I know a Skinnerian who calls Freudians followers of Sigmund Fraud." They're all wrong, but that's OK because they're all partly right too, and you don't have to sort it all out before you can do good therapy, which is a very good thing. I never know what to say when someone asks me what school of thought I subscribe to, and I usually give such a long answer that the person leaves before I'm done. He or she wanted a label with which to put me in a category, and I want to resist that. "Eclectic" is a reasonably good answer, but it can mean anything from "I fly by the seat of my pants" to "I'm a closet Jungian, but I'd rather not say so." The fact is, though, that all of us do have some notions about human nature and the kinds of problems that people face. It is probably useful to give a lot of thought and discussion to just what this implicit personality theory is that you hold, because it is going to guide your therapy to some extent; it will make you tend to select certain parts of the client's message over others.

But We Already Talked about That

One last comment on the content of therapy will be from a slightly different perspective. Your client will be talking about his or her unique content in exploring a particular problem and then will leave it to talk about other things. If this particular issue, however, is still not resolved or is still the cause of discomfort, the client will return to it. Often the same general topic will arise repeatedly in therapy. The client is taking repeated runs at the problem, dealing with it a bit differently each time, leaving it for a while, and then returning to it. Sometimes in discussing one of your therapy sessions with you, another therapist might observe "It sounds like he's worried about whether his son likes him," and you might respond "Yeah, but we already talked about that." It seems to feel redundant to the therapist; the issue has been tabled and dealt with, so why return to it? Trust the process; if the client is trying to return to the issue or is still troubled by it, it still needs to be faced. The person with anxiety-based problems *will try* to approach the issues that are causing the trouble, and if he or she is making that approach, your job is to hear it—to know that here is the appropriate content of therapy.

If your client says "Well, I've told you the whole story, and I understand it, and I'm still paralyzed. I still don't know what to do, and I still feel awful," you can safely say "If it still hurts so much and is still all so confusing, we don't know the whole story; there must still be things we don't understand." Actually, of course, this usually wouldn't have been the most helpful thing to say, since it doesn't prove that you understood. A better response might have been "I hear you sort of reaching out . . . where do I go from here . . . I'm stuck . . . help me with this, please." Most of the time, the client would go on talking after this. If he or she didn't, I might say something about there still being things we don't know and let's explore them further together.

INFLUENCING THE PROCESS

To say that this approach is directive in process does not mean that the therapist gives directions like "You have made an intellectual statement; now tell me the feelings behind that statement." It is directive only in the sense that the therapist behaves in a particular way that keeps the client looking at what he or she has said—that says that this is a process of intense mutual exploration. Thus, you don't usually have to do much in the way of direct teaching of the process—it just flows and happens if you start right out responding empathically after some general opener like "What can I do for you?" or "What's on your mind?" or "How are you?" Good evocative empathy is so rewarding to the client and so quickly feels productive that questions like "What am I supposed to do?" and "What's the point in this?" may not come up.

Teaching the Process

Sometimes, however, clients do ask these questions, and some clients have little or no idea what therapy is like. They may have been sent to you for help with their "nerves" and expect an examination and advice. They may not be oriented toward verbal problem solving. They may want to please you and be at a loss how to start. Or a client may spill words easily for a while and then get stuck, asking "Now what?" It can be helpful to teach something about the general process of therapy with words like "Yeah, it must be puzzling to know how talking is supposed to help—even to know what to talk about. I'll tell you a little about how I work, and if I miss something you'd like to know about, just ask. I see you having come here hurting and confused over how your wife seems to be changing so fast and really not knowing what to do or think or feel about that. Very complicated stuff, and something has to be done soon. What you and I can do together is to explore and talk and try to figure this out. My experience has been that if you will talk about whatever is most on your mind—the feelings, the ideas, whatever—then my job will be to help you explore that, and together we will discover things we don't understand now." If the client seems interested, I will very explicitly say just what it is that I do. "I think a lot of times a person can sort of vaguely understand and feel things, and what I'll do is try to hear what you're *trying* to say, and I'll help you get that into words—to get that clearer. Sometimes I'll be guessing as I try to understand, and I want to count on you to tell me when I miss. If I can count on you to do that, it'll be easier for me to make some guesses." I seldom would make such a long speech in a session, but all these ideas might come out at one time or another. Anything about the process that the client wants to know seems legitimate.

Getting a Word in Edgewise

One problem that arises occasionally is that a client will talk so rapidly and continuously that there are virtually no natural pauses in which the therapist can respond. When this happens, the therapist is clearly not providing any evocative empathy, and the client is not going through much self-confrontation. There is a way to intervene in the process without giving orders that violate the spirit of therapy. You can say, in a supportive but firm tone, "Wait . . . I want to make sure I'm understanding this part. If I understand what you mean, you want to be a calmer person, but you want life to be meaningful, too." You might have to be fairly persistent sometimes, but by intervening this way you clearly are expressing an intention to understand, and you are not making the client feel judged in the way you would if you said "Wait . . . you're talking so much I can't get a word in edgewise."

Requests for Advice

A more common problem is what to do with direct requests for advice. Many people come to therapy expecting advice and can be quite frustrated when they don't get it. It is easy to give in to the urge to give advice, especially under the pressure of the client's expectations and hopes, but if the client really does have to take responsibility for his or her own life, and if evocative empathy really is as powerful as it is supposed to be, there has to be a better way to handle the question "Well, I've told you what the problem is. What do you think I should do?"—or, even worse, "Nobody cares enough even to give me suggestions about what I could do differently. Please don't you be like everybody else and not help me." (Can't you feel the guilt as you say you don't give advice?)

You need a response that shows you understand the need for advice, that says you can't solve the client's problems, that says he is responsible for his own life, but that says that you *will* help—that there is hope. Piece of cake, right? You could say "It would really feel good if I could tell you 'Here, do this' and you could go do it and the problem would be solved. [Note: This empathic statement will probably help the client to look at what he is asking for and to know that even if you did say "Here, do this," he wouldn't do it.] I don't think I'm smart enough to solve your problems for you, but I think I do know how to help you solve them. I guess right now you feel so much at a loss that it seems like you could never figure anything out alone. Let's do that together." You are expressing both hope and confidence in yourself and in therapy as well as understanding and a trust of the client's capacity to take personal responsibility.

I had one client who must have asked me "What do you think I should do?" at least 100 times. There are just so many ways to say you don't give advice, and after a while he started following his question with "Never mind, I know what you're going to say." Later in therapy he said "I still wish you could do this for me, but I really do know that it has to come from me. I know what I have to do, and nobody can do it but me." (Remember that teaching is appropriate in therapy if the problem is simply a lack of information, but this is a much different matter from giving advice.)

SETTING GOALS

The client comes to therapy because he or she wants change. So one goal of therapy is always that things be different than they are. The difficult question is: change to what?

Goals Are Values

Just like the content of therapy, the goals of therapy can be stated in general ways, and this is a useful, even a necessary, thing to do. The particular goals of a particular client's therapy, however, are unique to that client and reflect that client's values. When we ask for the goals of therapy, we are asking for a description of the Good Life, and any such description is inevitably relative to the individual's culture and circumstances. Is individual accomplishment good? Most people in our culture would say that it is, but there are cultures in which the group good is valued more, and to praise a child for an individual accomplishment would be to humiliate him or her. Is it good to be open and honest in your intimate relationships? "Sure," you say, but the truth is more like "That depends." You aren't *completely* open and honest in your relationships; why not? Are you espousing values for your client that you don't really live by yourself? There are people for whom openness and honesty would be terribly self-defeating under some circumstances. How will you respond when your clients express goals for themselves that you disagree with, especially if you have a personal investment in the issue? You might feel strongly about sexism and have a client who says "I think women were meant to be passive. I don't want some woman who'll sacrifice her family for some ideal about independence." This client is struggling to define and pursue goals for his life. Can you let him do that? Your solutions are not the best solutions for everybody, and a therapist is called on to let the client find his or her own best solutions. There are limits beyond which each of us will not go—values whose violation we can't participate in— but these limits have to be wide for an effective therapist.

Describing the effective person is so difficult that only a few humanistic theorists have made a serious effort at it (Allport,1969; Maslow, 1954; Rogers, 1961). One way to summarize these descriptions of the effective person that is meaningful to me (Martin, 1976) is to say that she or he has four general characteristics: a quiet sense of personal worth; autonomy and a sense of competence; accurate, full openness to feelings and thoughts; and the capacity to be intimate. In a sense, these describe the goals of therapy for me, although each individual will find his or her own expression of these characteristics.

Another way to state the general goals of therapy that I will discuss in Chapter 16 is less positive in tone. It is to name the problems that bring people to therapy and say that the goals are the relief of these problems: reducing painful emotions, improving problem solving ability, reducing maladaptive behavior, and improving self-esteem.

These general guidelines are helpful, but the specific goals of therapy are determined by each client.

The Hierarchy Emerges

So the client finds the goals; how does this happen? It is quite clear that anxiety-based problems are so complex that the person entering therapy often does not know what the problem is, and so goals set at one point in therapy frequently change. A client recently said to me "I remember telling you I was a trusting person, and I really meant it. But I guess I'm not . . . I guess that's a big part of the problem." So now one of his goals is to become more trusting. To have said this was a goal at the beginning of therapy would have made no sense, because he saw himself as an unusually trusting person. It was threatening to him to know that he didn't trust very much, and only as we worked through other, less threatening material could we get close to this particular bit of truth. We worked on successive approximations of the truth—on a series of threatening thoughts and feelings naturally arranged in a hierarchy of how threatening they were.

The goals of therapy emerge from the therapy process. This does not mean that goals are unimportant or that there really are no goals. It means that goals are held and worked toward energetically but with the flexibility to know that they can change with new understanding. This flexibility seems essential to effective living and effective problem solving; your client will need both strength and flexibility to live well, and you give the client the chance to get both when you help him or her be the problem solver.

What Is a "Cure"?

I am concerned that what I have been writing will sound naive, as though evocatively empathic therapy were the key to the golden door that will let your clients live happily ever after. I need to say that I think human life is essentially a difficult process, with ups and downs and conflicts both within and between people. It is possible to live well and meaningfully, and good therapy can contribute to that. But there is no "cure," no goal to reach. Life is a process that one can live more or less effectively and rewardingly. You will enter your clients' lives for a limited time and have an influence that may change directions for them in some ways by helping them be stronger.

CHAPTER SIX

Relationship Issues

The power of the therapeutic relationship comes from its nonjudgmental nature. The therapist dependably accepts and values the person as worthwhile but does not judge what the client says as *either* good or bad. The therapist says, through behavior, that anything can be said or thought, without being either praised or punished. (There are, of course, limits on overt behavior that must be set.) The client is free to explore all of his or her experience and to find whatever solutions are best. It may surprise you that being nonjudgmental means not giving approval, just as much as it means not giving disapproval; as soon as you approve of a particular way of thinking or feeling, you are saying that you are in a position to approve and disapprove and that *not* feeling or thinking this particular way is not acceptable. Your client is having trouble crying in front of you because he is embarrassed and ashamed, and you say "Go ahead; it's good to cry; it's not to be ashamed of; feel free." Your intentions are helpful and supportive, but you have failed to understand what the client is trying to say, and you have said that it is not acceptable to feel ashamed of crying. You have, probably unintentionally, taken over the direction of therapy and subtly prohibited certain feelings. You could have given the support you wanted to give, without making the judgment, by saying "This is pretty painful stuff, and I guess it brings the hurt up into your eyes . . . but then you want to stop because it would feel so crummy for tears to come. I want you to know that it's OK with me if you cry, but I realize that's not the issue—it's not OK with you."

Clients will sometimes say to you "It really helped when I told you all that stuff about what I think, and you didn't even flinch. I guess I expected you to laugh or think I was crazy or awful or something." We all think disgusting things sometimes, and a common feeling that clients bring to therapy is "Although people may like me, if they could really know what goes on in my mind, that liking would turn to disgusted rejection." This fear leaves the person feeling unlovable and unworthy because what she *really is* feels unacceptable.

If I had only two words to describe a good relationship, they would be *understanding* and *acceptance.* To be accepted by someone who really knows you as you are may be life's most releasing experience, and that is what therapy provides. The therapist *proves* that she or he understands through evocative empathy and also communicates a dependable, nonjudgmental acceptance of the client.

This chapter is about the nature of the relationship that communicates that acceptance. So far, this book has focused on evocative empathy skills, almost implying that they constitute all of therapy. Evocative empathy will work, though, only in the context of a good relationship, and that easy-to-say phrase *good relationship* will lead us into incredibly complex areas. Now the going starts to get tough. I write this chapter uneasily, knowing that we are only going to scratch the surface of the issues and fearing that I am going to mislead you with some simplistic descriptions—knowing that I can only introduce a topic that you will be resolving for yourself for years. Evocative empathy is a skill that can be operationally defined and taught and learned with practice. Relationship skills depend much more on the kind of person you are and on the needs and distortions that you bring to doing therapy.

Remember all the things that evocative empathy is not: It is not sympathy or love or caring or agreement or disagreement. It is only communicated understanding of the other person's intended message. It often does imply caring and respect, but it is important that it not be confused with these other things. You could be evocatively empathic with a person with whom you totally disagreed and whose presence you could hardly stand, difficult as that might be to do. The relationship involves more than evocative empathy, and we have to tackle what that "more" is.

RESPECT AND PRIZING

Many attempts have been made to describe what it is about the therapy relationship that helps the client. Rogers's early term was *unconditional positive regard* (1957), but it led to a lot of misunderstanding because many took it to mean some kind of impossibly tolerant permissiveness in which no limits were set. Rogers clearly did not mean that, but rather meant that the therapist's positive feelings were not conditional on the client's thinking, feeling, and talking in certain ways and not other ways. He implies an acceptance of the person but sets limits on certain behaviors when he says:

> The effective therapist may feel acceptant of [antisocial] behavior of his client, not as desirable behavior, but as a *natural consequence* of the circumstances, experiences and feelings of this client. Thus the therapist's acceptance may be based upon this kind of feeling. "If I had had the same background, the same circumstances, the same experiences, it would be inevitable in me, as it is in this client, that I would act in this fashion." In this respect he is like the good parent whose child, in a moment of fear and panic, has defecated in his clothing. The reaction of the loving parent includes both a caring for the child, and acceptance of the behavior as an entirely natural event under the circumstances. This does not approve of such behavior in general [Rogers et al., 1967, p. 103].

Other phrases have included *nonpossessive warmth, prizing,* and *respect.* All of these imply that the therapist somehow communicates the message that the client is a worthwhile person, regardless of what he or she is experiencing. They all avoid words like *love* because the therapy relationship is a limited relationship, in some ways unlike any other, and the therapist cannot realistically offer love. He or she offers a chance to explore and think and feel in a context of acceptance and respect. Later we will discuss the notion that "you are not the solution," meaning that your job is to help your client live well and relate well in the world outside therapy. You will be dishonest and will hurt a lot of people if you implicitly promise your love as a solution—a promise that you can't fulfill for your clients.

So therapy is a limited relationship, but it is also a powerful one. Respect and dependable, nonjudgmental acceptance are incredibly helpful to the client. How can they be communicated?

Commitment and Effort to Understand

I said that evocative empathy is something different from acceptance, but your attempt to understand powerfully communicates that you value your client. You are saying with your behavior that she is worth intense effort on your part, that what she is experiencing is valuable enough to be worth a lot of work exploring, and that you are not afraid of that experiencing.

Certainly implicitly, and often explicitly, you say to your client "I am in this with you until we find new ways for you to be and to live. I have a commitment to helping you." You follow through on that commitment by being dependably involved. The way that you really communicate your commitment is over the long run, by your behavior—you really do stay with the person.

Expressing Acceptance, Explicitly and Implicitly

What you do speaks more eloquently than what you say about how you feel toward your client—partly because saying "I really care about you and value you" can be a cheap shot. Anybody can say such words; everybody knows that is what therapists are supposed to say; and besides, it's part of their job. Another problem with saying these words is that for many clients words like these have meant betrayal and undependable acceptance and have masked feelings of dislike and rejection. Words are easy; demonstrated respect is what counts.

This is not to say that you should never openly express respect and prizing for your client, particularly when he asks for or seems to need to hear some acceptance. The problem comes from thinking that the words will have much power and from taking the focus of therapy away from the client's exploration of his or her own experiencing. If the client says "I really feel that nobody cares anything about what happens to me or how I feel," and you say "But I care," you are saying that the client's feeling is not a valid experience and he should not be feeling it. You are trying to use reassurance and talk your client out of a feeling, and it won't work. If you really have to express your caring here (to be honest, your need to do this is partly just that—your need), you might say "That's a horribly lonely feeling . . . not to matter to someone . . . I want to say that *my* feeling is that you matter to me, but it really sounds like it doesn't feel that way to you . . . that you really are alone." In most instances, this response would have been more helpful without the explicit expression of caring. The client will likely appreciate the words to some extent, but you will also introduce a lot of other issues: "Maybe I shouldn't have said nobody cares, because she says she cares—how awful of me not to appreciate that; that's easy to say, but it's just the therapist's job; I meant nobody cares enough to love me, and that's not what she means, so she didn't understand; maybe that is what she meant, and she will be my source of love."

You absolutely must express your caring, but you do that most effectively with your intense effort to understand.

Belief in the Person

In Chapter 5 I was pretty insistent that the client be the problem solver, sometimes to the frustration of our clients who come to us for advice and solutions. One subtle but important implication of this is that we really do believe in our clients. We trust their ability to solve problems—a trust that clearly implies immense respect. One woman, for whom independence and personal strength were central issues, said near the end of therapy "You know, this really has been feminist therapy. You respected my ability to take care of myself. I remember when I came how desperately I wanted you to guide me . . . I felt like I was going to the doctor . . . and how angry it made me when you wouldn't. I know now that if you had tried, I wouldn't have done anything you told me to do and probably would have quit." The client I mentioned earlier, who said at the end of therapy "I did this myself," had knocked me down a peg or two earlier in therapy over this issue. We were well into therapy, and I think I had been pretty consistently letting him be the problem solver. But I made a clear error in judgment and behavior in therapy when he moved in with a new roommate. This roommate started verbally tearing at my client, trying every way he knew to make my client feel bad about himself. I directly suggested that the client move out of his new living arrangement and can still remember my foolish, protective worry that this creep was going to undo all the gains my client had made in therapy. My client nodded (he was quite surprised, although I couldn't see it at the time) and seemed to consider my advice thoughtfully. The next week he came in angry, saying "You didn't trust me . . . I can take care of this." I had to agree, and we discussed this for some time, but what it drove home for me was how important it was to him that I had trusted him—had trusted his strength.

Dependable, Nonjudgmental Acceptance

It is important that the therapist be immune to shock and embarrassment. The client is afraid to face his or her own experience, which is hard enough to do alone, and is afraid of shocking the therapist and losing his or her respect and acceptance. Very often a client will have enormous difficulty saying something and may take several sessions to get around to it. "I want to tell you," she will say, "but I just can't . . . God knows what you'll think of me." Finally, she will get around to saying it, and you will feel "That's *it*?" This is not to cheapen the client's pain at telling you, but what felt so disgusting and unacceptable to the client will be understandable and acceptable to you. The client then will be able to face this painful material and still feel acceptable, and the curse will be taken off whatever was so awful. If you flinch, however, and are shocked or embarrassed, you obviously will confirm your client's worst fears, and that part of her experiencing will be harder to look at.

This clearly requires that you be comfortable with a wide range of experience. This comfort will come partly with experience, as you hear and become used to more topics. It also can come from your own personal growth; if there are a lot of things that shock and discomfort you, you have some work to do, either in your own therapy or in discussions with friends or in thinking through what your own areas of discomfort are. If explicit sexual talk makes you blush or strong expressions of anger scare you, for example, you will have trouble helping your clients freely explore such issues.

Privacy

Another way that you offer respect to the client is through the confidentiality you promise. You imply that what the client has to say is important and personal and worthy of being taken seriously. Confidentiality in therapy is almost never total, of course, and I will discuss this at length in Chapter 11, but therapy does give a privacy in which the client can build enough trust to make himself or herself vulnerable.

SHARING YOUR EXPERIENCING

Therapy centers around the client's process of exploration, but there are times when the therapist can appropriately say how he or she feels about things, when the therapist's experiencing is shared through self-disclosure.

Benefits and Dangers

It may seem unnecessary to say this, but the therapy session is for the benefit of the client. It is not a place for the therapist to work on his or her own needs—to get understanding and acceptance from the client, to impress the client, to satisfy needs for power and control, or any of a hundred other purposes the therapist might use the client for. Some therapists cloak their misuse of therapy in the disguise of "honest and open self-disclosure" and spend a lot of time talking about themselves and "expressing" their "here-and-now reactions." It can also be disguised by "I know just how you feel . . . I've been through the same thing myself."

Self-disclosure can serve the purpose of being honest about your feelings in the relationship. It also can give the client some feedback on how other people feel when he says or does certain things or how other people react to particular situations. At least it can give this feedback about how one other person reacts, since when you share your feelings, that is exactly what you are sharing—your feelings. It is important that both you and the client know that this sharing is not sneaky advice about the way a person should react, and you might say in response to a question about how you would feel in a particular situation "Sure, I'll tell you how I think I would feel, but I want to be sure you know that it is just my feeling, and what might be right for you could be very different. I think I would be angry and a little self-righteous if someone told me that . . . but that's just me. It sounds like you would like to fight back somehow, but you immediately start doubting your self and thinking 'Maybe he's right.'" You have answered the explicit question about your feeling but immediately put the focus back on the client's reactions.

Moderate Levels Best

In orthodox psychoanalysis, the analyst is to remain a truly blank slate, to facilitate the patient's use of the analyst as a screen on which to project fantasies and transferences. This can be carried to extremes that deter the course of therapy; in one instance (Greenson, 1974), for example, the patient came to the session with a large head bandage and obvious serious injuries. The analyst, strictly following tradition, made no personal reaction to the patient's plight and waited for the patient to bring the topic up. This absurd insensitivity left the patient unable to continue. But Malcolm (1980) quotes an anonymous analyst who says that Greenson's story is "heartrending and affecting" but completely misses the critical point. This analyst tells an incident in which he profusely apologized to a patient for being late to a session. Looking back on it, he could now see that rushing his own feelings into the situation prevented the patient from reacting to the analyst's lateness. Greenson's point with the bandage story was to say that complete disengagement is destructive, and the anonymous analyst's response does not take away the truth of this. What it does do, though, is show a subtle (and therefore too common) way that "self-disclosure" hampers therapy by taking responsibility away from the client and by turning therapy to meet the therapist's needs. If you apologize profusely for being late, you almost cut off your client's freedom to be angry or hurt or confused by your behavior. You are protecting yourself from that at his or her expense.

You and the client are in an important human encounter, but one with an unusual one-way structure. You are there to serve the client's personal growth. In some cases, your disclosure of how you feel will serve that growth, but you should be quite clear exactly how your self-disclosure is going to be helpful when you do share your own experience.

GENUINENESS

The "core conditions" of therapy discussed in Chapter 1 included empathy, concreteness, respect, and genuineness. The last is the most difficult to define and to measure. Several phrases that capture some of its meaning are "authenticity," "being the person that you really are in the therapy relationship," and "being congruent with yourself in the relationship." None of these, however, is very helpful to the therapist struggling to know what to do in therapy to be genuine. It is easier to say what genuineness is not: it is being not-phony and not-artificial; it is not playing a role, pretending to be an expert; it is not acting as though you feel something you don't. The idea is easier to grasp this way, although it doesn't sound nearly as marvelous as being "authentic." The word *congruent* (Rogers, 1957) captures part of this not being phony, because it means knowing how you really do feel in the relationship, being accurately in touch with your own experience, and acting in ways that are consistent with that.

Facilitative Genuineness—Not Just Self-Disclosure

Probably the most common misunderstanding of genuineness is that it involves a blurting out of whatever the therapist is feeling, rather than just that the therapist is aware of what he or she is feeling and acts in ways consistent with those feelings. When self-disclosure is confused with the notion of genuineness, some therapists use it as an excuse to be "open and honest" in an attacking way. Carkhuff and Berenson note that "many destructive persons are in full contact with their experience; that is, they are destructive when they are genuine" (1977, p. 12). It is important to be open and honest and not be playing a role with your client, but it is also important to remember that the expression of your feelings is appropriate in therapy only if it facilitates the client's process.

I have talked about instances in which your expression of positive feelings could help but also could hinder therapy. The more obvious problem is with negative feelings you have toward your client. The expression of these feelings can quite obviously hinder therapy, since they usually carry a strong implication of judgment of the other person's worth and character. But the notion of judgment also gives a clue to when the expression of your negative feelings can be helpful in therapy. Your reactions can be an important lesson for the client in knowing how he or she affects other people with particular actions and words. If you can express your negative feelings without judgment of the client's character, your reaction can be helpful. This requires great sensitivity and skill, since negative reactions usually imply rejection and judgment in our everyday lives. But if you have a relationship in which your client trusts your acceptance as truly dependable, you could say "I want to share my feelings when you keep saying 'That's your opinion.' I'm not sure why, but I get irritated . . . like you're slapping me down." Quite clearly this statement is not empathic, and in most contexts it would imply judgment and advice about what the person should be doing. If, and only if, you have laid a strong foundation in which the client knows you do not take over as the problem solver or judge his or her personal worth, then a comment like this could be a helpful piece of information for the client. These conditions tend to be met only later in therapy, and this kind of response would probably still be fairly rare.

An interesting problem that we will face more thoroughly below is that of your own distortions as they relate to "facilitative self-disclosure." You have to be pretty humble about the accuracy of your own experiencing. The feedback in the last paragraph was to help the client know how "That's your opinion" affects others. Who's to say that your reaction is typical and doesn't come primarily out of your own needs and blind spots? Something to think about.

Being Caught Off Guard

One of the most severe tests of your genuineness will come when you are made uncomfortable by something you have said or done or by something the client says that catches you off guard. A common reaction is to want to cover up, acting as though nothing both-ers you, trying to save face. You will have to be pretty smooth not to be seen through, and it is probably better just to comment on your own discomfort and lack of infallibility and be sensitive to the client's reactions to the incident. The importance of the incident is not in your reaction to it anyway. This situation is especially likely to plague you if you are hung up on the need to be seen as an expert; if you make a mistake, there is no need for a lengthy defense of yourself, but trying to avoid it will surely establish you as a phony.

IMMEDIACY—DEALING WITH YOUR RELATIONSHIP

In good therapy relationships, you will become very important to your clients; you will be a significant part of their lives. It is almost inevitable, then, that your relationship will become an issue that needs to be explored. There are important things that your client can learn from your relationship—trust, what it means to be listened to, how to listen, and that your acceptance makes self-acceptance easier. Your client will often try to talk about these issues and some-times about more complex issues such as intense attachment to you, a very difficult problem. These relationship issues are about as "here and now" as you can get, and dealing with them is often called "immediacy" in therapy.

An Empathic Context

In one sense, talking about your relationship is no different from talking about any other topic that might come up in therapy. It is part of the client's life and experience and is involved in his or her problem solving. It should be dealt with in the same evocatively empathic way as any other issue; the focus is on the client's implied experiencing and attempts to understand and take action, and your job is still to hear what the client is trying to say about you and your relationship but can't quite say.

Your Troubles Hearing Immediacy Issues

That last paragraph was so easy to write, but talking about you in therapy is going to be a lot more difficult than talking about test anxiety. It is here that your third ear will be most needed and most difficult to use, because the implicit message touches you; it can threaten you if there are negative feelings and even (or maybe espe-cially) if there are positive feelings. If your client wonders just how qualified you are or how old you are or whether you're happily married or why you get so uncomfortable every time he mentions you-know-what, you will likely be reluctant to hear the message and even more reluctant to put the message into words in an evocative way.

It's easy to be afraid of getting egg on your face when you respond to what you think are the client's attempts to talk about your relationship. Imagine this situation: The client says "I really like coming here and being close . . . to . . . well, sort of, I guess, things that mean so much." You respond "It means a lot to you being able to be close to me, it sounds like, in a way that lets you talk easily," and the client draws back a bit in the chair with "No, I didn't mean that. I meant get close to talking about how much my family means to me." Normally when you miss the message this way (or maybe you heard something accurately but went beyond what the client intended you to hear), you can just back off and correct yourself. This time is different, however, because you and your feelings are involved. You will have to deal with your own awkwardness somehow, without getting defensive and ungenuine.

Successive Approximations

Issues that you are involved in will be more difficult to deal with, and so it is very likely that you will avoid them, consciously or unconsciously, unless you make a pointed effort to listen for them. They must be dealt with. It is easy to see that if you consistently avoided responding to some other issue in therapy, you would be communicating that this aspect of the client's experiencing was somehow taboo and unacceptable; it was too frightening to be dealt with. The same principle applies to immediacy issues. They must be dealt with if they are important to the client.

I probably can't help you very much in this book with the problem of being able to hear when the client is trying to talk about you and your relationship; you should deal with this issue by being supervised or by sharing your therapy experience with another therapist/friend who will help you explore the issues that give you trouble. But I can say some things about what you do with the message once you hear it.

In our unnerving example in the previous section, the poor therapist is probably imagining the client saying to someone "My therapist is pretty hung up on himself. Everything I say makes him think I'm in love with him." Almost certainly, the client wouldn't have reacted this strongly, but the experience might well have scared the therapist off from openly discussing immediacy issues in the future, to prevent more hoof-in-mouth disease. But these issues must be dealt with.

It is here that using successive approximations is an especially helpful way to respond. Be cautious but tenacious, sensitively wording your response so that the client will be able to react internally with "Yes, that's what I meant," but at the same time don't let go of the issue easily. This may mean that you will make more statements than you might about some other topic, each statement conveying a more finely shaded meaning; take more but smaller steps to go the same distance.

Your client might say "My brother fell in love with his therapist, and it really hurt him when she wouldn't have anything to do with him outside therapy." You quietly catch your balance and say "That obviously meant a lot to him . . . and it sounds like you could really tell how strongly he was feeling." I think this is about as far as you can go with what the client has given you, without eliciting a threatened denial that the comment had anything to do with your relationship. We're pretty sure the client is trying to say something about being attached to you, but the actual statement made no mention of any of the client's feelings. In your response, you skillfully got ahead of the client, heard the implicit feelings that the client intended—how strongly he felt for his brother's strong feeling—and put that into words. You have acknowledged the importance of what was said for your client, and you have opened the door for further exploration. In fact, you have done more than just open the door; you have faced your client with his immediate experiencing in a way that virtually demands further exploration but demands just enough to be difficult and challenging without being threatening.

Now the client might say "Yes, I do . . . in a way, that didn't seem right." You are still scrambling; you can't let the issue die, but you don't want to step right in the middle of something untoward. "It confused and hurt him," you say, "and I think it puzzles you too." (Notice that you have said the brother is "confused and hurt," words that the client probably wouldn't accept about himself; but you use your vocabulary of shadings to acknowledge and articulate similar feelings in your client with "puzzles you.") "Sort of asking 'Why can't there be more in a relationship like this . . . if a person feels strongly?'"

You are "working your way toward the truth" with successive

approximations, just as you do with any difficult issue, but immediacy talk takes special sensitivity and skill.

A Place to Work Out Issues

One of the values of immediacy talk is that it can give the client a chance to come to terms with the way he relates to others in a nonthreatening atmosphere, where the consequences of mistakes aren't devastating and words can be taken back. Many psychoanalytic therapists would say that interpretations of the "transference relationship" are the foundation of therapy. Most other therapists seem to feel that such issues can be important, but helping the client deal with life outside therapy is more typical.

Anger between You

Anger and the fear and anxiety triggered by angry feelings are some of the commonest problems clients bring to therapy. In effective therapy, the client will often feel anger during the therapy session as she talks about people and situations in life outside therapy. Sometimes, though, she will be angry at you, and sometimes you will probably be angry at her. If you have any of the discomfort that most people feel when someone is angry with them, it will be difficult to listen accurately, but you obviously must do so. All the things I said about immediacy apply here, but there is also your need to know whether the anger was something you earned in some way you are unaware of or whether it is coming from the client's distortions and problems. It is easy to lay all this at the client's doorstep and presumptuously talk about his or her defensiveness and inappropriate reactions, but it is also a good idea to be as open to your own contribution as possible. A client who is quite angry with you is probably a good cue for you to consult with another therapist for another view of what you are doing in therapy.

The point I really want to get to is that some therapists advocate provoking the client's anger—with the best of intentions, but with some unintended results. They argue, quite correctly, that an important lesson for a person to learn is that anger does not mean the loss of the relationship or rejection—that anger is not to be feared. For many people, anger does mean loss of love, and the fear of this loss becomes so overwhelming that they avoid anger at all costs—costs such as failing ever to assert themselves, feeling helpless and depressed, and being devastated by fear of their own angry feelings.

The skillful therapist very often *evokes* anger, as the client tries to deal with experiences from real-life situations and relationships. In order to *provoke* anger as a technique, however, the therapist must be manipulative and dishonest and take on the role of the expert master of the treatment process. Therapists obviously can't tell the client why they are goading and attacking, or it won't work. A powerful and experienced therapist might well pull off such an encounter so that the client ends up feeling that he did survive an angry outburst and the therapist is still there, but this lesson has been won at a cost of putting the client in a subordinate role in therapy. The therapist becomes someone who does things *to* you, and the client is the recipient of treatment. The client must also, consciously or unconsciously, view the therapist with suspicion from now on: what clever tricks await in the name of therapy?

All the benefits of this provocative approach can be won without paying these costs. The point is that the person face his or her own anger, experience and think more accurately, and use the resulting new understanding in life outside therapy. The whole point of evocatively empathic therapy is to confront experiencing; your client will be facing a lot of anger, if that is part of the problem, and then finding ways to deal with that anger and express it constructively. This process may include anger at you, but if it does, the anger will grow honestly out of your interactions. If the client gets angry at you for some mistake you've made, then it's a real interaction, and you're still trustworthy—clumsy maybe, but trustworthy—and not cleverly manipulative. If he or she gets angry because of personal needs and distortions, then it's still a real interaction in which the anger will be explored.

This discussion of provoking anger points up sharply the more general issue of how the therapist's approach to therapy is very much a relationship issue. You will read and hear many ideas about therapy that are inconsistent with an evocatively empathic approach—ideas about giving clients paradoxical instructions and using therapeutic games or environmental interventions. There are times when some direct interventions are called for (see Chapter 9), but I think these times are rare. You must be clear about what the goals of therapy are and sensitive to how the nature of the therapy relationship affects those goals. If you want your client to gain independence and to be honest in relationships and to be able to think clearly, you must relate in ways that facilitate these things, both directly and by your example.

I-Messages

Of course, the issue of your own anger at the client is also important here, and I discussed this earlier when I talked about self-disclosure. The expression of your feelings can be helpful under the special circumstances of a strong, trustworthy relationship.

What we haven't looked at is why you feel your anger. The first glib thing we think is that the client provoked it with inappropriate behavior, but it is important that you find someone to help you explore yourself through to an understanding of how your needs play into your interaction. In one way, it makes no sense for you to feel anger toward a client. You are in a one-way relationship in which you are not directly involved in the client's outside life, and so the client's behavior affects you only within the therapy session— a session in which blame has no place and where the client is expected to deal with inappropriate behavior. You understand the client's experiences and actions as the result of his or her life and don't see them as somehow based on evil intentions. Why are you so angry?

Of course I'm not saying that you should never feel anger; that would be imposing on you the same impossible demand to avoid anger that your client is trying to get free of. Just recognize that your anger comes partly from you, and it would be worth knowing yourself as well as possible by finding someone to talk it through with.

When you do express your anger in therapy (or in any relationship, for that matter), Thomas Gordon's (1976) advice about delivering I-messages gives a very helpful structure. A you-message lays blame on the other person's character and motives: "You are so insensitive and don't care anything about me!" You-messages are so laden with judgment that the other person almost has to defend against them with denial and returned blame and judgment. An I-message gets the same point across without the judgment by including three elements (not necessarily in this order):

1. Name your feeling or reaction.
2. Name the other person's *behavior* (not motives) that makes you feel that way.
3. Name the tangible connection between the behavior and your reaction.

Rather than say "You're insensitive and don't care," an I-message would be "I feel hurt and angry when you read things while I'm talking to you because your not listening shuts me out."

When You Disagree

The foundation of therapy is evocative empathy, in which you neither agree nor disagree with the client's statements; you nonjudgmentally facilitate the client's exploring. Perhaps it would be more accurate to say that you neither approve nor disapprove, since there will be things that you personally believe that your client will not. Usually, as you know by now, your opinion on these topics doesn't matter much in the therapy process. Sometimes, however, your client will ask your opinion, and a useful response might be "I think I see this differently than you do, but I don't think my opinion is the important thing here. It seems to me that people in general are neither bad nor good inherently, but the important thing is that from your perspective, people should be and are basically good . . . that when they do hurtful things it's because they are hurting." You have not dodged the issue, but you have kept therapy focused where it needs to be—on the client.

RELATIONSHIP WEAKENERS

You already know that the power of the therapy relationship comes from being nonjudgmental, and so the quickest way to weaken the relationship is to make judgments. But there are others.

False "Understanding"

Saying "I understand" when you don't is risky because you will often be called on to prove that you understand by your client, who may sense your puzzlement. Your words will become empty if this happens very often, and when you're puzzled, you're probably better off just saying so. "Keep talking . . . I don't really have all that yet . . . I'm puzzled right now because I'm not sure what you mean . . . help me get a handle on that . . . I thought I understood, right up to the last two sentences, and then I got lost" are all things you could say and still be expressing your empathic intent—your desire to understand and to explore with the client.

A friend of mine who is a counselor suffered a personal tragedy and afterward said she was ready to write a book on "how not to be helpful." Things she had often said to people felt very different when she was on the receiving end, and at the top of her list was "I know just how you feel . . . I felt the same way when I lost my job [or whatever]." She had the strong feeling that the person didn't understand and was distorting what she was feeling to fit the listener's quite different experience. An empathic response would, of course, have demonstrated understanding by articulating her feeling. A high school student said that when she felt down and tried to find someone to talk to, the person usually started out, "I know just how you feel. I felt the same way when . . . ," and then the rest of the discussion centered on the other person.

Most Reassurance

One of the hardest things to grasp intuitively in therapy is that reassurance almost never works, and it often slows therapy down. Our faith in reassurance must have something to do with how often people in our lives use reassurance to deal with others' painful emotions; it becomes the only way we know to respond. When your friend feels worthless, you say "Come on . . . you're a good person. Look on the bright side of things." When you feel worthless, and your friend says the same thing to you, it annoys you. How do you think your friend (or client) feels? I guess, more accurately, you appreciate your friend's concern and are glad he or she feels that way about you, but you also feel quite misunderstood, thinking "That's easy for you to say because you don't really understand."

The principle is that reassurance implies that you are not supposed to be feeling the way you feel—that your experience is not acceptable or even a valid way to feel. Reassurance says that it doesn't make sense to feel the way you do, and so there is even some blame implicit in it. "Don't feel that way," reassurance says, as though persuasion could change your feelings.

Until you trust the therapy process, though, you will be overwhelmingly tempted to give reassurance, especially when you see your client hurting over things that seem to you so clearly not worth hurting over. Maybe you will be afraid that if you don't somehow pull your client out of the feeling, it will get worse. All you will do is cut off the therapy process and prevent the facing of experience. It is unnerving, though, not to give the reassurance that you so much want to give, unless you have something more effective and more powerful to do instead. It will take time and experience to fight against the intuition that you want to save the person and to build your trust in the power of evocative empathy, but it will be worth the period of awkwardness.

Detachment

I have used terms like *intense involvement* and *focused listening* and *effort to understand* and *respect* to describe the therapist in the relationship; this is hard work. The opposite of these qualities is found in the therapist who is just doing a job and going through the motions of technique. It is nearly impossible to be evocatively empathic and to remain detached, although it conceivably could happen, since empathy is theoretically only communication of understanding of the intended message. Involvement in the relationship is communicated by the intensity of the therapist's effort— by caring enough to be working hard. Later I will discuss a kind of distance the therapist keeps because of the limits of the therapy relationship, but that is quite different from an uncaring detachment.

Intellectualizing and Jargon

My past discussions of intellectualizing have been about honest attempts to understand that dampen therapy but don't necessarily weaken the relationship. Show-off intellectualizing, however, is a sure-fire relationship weakener. Playing the doctor, with marvelously impressive jargon, may wilt the client into acquiescence and "yes, doctor" reactions, but it will do nothing to facilitate the client's experiencing and will almost certainly prevent the client from learning to trust you to hear. The use of jargon is a reliable indicator of a therapist who is meeting his or her own needs for admiration or who is covering up insecurity with self-deceptive pomposity.

Moralizing

There are limits to what the effective therapist will accept on moral grounds, but those limits recognize that there are thousands of ways to live effectively, and the therapist's way isn't the best way for everybody. The limits are wide, and if you are not comfortable with this, you are probably headed in the wrong direction by becoming a counselor or therapist. One trainee used to describe his clients as "wholesome" and "unwholesome" and spent considerable time in therapy discussing his client's experiences in moral tones—preaching, in a sense. There is a place for preaching and moral training, but it is not in therapy. Quite obviously, the problem is that moralizing is judgmental in the strongest possible way.

DEPENDENCY AND ATTACHMENT

In one way, evocatively empathic therapy prevents dependency on the therapist. It tells the client that she or he must do the work and cannot depend on the therapist to guide the process. In other ways, however, the therapy relationship can lead to the client's dependency and attachment on the therapist. This is understandable, since the therapist is probably one of the few people ever really to listen to the client and also gives the incredibly rare experience of dependable acceptance. Therapy offers part of what a mature love relationship offers, but it is definitely not a love relationship; it is a limited relationship, and these limits can set up some confusing tensions for the client.

I said at the beginning of this chapter that we were entering deep water, and it will probably be these relationship questions that will take you the longest to become comfortable with. This book can only get you started.

You Are Not the Solution

You will need to be clear for yourself exactly what the nature of the therapy relationship is, or you will become involved in ways that will startle and bother you, and you will promise your client things that you cannot and will not deliver. You can do a lot of damage this way. It is tempting to think that your love is curative—that you will give your client the relationship that he or she has missed out on. That is partly true, but only in a limited way, and unless those limits are clear to you and to the client, you may seem to be offering yourself as the solution to the person's problems. You cannot possibly follow through on this offer—you cannot be the solution—but you can help the person find solutions in life outside therapy. In purely practical terms, you cannot be the most significant person in very many people's lives, and if you try you will burn yourself out, damage your own relationships, and ultimately hurt your client when you pull out.

It seems paradoxical that the therapist is supposed to provide warmth, understanding, acceptance, and intense involvement—all parts of mature love—and at the same time maintain a distance that says: I am not part of your "real life"; I am part of your life here in therapy and give you some very powerful and helpful things, as your therapist; but that's exactly what I am—your *therapist*. The resolution of this paradox and ways to deal with it come clearer when we think about the functions and setting of limits in therapy.

Limits of the Therapy Relationship

You provide your client with remarkably attentive listening, intensely worked-at understanding, unusually dependable respect and acceptance, and the freedom to deal with all kinds of thoughts and feelings. You provide these qualities at a level that you could not maintain continuously, and so you set limits that prevent behaviors and demands on you that would force you to pull back. At the extreme, if the therapy session might last anywhere from one hour to seven, and the client were free to call you at any time to talk as long as he or she wanted to, you would have to pace yourself quite differently than if you know how much is going to be asked of you. Setting limits frees you to give more fully in the session.

There is no limit on what may be discussed in therapy, but, for example, the client is prohibited from harming you physically; this knowledge frees both the therapist and the client to deal openly with feelings and thoughts of hostility toward the therapist. Thus, although the primary function of limits is to permit the therapist to function more fully as a therapist, a second function is to provide the client with a similar reality-based structure that frees him to deal more fully with thoughts and feelings, secure in the safety of knowing that both he and the therapist are prohibited from acting in certain ways on those thoughts and feelings.

Knowing what your own limits are and being able to set them clearly will be partly your own idiosyncratic responsibility. Partly, though, limits are implicit and explicit in such documents as *Ethical Principles of Psychologists* (American Psychological Association, 1981) and similar standards of professions that include psychotherapy. Therapists, for example, avoid "dual relationships" with their clients by not treating colleagues, close friends, and relatives. Clearly this limit permits the therapist to stay uninvolved in making judgments in a way that he or she couldn't otherwise. The statement "Sexual intimacies with clients are unethical" (American Psychological Association, 1981, p. 636) is a clear limit. You are unquestionably required to study and follow the ethical standards of your profession.

But it is the idiosyncratic nuances of limits that will require you to do some hard thinking. Surely if your best friend wants to talk to you, you will respond therapeutically—but somehow without becoming his or her therapist. Is it clear to you what you will do when a client invites you to dinner or to a party or asks you to teach him to swim? The principle is that you remain as the person's ther-

111

apist; how you do that is a complex business. At the risk of looking a little naive, I might ask you exactly what "sexual intimacies" are. Do they include putting your arm around the client's shoulders supportively when he or she cries? Of course not, you respond, that's silly. But where is the limit for physical contact between you and your clients? Is it the same for all clients? Why or why not? More important, is the limit clear to you and to the client? If it is not, uncertainty floats between you about what will happen if the client says "Sometimes I wish you would lie down with me here— not for anything sexual, just for the comfort and support of feeling you close to me." Not knowing where the limit is might well make it more difficult to talk about such feelings.

Most limits get set implicitly. It may be standard practice at the clinic you work at for sessions to last 50 minutes and for all client calls to be handled through a switchboard. Your client may just assume that these and many other limits exist, and they will never arise in therapy. Many other limits will be irrelevant to your relationship with particular clients. The problem is in setting limits of which the client is unsure, which matter to him, and which he only hints at wondering about. As with any other issue, you are listening for implicit messages about testing limits, and we might continue with our client from several pages ago who said "My brother's therapist hurt him by not having a relationship with him outside therapy." You skillfully respond in increasingly complete ways until he finally says "Yeah, I do think about you a lot. You've been good to me and helped me so much, and you're just the kind of person I've always wanted for a friend . . . could that . . . well . . . I wish. . . . " He's asking in a way that touches you and makes you want to reach out and help him, but you know that you are his therapist, not his friend. You combine limit setting with empathy by saying "I guess you're asking me . . . in a way like your brother . . . and wanting to have a different kind of relationship with me . . . more than therapy . . . and it feels like that would mean a lot to you. I think you've told me this will hurt you some, but for me it is quite clear that our relationship has to be here in therapy. I say that largely because for me to be your therapist—or anyone's—I have to know what the boundaries are. And the boundary I'm comfortable with is that therapy not include other relationships." Now you've probably said enough and will tune in to hear the effect this has on your client, but you will likely return to this problem again. I hope that, in reading this, you can see how you have to have your feet under you to set limits without dropping a brick on your client. Only by thinking through ahead of time what your limits are will you be ready.

Transference

The term *transference* has taken on a great many meanings. Originally, it was Freud's characterization of the patient's irrational (that is, having no basis in the reality of the therapy relationship), intense attachment to the analyst. Since, he argued, he had done nothing to elicit this attachment, it must be feelings held toward other significant persons and transferred to the analyst. Negative transference was equally unearned hatred and anger felt toward the analyst. Many people now use *transference* to refer to virtually any feelings the client has toward the therapist, and the therapy relationship is, almost by definition, a transference relationship. Others react strongly against this denial of the therapy relationship as a real relationship, arguing that of course all relationships are based in part on past relationships, but it is avoiding the real human encounter of therapy to dismiss it as transference.

Whatever the merits of these arguments, Freud's original observation is worth understanding accurately. Most psychoanalysts argue that an irrational transference attachment is inevitable in therapy, and some argue that it is essential and that the only good interpretation is a transference interpretation. Most other therapists would say that transference attachments do happen in therapy sometimes but that they are neither inevitable nor essential. On the contrary, many clients will use therapy and the therapist to solve their problems outside therapy, appreciating and liking their therapists, but not out of proportion to the quite realistic positive feelings that grow from such a good relationship.

However, transference attachments do occur in nearly every therapist's experience, and you do need to be ready to deal with them openly and helpfully. The client will want you to break the limits and to be more than a therapist. Sometimes clients will drive past your house, feeling strong infatuation; sometimes they will phone you repeatedly, perhaps begging you for a more complete relationship. You have become part of the problem. Your response should include firm and consistent maintenance of your limits and empathically helping your client work through the attachment feelings. Strong attachments take a long time to work through, and a new element in the problem is that now your client has a strong motive not to improve, because if he or she no longer needs therapy, he or she loses regular contact with you.

Your Own Distortions and Needs

Psychotherapy is a complex interchange, and your own blind spots and open nerves will interfere with it—unless you never distort anything, of course. The extreme expression of this is "countertransference," the therapist's irrational attachment to or anger at the client. Fortunately, this is less common than transference, but it does happen, and you should be alert to the signs of it in yourself so that you will know when to find a trusted therapist/friend to help you figure out what's going on for you.

Unusually strong feelings toward a particular client are your most important clue to countertransference. You may feel that only you can really help this particular person or have powerful "rescue fantasies" that a relationship with you will change the client's life, or you may have frankly sexual feelings toward the client. Especially looking forward to or dreading sessions with particular clients is a sign that something may be wrong, or getting inexplicably sleepy during sessions can be cause to wonder.

Beyond the rare strong instances that can really be called countertransference, there is good evidence that nearly all interactions with clients are affected by the therapist's emotional involvement. My goal is to alert you to these influences and encourage you to think and talk about them. A good summary of both clinical and empirical investigations of countertransference is presented by Singer and Luborsky (1977).[1] Their conclusions from the clinical literature include these:

> Countertransference is a hindrance to effective treatment of the patient. . . . Countertransference hinders the treatment by preventing the therapist from properly identifying with the patient, a necessary part of the process of understanding. . . . One of the marks of the occurrence of countertransference is an inordinate intensity or inappropriateness of sexual or aggressive feelings toward the patient. . . . Avoiding countertransference problems can be aided by self-analysis or by discussion with a supervisor or colleague [pp. 447–448].

[1]From "Countertransference: The Status of Clinical Versus Quantitative Research," by B. A. Singer and L. B. Luborsky. In A. S. Gurman and A. M. Razin (Eds.), *Effective Psychotherapy: A Handbook of Research.* Copyright © 1977 by Pergamon Press Ltd. Reprinted by permission.

Their conclusions based on research deal more with the general issue of how the therapist's emotions distort the therapy process, rather than the intense instances of countertransference. These conclusions include the following:

> Therapists are more inclined to avoid patients' feelings, especially anger, when they are directed against the therapist than when they are expressed toward someone else. . . . Therapists are much less accurate in reporting their own and their patients' behavior in psychotherapy when the issues are related to personality conflicts of their own—less accurate in terms of a greater discrepancy between their own report and a judge's report of what happened. . . . More experienced therapists tend to show fewer indications of countertransference in their work than do inexperienced therapists. . . . In response to client hostility (versus friendliness), counselors use more avoidance behavior such as suggestion, disapproval, and information giving, and less interpretation, elaboration, and reflection [p. 448].

These lists of conclusions are only a sampler, and you would be wise to read the whole article. What our sampler does is point out that you and your personality are deeply involved in what happens in therapy; and your involvement will often escape your conscious notice. Feedback from another therapist is essential to your continued growth as a therapist and diminishing of countertransference effects.

I have repeatedly recommended that you explore your own experiencing with a therapist or friend (or both), and an important issue you should think about is whether therapy for yourself would be helpful. Another of Singer and Luborsky's conclusions from the clinical literature was "The therapist's emotional maturity is a deterrent to his potential countertransference needs which might interfere with the relationship, and psychotherapy or psychoanalysis is usually necessary to achieve this emotional maturity" (p. 448). We all have anxiety-based problems and distortions, and we all could grow in a good therapy relationship. A therapist is especially called on to be clear and congruent with himself or herself, but there are other reasons for seeking therapy for yourself. Several other therapists and I have shared the feeling that it is a remarkable experience to be in the other chair, to feel what it is like to be deeply understood, to feel the release of saying things that have choked and haunted for years, to face the pain of looking at ourselves and feeling clearer and cleaner afterward. It can teach you a lot about doing therapy because it so strongly lets you get closer to the client's experience. Peebles (1980) reports evidence that the number of hours therapists had been in personal therapy significantly correlated with the level of empathy and genuineness they offered their clients, as rated by other professionals applying rating scales to tapes of therapy.

Whether it makes you a better therapist or not, you deserve a strong sense of your own worth, to feel stronger and more autonomous, to accurately experience yourself, and to be able to be intimate. Just be sure you get a good therapist.

Sexual Issues

Our culture is not exactly forthright and mature about sex, and so a lot of your clients will need to talk about it; for the same reason, you will probably have some discomfort hearing and articulating sexual messages. In one sense, sex is no different from any other difficult topic that you help your client "take the curse off" by your comfortably using language that explicitly says what your client implies. In another sense, though, sex has a special status because it so often intrudes on the therapy relationship in ways that other issues don't. This is especially clear when transference and countertransference develop, but we call these situations by special names only because they are so obvious. The same processes are operating to different degrees in all close relationships. It would take a lot of denial to think that warm, intimate relationships don't carry some implication of physical closeness, and whether our culture is forthright about this or not, you will need to be forthright about it in therapy.

You will need to make a special effort to hear your client talk about sex, and you will need to be sensitive to what you are communicating to your client. You will become very important to your client, and what you intend as a supportive physical gesture (let's assume you're not distorting your intentions) might well seem very different through the client's eyes.

VALUES AND EXPECTANCY EFFECTS

There is some evidence that clients' values shift in the direction of their therapists' values over the course of therapy (Rosenthal, 1955; Welkowitz, Cohen, & Ortmeyer, 1967). This may well be because therapists tend to have more mature values, and clients naturally move in their direction as they become more mature. It is also remarkable, though, that clients of Freudian therapists have Freudian dreams, clients of Jungians have Jungian dreams, and clients of Ellis turn out to have problems that fit his theory.

It's difficult not to think that therapists subtly influence the course of therapy, beyond the ways that they think they do. Rosenthal's work on expectancy effects, or self-fulfilling prophecies (Rosenthal & Rubin, 1978), makes it clear that we reinforce in others what we expect them to do. If they do things we don't expect, we tend to ignore it, even though we would deny having done so. The danger that this apparently inevitable process poses for evocatively empathic therapy is that we may be fooling both ourselves and our clients into thinking that we are permitting freedom and autonomy to grow, when in fact we are being quite controlling. In a sense, this is a countertransference issue because, although some such unintended directiveness is inevitable, the greater the therapist's distortions, the greater the danger. The (partial) solution is to build in the safeguards of getting feedback on your work, listening critically to your own therapy tapes, and knowing yourself as honestly as you can—perhaps through your own therapy.

SEX ROLES AND THERAPY

One last relationship issue for you to think about is raised by books like Chesler's (1972) *Women and Madness.* Chesler argues that psychotherapy is structured in the same way as the generally oppressive male-dominant culture that gave rise to therapy. Her complaint is largely with psychoanalytic therapy, which does have considerable sexism in its theoretical base. But the general argument is that the expert male therapist tells the passive female client (in the usual arrangement) that her psychological health lies in accepting her role as a woman. Broverman, Broverman, Clarkson, Rosenkrantz, and Vogel (1970) reported a study in which therapists seemed to stereotype men and women, to the detriment of women, but Stricker (1977) seriously criticized their methodology and interpretations. Stearns, Penner, and Kimmel (1980) found "little support . . . for many of the widely held assumptions about sexism in psychotherapeutic practice" (p. 548). Whitely (1979) reviewed the literature and concluded that "whereas [mental health] professionals share the sex role stereotypes of their lay contemporaries, the professionals are unaffected by them in making mental health judgments and in setting therapeutic goals" (p. 1309). The debate still goes on about how sexist therapists are, but in general they are looking pretty free of stereotypes. The point for us, though, is not whether therapists are sexist in general, but whether our therapy is sexist.

Done well, evocatively empathic therapy is quite clearly not sexist. The goals are autonomy and self-esteem and accurate experiencing and good relationships—generally that the person find the life that's best for him or her—regardless of gender. I mentioned a client who said "This is really feminist therapy." That was right for her, but I would rather think of it as nonsexist therapy. A female client can take charge of her life, and so can a male client; a male client can become more sensitive, and so can a female client.

PART TWO

Putting It Into Practice

Getting Started

The only way to learn therapeutic skills is through practice. You must make yourself articulate responses, feeling all that initial awkwardness, until it becomes second nature. It is difficult, though, simply to read descriptions of what good therapy is and then start out doing it; you may find it helpful to begin with some pretty mechanical exercises. Jacobs (1981, in press) showed that students could be taught, with an hour of instruction, to respond to written "client statements" in a way that would be rated as highly empathic on Guerney's (1977) Acceptance of Other Scale, a rating scale for empathic responding. One of Jacobs's points was that if it is this easy to get high empathy scores on such tests, it is amazing that the bulk of experiments on training report low empathy levels among their trainees. We can't know whether Jacobs's subjects were truly empathic in the sense that they could have made a client feel understood, but his training procedure does give you a way to get started.

WRITTEN EXERCISES

You can start out all alone in your room where nobody will know what you're doing. In Chapter 8 are transcripts of therapy sessions from which you can select client statements. Choose a few fairly long statements (so there will be more to respond to) and take your time formulating an empathic response. To be rated at the minimally facilitative level, Jacobs would tell you simply to paraphrase the content of the client's statement. This will probably feel inane to you, as it probably would to an outside observer. Surprisingly, though, such a paraphrase often has powerful effects on a client. Gendlin (1974) quotes a person in a training group as saying "It feels so odd to repeat what someone said, but it feels so powerful when someone does it for me" (p. 220). I frequently hear from trainees "People really are solving their problems, but I'm not doing anything. I'm just listening." *Just* listening! Learning to paraphrase is an important first step in your skill development, and it will help to compare your written paraphrases with a friend's.

Jacobs instructed his subjects that they could get a higher rating by making a *plausible guess* at something the talker was feeling. (Remember our first "formula" response in Chapter 3?) To get a higher rating, make a plausible guess at a feeling *and* at something the person is saying he or she wants, wishes, or hopes for. (Here's the second "formula.") Plausible guesses at two feelings will earn this higher rating in lieu of wants or wishes. You can also raise your ratings by using introductory phrases such as "Sounds like . . ." and "It seems to me that you're saying . . . ." Jacobs was demonstrating some serious problems with rating scales for empathy, since his subjects could earn high scores with one hour's training and rigid following of a few rules, whether they understood another person or not. You can use his procedure, however, to get started with written exercises.

ROLE PLAYING

My experience has been that beginning therapists make their greatest strides in confidence and skill by role-playing therapy in groups of three with other students. One person plays the therapist, one plays the client, and the other sits as a silent observer until the end of a role-playing session, which may last from 5 to 20 minutes or so. The observer can then join in a discussion of the session from a different perspective than either of the direct participants. The advantages of role playing are that threat is low (unless a teacher or supervisor drops in to observe), mistakes don't cost anybody anything, and you can sit as long as you want to formulate a response. At first, it's easier if the "client" plays some other person or some composite person with a problem. This makes the situation artificial, but it also lowers the difficulty. After a while, though, I hope you will be able to move toward discussing real problems. These don't need to be deep personal problems, which might be quite inappropriate to discuss with other students, but to the extent that trust can be built, you will benefit more as the therapist and as a person who can experience the releasing power of being understood.

THE VALUE OF TAPE WORK

I consider both audio- and videotapes of therapy to be essential parts of training. They permit you to learn by observation, as you will in Chapter 8; they give you an accurate version of what you did, as opposed to the well-filtered version that any therapist gives of a session; and they provide the opportunity to receive feedback from others who can observe your work. Threatening as getting feedback can be, it is essential.

There are several ways you can use the tape that comes with this book. I would simply listen to the sessions one time through at first and then stop the tape occasionally to formulate and articulate possible responses to particular client statements. Doing this with a friend or in a group will be a sobering experience, as you hear the variety of messages different people hear, but it will be good feedback on the accuracy of your own perceptions. The therapists represented on the tape are all pretty good therapists but are not perfect. You can improve on their responses by taking all the time you want.

One of the most instructive ways to learn from a supervisor is to have him or her listen to a tape of you doing therapy, stop the tape at the end of particular client responses, and have the supervisor give a hypothetical response. This will probably be a good experience for both of you, since many experienced therapists have become so comfortable with their style that they often give very helpful responses but can't say why. Having to explain a response to you may also help the supervisor to stay sharp and to improve.

Beginning Therapy: Reflections of a Novice Therapist, **by Michael Stambrook.** For me the process of beginning training in psychotherapy was one of the most demanding and eventually rewarding challenges I have encountered. What I hope to do here is to communicate and share my experience of being confronted by clients who have come to me for help.

The initial hurdle I needed to overcome was to become comfortable with my role of supposedly having expertise in the process of helping my clients find the solutions that work best in their own lives and resisting the pressure to provide what clearly would be gratuitous advice. This pressure, I believe, was due to my feelings of uncertainty and anxiety related to my new role as a neophyte therapist wanting to do the best possible job for his clients. I found it difficult and sometimes two-faced to communicate to my clients that they should trust me and the process so that in time, through ɩ collaborative exploration, they would come to face what was most troublesome and work out the best possible solutions. Further, although sincerely acknowledging the distress and pain my clients felt, I was unwilling and unable to impose on them my unique solutions in the form of advice.

For me there was an additional and powerful source of uneasiness, which was due to my having to take on faith, and what seemed to me face validity, that the process that I was learning to use did work and would be very successful for me. Part of this was learning to trust that through the use of evocative empathy the client would in time get to where he or she needed to go. It seemed sort of paradoxical that before I was able to have the implicit faith and trust in my clients' own resources to reach their own solutions, I had to see firsthand that such faith and trust were warranted. Bluntly, I had to *learn* to have such implicit trust and faith so that my clients could increasingly approach what they feared most through my reinforcing their approach attempts in active but nondirective, nonthreatening manner.

In terms of actually learning to respond in an evocatively empathic mode, one of the most difficult aspects was attempting to get beyond the content of what was being presented, to what were the reactions to what was said. It was as if I had a task of attending to and responding to multichannel input, but I was so skilled in dealing with only one of the channels that at first it was almost all I heard.

Based on my academic training in psychotherapy, I was skilled in thinking and responding that was predominantly content-oriented. Initially I found it surprisingly difficult to keep these intellectualizing and analytic modes of thinking and reacting in check. While I had to stay very much in tune with the content of my clients' verbalizations, I somehow also had to keep track of all the verbal and nonverbal affective cues that gave the content its life. Because clients need to face the emotional impact of their experiencing, the goal for me as the therapist was to help them confront the experience fully without resorting to defensive avoidance maneuvers. The demanding and difficult task for me was to attend to these affective cues that were behind the explicit verbalizations and help my clients confront them immersed within the content of what was presented.

I have already identified one of the reasons it was hard to attend to the affective components of my clients' messages—that is, the need to break from that deeply ingrained and well-reinforced intellectual mode of reacting; but for me there was another reason, related to the fact that for the most part the emotions dealt with were very painful. It seemed at times that confronting clients with that which was implicit in their message, even though they had almost stated it, would hurt them more, and there was a tremendous urge to back off.

For me there were two parts to this desire to pull back, both of which are clearly countertherapeutic. First, although this urge not to further expose my clients to the distress they felt was due to my wanting to see them free from anguish, it would not have been respectful and would have demonstrated a lack of trust and confidence in their ability to face what troubles them most and be able to come through the experience intact.

The other part of not wanting to hurt my clients more by confronting them with their experience was self-protective. That is, to help a client get to where he or she had to go, I had to be willing to go there myself and be able to face with the client the full impact of the experience. Although for my part this sharing of the experience had an "as if" nature, I had to be willing to see and experience in myself similar painful emotions to be able to be useful. I felt that if I was not able to deal with issues of competency, dependency, intimacy, mortality, and so on, I would not be able to help my clients deal with such issues in themselves. That is, if I could not face in myself some issue my client was struggling with, I doubt I could help my clients confront the full impact of their experiencing, because it would be too threatening *to me*. In many instances during supervision sessions, I have needed to talk about my reactions to the experiences clients have presented, and it was always a shock to me for a therapy supervisor to point out issues that at first I was blind to which later became glaringly obvious.

At present, I believe that the first part of not wanting to hurt clients further has been dealt with by my increased maturity and experience in that I have discovered that I can trust my clients to live through the worst of their experiences. I believe the second part, however, is something that will be in effect insidiously throughout my career practicing psychotherapy; effort and attention will always have to be given to preventing clients from building defenses based on my own defenses. To put this into the perspective of beginning psychotherapy training, these issues forced some rather intense and sometimes painful self-exploration in which I felt impelled to examine parts of myself that I had previously avoided. To this end I was lucky in having the opportunity to be in a "growth group" with fellow students who were also beginning therapy training: we could explore these issues and common concerns in a non-threatening environment. It was extremely reassuring and supportive to learn that what I was experiencing was not unique to me but was shared with my colleagues.

Looking back now from the perspective of having three years of training and experience in psychotherapy with many kinds of clients, it seems as if the issues that before felt so acute are no longer as troublesome. Although much remains a mystery, I feel confident in what I do in therapy and strongly believe that I have something valuable to offer my clients. I have found that writing this has been difficult because I have not been able to recapture, in all its vividness, the unique experience of beginning and taking the first steps as a therapist.

Through continual discussions with my fellow students and countless hours of intensive tape-work supervision sessions that involved role playing and learning by shaping, I no longer feel that I have to consciously and strenuously force myself to attend to that which my clients are implying and can't quite face—somehow, although it is still an active process, it feels as if it comes more naturally.

CHAPTER EIGHT

Observing Others

One student told me I should never let people read what I have written about therapy unless they also hear a session. Many students react with, "Oh! Now I see what it means" after they hear a session, and I have given you a lot of advice about the value of tape work. This book comes with a cassette tape illustrating therapy as done by five therapists, but I realize that some of you may not have access to this tape for some reason. This chapter presents written transcripts of part of each session on the tape, along with comments by the therapists and one of the clients involved. Thus, the book can stand alone as an (incomplete) way to observe the work of others. You can also use the typed transcripts as a sort of programmed text by moving a piece of paper down the page, stopping at the end of each client response, and formulating a response you might have made. You can compare your response with what the therapist actually said—which may or may not have been the best possible response.

It is best, of course, if you can also use the tape, because you will have some of the nonverbal cues such as timing and voice quality. You can also use the pause button on your recorder to practice responding. Just stop the tape where you feel like responding and take all the time you need to hear the implicit message and formulate a response. If only clients came with pause buttons.

Observing Bob Lee—*Multi-Cultural Counseling and Consulting Center, San Diego, California.*

This therapy session was conducted as a demonstration in front of a group of other therapists and counselors at a workshop on therapy. The session itself interestingly illustrates therapy, and the discussion that follows gives a fascinating glimpse into what the session felt like both to Bob, as the therapist, and to the client. At the time,

Bob and the client did not know that the session might be used as part of a book, but the evening after the interview, the client had written down her reactions, and some of her comments follow the transcript of the session.

THE INTERVIEW

Client: My nervousness is mostly related to the group, I think. Sometimes I have a . . . a hesitancy to volunteer because I . . . I always want to jump into things all the time. And sometimes I talk too much, and it . . . uh . . . don't let other people have a chance. That's why I've been waiting [Mm-hm]. . . .

Therapist: It's like there's some kind of . . . uh . . . enthusiasm or excitement to kind of get in there and get involved, but it's also a conflicting thing because part of you says "Hey, let's let some other people have the . . . have some time."

C: I have been told a lot, even as a facilitator, I step in too much . . . and, um, . . . I want . . . I'm trying very hard not to do that . . . I'm getting better at it, but I'm hesitant. Also, something that's coming up—that I realized when I was sitting there was . . . the problem that I have . . . I can almost start crying about it right away because . . . but I don't want to do that.

T: Maybe right now you're doing some of that . . . like you're coming on a little too fast for your own self . . . and you're saying, "I want to step back a little from this and . . . "

C: Well, it's something that I . . . I've dealt with with many therapists and I've gone through it a lot [voice breaks] and, uh, being in a therapeutic setting with people who are doing it, I start to think about my problem. Whereas, you know, normally I can go through the day and not think about it [Mm-hm] and, uh, being around so many people who I know are good counselors, part of me wants to talk to 'em about it, and . . . and part of me says "I'm sick of talking about it." [Mm-hm] It's, uh, well, I want to tell you what it is, so you won't just be responding to this vague problem and it . . . the label for it was originally called "anorexia nervosa." And I don't know if you know what this is. [Mm-hm]. . . I think the label upsets me . . .

T: It's like you're having to live with some label . . .

C: [crying] Sort of . . . I don't think other people label me that anymore, but it . . . on the outside it looks like it's gone, but it's not . . . on the inside of me it's always still there [Mm-hm] and, uh, I feel like it's . . . You know what that is, don't you? [Mm-hm] I don't know if we should . . .

T: Do you want to say more about that? Maybe we . . . it would be better if you just said something about it . . .

C: Well, uh . . . it's something that happens to you that you don't realize is happening to you in the beginning and, um, it started with me a long time ago when I was in college [voice breaking], and I just . . . went on a diet, like a lot of other people go on diets, but I . . . just, for some reason I couldn't stop doing it . . . I . . . It was almost like I had to have complete control . . . but anyway, I didn't realize what I was doing, and I had some doctor, my doctor, you know, say to me, gave me this book to read about it, and I said "Naw, that's not me," and eventually I realized it was me, but I still couldn't stop it . . . and now, even though I've gained the weight back, I'm terrified by the idea every day . . . It's, um, it seems like there was another person inside of me, always talking to me [Mm-hm], and I want to get rid of it so bad . . . and I've talked to so many people, and I wasn't going to talk to anybody here because I've decided I can only get rid of it myself . . . but I guess every little discussion about it makes it get a little better, so . . . I volunteered . . .

T: Like there's still something compelling in you to tell somebody else about it, and hopefully this time maybe . . .

C: Somebody else who might . . . who might be able to help me understand it a little better because I could go around and talk about it sometimes. Sometimes I can talk about it very . . . like, therapist. And I've been asked to work with people who've had it, and . . . and, and I can't do it because what happens is I get jealous of the patient . . . [crying] That's hard for me to admit. [Mm-hm]

T: It's like that's something you don't like about yourself that you do that . . .

C: That I get jealous?

T: Jealous of the patient.

C: Yeah, I think, it's crazy . . . but on the other hand, if I see someone who's really thin or working with someone, and I think "How come I can't do that?" . . . and I used to have so much control, and I used to be able to not eat, and I used to be able to turn down certain things and stuff, and now I don't have that anymore, and I get jealous of them, and I . . . feel a little crazy . . . now I can go around and have a normal life and no one would guess, there's a former anorexic walking the street, but it's . . . it's still there, it causes a lot of problems in relationships . . .

T: Like you can disguise that from most of the world most of the time pretty effectively, but inside you know that it's still there . . .

C: I can't seem to exactly turn it off, my, uh, my behaviors are changed—I'll sit down at the table and eat, but almost the entire time, I'm . . . someone's talking to me, . . . it's like "You shouldn't eat that, you should eat that, this has that many calories, you can't eat the whole day if you eat that," and I just want it, just "Shut up" . . . I guess . . .

T: "Shut up, leave me alone," those voices just keep hounding you.

C: I mean, sometimes it's from the minute I wake up . . . and sometimes it's . . . it's not this bad . . . as bad, I mean . . .

T: Like when you come into therapy, you talk again about the problem, why, then it . . .

C: Yeah, yeah, exactly. . .

T: . . . then it's exaggerated . . .

C: In this kind of setting, when you talk about people's problems and helping people and stuff like that, I start thinking about it, and it gets . . . builds up more and more and more . . . and, well, you know, the bottom line is that what I think is that nobody else can do anything about it. Uh, I don't know . . . uh . . . I'm reluctant . . . uh . . . I been wanting to seek therapy again for it . . . because it's not just the anorexic thing, I think you get that from a lot of other reasons—being insecure or whatever—but when I start being in therapy, I start talking to someone about it, I become more aware, like, after this session, when I go to the cafeteria to eat, number one, I'm going to be a lot more aware of it, and number two, everybody else who's in here is, I feel like they're gonna watch and see if I eat! [Laughter]

T: Yeah. Which is just going to make you more aware of it. It's like a vicious circle.

C: [Long pause, sighs] And sometimes I . . . sometimes I'm even a little embarrassed because I'm almost . . . a little proud of the fact that I was one . . . I was one [Mm-hm]

T: Like, I was something, I was this . . .

C: Uh-huh . . . That's exactly it. It's, at the time you think in a strange way that you're special. That you have something that nobody else has . . . And people talk to you about it . . . In the beginning, "Oh, you're so thin, how did you get so thin?" and then it becomes "My God, you are thin," and then . . . but it's still . . . something special . . . [Mm-hm] and I think . . . I don't want to lose that . . .

T: Yeah, and it's really hard to let go of that . . . On the one hand, you want to let go of it, because it's very tormenting . . .

C: It's not healthy. . .

T: Should do this, should do that, wake up in the morning with it . . . and on the other hand, there's something special . . . [Mm-hm] like in some weird way it's an old friend, been with you a long time . . .

C: I think everybody wants to think they have something special, you know, about them [Mm-hm] . . . but . . . So then, there's another thing that comes in, you know, that, do I really want to talk about it, you know, because did I just get up here because I want everyone to know that I once was one . . . or do I really want help . . . you know, sometimes I can't decide, I don't even know what I want, you know . . . I'm not sure exactly why I came up here, I would hope to think it's because I really thought maybe I'd get something out of this . . . but there's another little part of me that says "Oh, you just want to tell . . ."—that you were once one . . .

T: It's like, on the one hand, you're just compelled to do what you're doing . . . and then when you stop and look at it, you say "Well, what did I do that for . . . what am I doing those things for?" . . . and sometimes maybe you have some answers, and at other times it's just like "I have no idea . . . but there I am again . . . there I go again . . ."

C: Yeah, and also it's a good excuse in a sense, because, you know, nobody else volunteered, so that made it a little easier for me . . . [Mm-hm].

T: Yeah . . . It's like maybe some others could wait longer, but it's like whatever that compelling thing in you—

C: I was almost crying sitting down there [Mm-hm], and I was afraid to get up because I thought "As soon as I hit that chair, I'm gonna cry. . ."

T: Yeah. Yeah. Like something takes over and it just starts working itself automatically.

C: I don't know . . . I wonder if things like that ever leave, you know. I wonder if they're always old friends that stay around, and maybe I just have to accept it as an old friend . . . I don't know . . . Maybe if I accepted it more as an old friend instead of trying to fight it . . . then I would be better off [Mm-hm] . . . like . . . that feels good to me, that thing about being an old friend, because, like when it comes knocking on your door, even though they may have done a lot of bad things to you, you let 'em in.

T: Yeah, like it has a home in me, maybe if I could just become friends with it . . .

C: I always let him in . . . I'm worried about my health . . . and, um, doesn't seem to me to be a healthy friend to have.

T: It's hard to welcome it as an old friend and to really start maybe embracing that part when maybe it's really injurious to my health . . . That could be a mistake, I wouldn't wanna do that . . . So it throws me into another quandary about what I should do, try to keep it, let it go . . . [Mm-hm]

C: Yeah . . . it's interesting 'cause sometimes I do want to keep it, and sometimes I just . . . [Mm-hm] . . . What I almost just said is "I want somebody to take it away" . . . that's what I almost just said, and that's like what I really do want . . . because I don't seem to be able to say "Get out of here" myself . . . I wish someone would just come take it away . . .

T: I guess you were asking me earlier "Bob, could you take it away?" and then sometime later you said "I don't think you can . . ." Maybe even you would give me a fight . . . 'cause it's special in some way . . .

C: Yeah, I gave a lot of therapists a lot of fight, yeah . . . I mean, in one of the first this, this, God, this Freudian analyst I saw, after the very first session, offered me a Coke . . . and I was so pissed off at him. I thought he was trying to get me, you know . . . and I'd lie to them . . . say I ate when I didn't. Even though I kept going to therapy, you know, I kept going 'cause I wanted to be cured, but I lied . . . That was stupid . . .

T: I'm hearing you say "Bob, on one hand, I want you to take it away, but on the other hand, I don't . . . I'm going to have to let go of this myself, and yet I'm not sure I can do it . . ."

C: Well . . . well . . . that's not exactly it. What it exactly is is that I want you to take it away, but I don't want to know when you're coming to do it. And I just want to quit . . . because if I know you're coming to do it, I'll fight you . . .

T: Yeah, yeah . . . okay . . . yeah . . .

C: Y'know, and I know, being a counselor, know that's not possible. I know, like I would say that, you know, if the situation were reversed and I was trying to help you, I would say that I would be doing the kind of things to try to help you help yourself. But being in this seat now, I don't want to do that, I don't want to help myself, I want someone to take it away. It wasn't as scary then as it is now, looking back at it . . . you know, I look at pictures of myself and I cannot believe I did that to myself . . . I . . . It . . . It feels like the same person, but . . . but when I get the image in my mind of who I was back then, and I think of myself back then, it feels like the same person—when I see a picture, it's not the same person. [Mm-hm] But the . . . the competitiveness, or the compulsion I have to do certain things, is almost exactly the same, but it's channelled in other ways. It's not channelled in food anymore; that one I've pretty much conquered—I won't want to eat it, but I will—that kind of stuff, but it channels out in other areas . . .

T: So I've found ways to channel this away from food but I still feel that strong compulsion, that competitiveness, in . . .

C: Yeah . . . yeah . . . See, I don't see that it's gone . . . a doctor can see that it's gone because I'm not, you know . . . 83 pounds or whatever . . . And I don't really see that it's gone. I just . . . I put it off into other places. One of the things I started doing was, when I started eating, I decided well what I have to do is exercise . . . So, you know, I was so compulsive about it, uh, well, I just, you know, I kept injuring myself . . . I'd hurt myself and not want to stop . . . I'd say "Oh, you big baby," and I'd keep going . . . I was working with weights, and I'd say "Oh, you know, don't be a baby just keep going," and I'd keep going and ended up on crutches . . . And I've done those things a few times . . . And I can't stand it anymore . . .

T: It's like there are two people in there, and one is like a baby and the other is older than that baby and kinda chides that baby, kinda harasses that baby . . . "Oh, you big baby, come on, you can do that" . . . And the baby kinda goes ahead and until it gets hurt . . . and then it can stop.

C: [crying] You know, people . . .

T: It's like you'd like to not have to go so far that you get hurt.

C: Uh-huh, uh-huh . . . I'm learning it, I'm getting better at it . . . But it's still there . . . I . . . You know, people tell you all the time . . . I said this to somebody here and we were joking about it and they didn't know the seriousness of it; now they're probably thinking about that, but I said: You know, when you go into a spa, they always have signs up that say, "No Pain, No Gain," so in my mind I always think, well, it's supposed to hurt . . . I'm afraid if I stop too early that I'm not being good enough . . . I'm not doing it the best . . .

T: Well, like that voice says, like, you're not good enough, you're not doing the best, come on, you can do it . . .

C: Uh-huh . . . Oh, I always have thought that I can do it, if I ever really want to do something, I can do it . . . And so I push myself to do the best, and I'm afraid to stop, because I'm afraid I haven't really given it my best shot. [Mm-hm]

T: Like, just one more push, one more try, and I'll get there . . . if I stop, I'll never get there . . .

C: Yeah, yeah . . .

T: I'll be right there where I was . . .

C: It'll be a waste . . .

T: It'll be a waste . . .

C: I won't ever grow . . . [yeah] . . . so I've been searching for a lot of people, like, it's almost like I have to have a doctor tell me, "OK, you can't run. You can't run for a month," and it's almost like they have to tell me that, and sometimes I go in there, and I want to say "Please tell me I can't run." You know, because if you don't tell me, I'm going to do it. I'll run on my knee and hurt it again. And . . . the problem is . . . you know, I feel like I'm a pretty intelligent woman, and in my life and in my work, you know, people look up to me and stuff like that, and I can't understand why I keep doing this. It doesn't make . . . it's not . . . it doesn't seem like me.

T: It's like it's not me that keeps doing this. There's something in here that's just doing this . . . going on and it's not me . . . and yet "me" goes with that . . . "me" doesn't have any choice not to go with that.

C: . . . Rationally I know that it's me, but I can hear it . . . talking to me . . . Sounds pretty weird, but I hear it saying things like, y'know, "Oh, you baby" or "Don't eat that."

T: It's like it's on a tape or something . . . like it's recorded in here . . . and once in a while somehow the tape gets thrown on. Says that to you . . . and the you that's like this little girl . . . this little child starts obeying, starts following its commands. And like there's another you that's standing and saying "I don't want to do this, and" . . . but it's like that part is lifeless. It has a voice, but it doesn't have any power to stop this kind of . . .

C: It doesn't have enough. Um . . . I think it's afraid to be by itself . . . the other part, the part that doesn't have any power. I

133

think it . . . well it goes back to that being special. I'm afraid without it, I'll just be this normal person walking ar . . . like everybody else is.

T: Yeah, "I like being special" . . . that's a part of it.

C: Yeah. I mean too bad it had to come out in that way. [Yeah] No, I . . . people I'm really close to tell me "Oh, you're special anyway. You don't have to have that . . . I liked you when you weighed 150 or when you weigh what you do."

T: They tell me that, and I hear it, and I even know that many of them are sincere in that, but boy it's sure hard for me to . . . [Yeah] to let that make much difference to . . . to that part of me . . . just goes on.

C: I, uh . . . it is hard for me to believe. It's hard for me to believe when someone tells me now that I look nice or I look thin. I don't . . . and I don't think they're lying to me. I just don't see it . . . I want to see that. I think that . . . what I have said to other people is that once you look in the mirror and you weigh 83 pounds and you like yourself, then anything else over that is going to be gaining weight . . . being big, you know, so I constantly, when I look at myself, I berate myself all the time. Why can't you lose weight . . . and . . .

T: Why can't you be that 83-pound beautiful woman again?

C: Well, it's more not why can't I be that. Why can't I . . . It's not to get there. I don't think about being 83 pounds, because I don't want to be. What I think about is why can't I have the control I used to have then . . . why . . . sometimes I feel like I've lost a certain amount of willpower or control I had then. I mean I could . . . You know, people couldn't understand how I could do it. I had sort of a pride in that. Like people who fast, you know.

T: It's like that's something I could do for myself. Like there was a me that could do that for myself. I did it for myself . . . not the little girl . . .

C: Yes, exactly . . . I did it. No one else had anything to do with it.

T: I was the power, and yet there's this other where this little girl was told do th- . . . you know, keep going, push some more.

C: It's like no . . . you know, that something you do all by yourself. No one else is going to starve you . . . well, maybe, but, you know in a sense . . . And I didn't feel like I was starving then, I really didn't feel like that. What I felt like was that—we don't need to eat as much as we do . . . these people are . . . look at all this shit that they eat, and I don't need to do that. That was basi-cally it. I never thought about being 83 pounds. I never wanted to be. I even hided the fact.

T: Yeah. You were sort of telling them "I don't need to do that. Look, I'll show you I don't need to do that." And then you showed yourself—I don't need to do that.

C: I was afraid . . . and I'm still afraid of . . . if I let go of a certain amount of control, that everything is just going to go all haywire . . . and it hasn't, . . . but each step of the way, the pro-gression I made, it . . . everything hasn't gone all haywire, but I still maintain that in my mind that it's going to. I think . . . of everything that we've said, that the specialness part sticks out the most.

T: That I'm somebody special. That "she" inside is somebody special. It's very hard to let her go—to say goodbye to her. It's like she's in control in a way—like she was in control—not so sure now, maybe, but she really knew she was, and that's sort of where the locus of the control is still. And it's like you don't want me or anyone else to do anything to take that away, 'cause that's like taking away that control . . . You're saying you need help for you to kind of sneak up and get it, because I don't know if I can let it go now. Like I've done such a . . . good thing of being in control that—like I'm a master at that—boy, hey, world, if you want a master on that subject, come to me, but the other side of it secretly is, like we're sharing here is that, will somebody please come and take this away.

C: And that exact thing happens in other areas . . . you know of my life—that secretly I don't want to be in such control all the time. I don't want to have to be . . . I don't . . .

T: It's a real burden [Yeah] . . . I thought you said too, [client's name], that it kind of scares you to let it go, and it's almost like having gotten so much control now, it's kind of scary to let it go. [Uh-huh] That will go, and then I could lose . . . then I could lose control [Uh-huh] I could just . . . God, who knows how nutty I could be or wild or whatever would happen.

C: Yeah. It's interesting 'cause in a, in fact I've actually said both, you know. I want someone to take the control away, so I don't have to be in control, and in other words, I don't want to lose control. I didn't even notice I did that, but that's exactly what the problem is, because I don't . . . you know, there's a thin line that you walk in a lot of things, like when you're being a therapist and you're dealing with somebody. How much control do you want to have in that situation and how much do you want to back off? And I don't . . . what I feel like is I don't really have, many times, the internal mechanism that is able to decide [Yeah] . . . Like when I'm starting to injure myself. I don't know when pushing is pushing for the good of me and when pushing is going to hurt me. And, God, I don't know why I can't decide that. I mean that seems like a decision that you learn over experience. And I always err on the pushing-to-hurt-me side. I always err . . . I always go a little too far, rather than back off a little bit. It was the same way in school with grades, you know. I would study so hard that sometimes I would lose sight of the general feel of the class. Like if it was sociology class or something, I'd study everything in such complete detail that I would know it so well . . . and I always lost something that . . . and I'd say "I'm not going to do that next time," and I'd do it next time. I'd be afraid . . . if I was studying for a test, I'd study so hard that I knew everything. Then I'd take the test and there would be so much extra stuff I studied, and I'd say "I'm not going to do that again." But when I go again, I'm afraid if I leave off one little part, that's exactly what they're going to ask, and I'm going to look stupid . . .

T: Yeah, like I have to cover it all, and then maybe they won't ask, and I won't have to look stupid, but boy, is that a lot of work.

C: Yeah. Constant work. I feel that every day I'm constantly working. I can't . . . it's hard to relax. I always feel I should be doing something. You know, if I go down to the beach, I should take a book down to the beach, you know. I hate that . . . If I have a break, you know, I should do something during the break . . . God!

T: Like, I think you're saying "Please, whoever you are in there who keeps demanding these things of me, let me relax."

C: It's funny. I want to keep telling you how much better I'm feeling. I almost said it again, because to me right now, it sounds a lot worse than I feel that it usually is. Heightened—really heightened at this point. [Yeah, yeah] But it's always there to some degree.

T: So I'm getting better in a lot of ways. There are a lot of ways I'm doing a lot better than I did those years ago. But there's still some more work . . . you know, there's still some more work. And it's only here in this kind of situation that it gets so exaggerated. It gets so magnified.

C: Uh-huh. And it's been a long time since I really talked to anybody extensively about it. 'Cause some of my friends knew I had it . . . you know . . . It's old to them and everything, but it isn't to me. It's constant to me. [The interview continued for a few more minutes.]

Discussing the Session

After a brief rest, Bob, the client, and those observing discussed the session. An edited version of that discussion follows.

Group member: Bob, I've known you over the past year [in a study group], and it was really good to see you work. And I saw, more than I ever have, your ability to help another person appreciate . . . recognize . . . the edge of ambiguity. Like, rather than getting out of a double bind, or trying to . . . structure your life so you never get in them, it's like that . . . to help a person really see that they feel this way *and* that way . . . And I don't think I've ever seen quite as skillful an appreciation of that "edge." Boy, I recognize it in myself, and I think you really helped [client's name]— I don't know how to describe it—embrace that or see that it's there and accept it more and more . . . I also appreciated the way you identified with [client's name] by actually using the first person often. You didn't always use it. The first person, saying "Well, I really feel . . ." as if you were actually a mirror. Those were the two main things I noticed . . . very helpful demonstration.

Therapist: Let me say the question here was what was helpful to [client's name].

Client: I have never been . . . I realized right now as it opened up . . . I have never been to a client-centered person about this, and I never was able to talk so much. I never was able to . . . you said a few—like the "old friend" thing. I was trying to figure out what that was; the "old friend" thing just really fit. And I guess I said that somehow, but I didn't know that I had said it to you . . . There were a couple times when you had said something back that I didn't feel was exactly right, but I really felt free and easy to say "Naw . . . that's not exactly it," whereas before, I remember a couple of times before in therapy when they told me something, and I . . . I didn't tell them . . . it didn't feel right, but I let them go on for a while on that thing. A great one was that I was embarrassed about having sexuality, like having breasts, and so I was not eating to hide that. And that didn't fit at all, but I said "Oh, well . . . that may be . . ." I went on for a long time thinking about that. I really felt like you were a friend, and I could say, "Naw. . ." [After some discussion from the group, she continues] To see client-centered therapy being done is a lot different from all of a sudden feeling it. As soon as we started talking, I wasn't aware of you as a therapist trying to "technique" me . . . but watching other people here, I was trying to figure out the client-centered technique. So it's totally different once you sit down in a chair and start doing it. I learned so much more just now, even about the technique, by having it done to me.

GM: It seems to me that one of the differences is that when I am a client in client-centered, I feel I have no obligation to understand anybody but myself. And somehow, in other kinds, I feel I have an obligation to understand the therapist.

C: Yeah, if they say something to you that you don't understand, you want to sit there and try to get it.

GM: Bob, can you say what's in your head as you're doing that? What your experience is like?

T: Sure . . . Somehow, over the years, I've really come to . . . it's been a process of what I have to say doesn't matter, when I'm in this kind of setting. It's just so clear to me it doesn't matter. And also, going with that, I really want to know you.

GM: One thing I noticed was that ambiguity seems to be at the core—both of the problem as well as of the session itself. And I wondered whether that was the technique.

T: Yes, and one thing I'm helping [client's name] learn—and everybody learn—to pick up on the earlier comment too, is ambiguity—to live with ambiguity. That's one of the critical things to me about client-centered therapy. Where in the world do people help you learn to live with ambiguity, and life is just full of ambiguity. I don't know of any other place. Other therapists get involved in their own way—and you learn other things. I want to say that too. I did. I've been in Gestalt and all that. But nobody got out of the way and just let me stay in an ambiguous state and work through it.

C: Uh-huh . . . just having someone let you . . . actually, it was almost like I felt you felt what that feels like . . . When you said it, I almost felt like, He *knows* what that feeling's like. You know when you said "It just seems like . . ." and I think you even hit your knees one time, and I felt like that was me saying that—like, you *know* what that's like. Whereas before it was more like they were saying, "You're *saying* . . ." I felt like they were telling me what I was feeling, but they didn't really know.

GM: I first started listening, and I'd hear all these clues as to what the problem was, and I'd wonder "Gee, why doesn't he get into that?" And I realized that the simple thing is that it's her thing and what you're trying to do is help *her* get into it. And she jumped a lot . . . and she kept jumping back to the same things, but you didn't try to push her into it. She needs to do that, and if she wants to jump then that's where she is . . . And I really appreciate the word *ambiguity* that started this off, because it helped me see how simple it is.

T: There were times in this session I had the very same thoughts you did. So you'll have those thoughts. I just let them go. But I do have those thoughts—that's something I know is going on inside me . . .

C: You mean the thought that . . .

T: That I know what this is . . . that I can get her to the place . . .

C: I can see now that I was jumping around a lot . . . but as long as you understood what I said when I jumped, then when I thought about it for a minute, I remembered the biggest thing I felt, and I went back to it. But if you hadn't understood what I meant when I jumped, I would have gone on and tried to make you understand and maybe been lost . . .

GM: There was one statement she made that I wrote down . . . and your answer . . . she said "I don't want to be in control. I don't want to have to be in control." And you said "Yeah, it's a real burden." At that point, I would have been real tempted to say "Yes, I don't want to be in control, but I'm afraid if I give up my control, I won't be special. I won't feel special." And I'm wondering why you didn't . . . if you had that choice, would you have said that? Did you just not think about it?

T: Yes, and other times I think I did say that. So the answer is yes, and if at that very moment, that were there, I would have said it. There are a lot of responses we could give at any one time. It would be fascinating if we all wrote down and compared our different thoughts . . . and they all have a validity, and the checkout is [client's name]. She would say "Nope, that's not it." or "That's close," like sometimes you said "Well, that's like it but not quite." One of the keys of the process is that I relinquish that to the client. "Boy, forget about what I said; let's go with what you're saying."

GM: To offer a friendly criticism, it seemed to me that you were doing something in the way of cognitive structuring by going along with this idea that there are various "parts" [to the client]. You picked up on that and even extended it. So then there was this notion that there was one part doing this and one part doing that . . . To what extent do you go along with the way people present themselves as "I have this part and that part."? Really, do we have these parts? Or it's a way that I interpret myself or it's a way that I construct myself. The therapist might even respond in a way that makes it more ambiguous, but really, what do we know?

T: Well, I *don't* know. And I could have been way off, and she would have said "Gee, what are those parts you're talking about?" And I would have said right then . . . I wouldn't have defended that or said—say, as in Transactional Analysis, there's a Parent, Adult, and Child [in each person]. I would have just said "OK, well, help me with that. I'm not clear about what you said."

Same GM: I'd like to make another point, which is a paradoxical thing. In a situation in which there is a . . . a struggle . . . an issue around control and self-control—that clearly kept coming up again and again—who's in control? Who's in control of me being in control, and so on? I would imagine that if this client felt that the therapist was very invested in taking away the symptom, then the only course you would have would be to resist . . . You know, it's an attack against the self. . . it's not a symptom [to the client]. Paradoxically, the structure of client-centered therapy is perfect for that. You immediately begin to pick up that he wasn't interested in taking away your symptom.

C: That's true. It's a friend.

Same GM: Yeah, it was you [Bob] who suggested the metaphor of the old friend, and you [the client] loved that. "Oh! He's not mad at me that I like to diet," or whatever, and that seemed to me to be very, very helpful, and a way of avoiding a lot of that, uh, [power struggle].

GM: I want to ask a question about staying with the client and about reflection. There was some point that I might have been tempted to say "You're concerned in a very serious way about losing control, and it looks like right now you're kind of trying to reassure yourself. You know, kind of calming down; pulling away from it a little bit, reassuring yourself that things aren't so bad. Things are OK. I really do have control." Well, that's not reflecting what the client has said, but it is aiming at what you're experiencing right now, and I wonder if you have some general feeling about how free you feel to make remarks like that.

T: I feel very free to, and you said a key word there for me. It's *aiming at.* I always remember that I'm pointing towards or aiming at [the client's experience]. That's all. Then she says "That's it, jackpot" or "Boy, you hit the mark."

C: . . . It's interesting . . . how much do you reflect just the words that they say or the body posture . . . that's kind of reflecting . . . not what I've said, but what I'm doing.

GM: What I've heard a lot of people speaking about seems to me to be the difference between reflecting and interpreting. There seem to be slight differences in degree that can or cannot be incorporated into client-centered therapy, depending upon the personality of the particular therapist.

T: But there's a "spirit" here. It's an attitude—that's a better word—that's the core. And then I have a style, and I have a personality, and all that comes into play, but I'm really loyal to that attitude . . . I'm having trouble saying what the attitude is . . .

Same GM: Well, I assume it varies at points in time, too.

T: Yeah, and yet there's some kind of a core that I don't want to be wishy-washy about. I want to be stubborn about it.

Same GM: My interpretation was that you stopped just short of an interpretation.

T: Yeah, and I have those inside of me, as I said earlier.

GM: Does your loyalty to client-centered therapy allow you to incorporate some of the other approaches that you use—with the same attitude, the same respect for the client?

T: Yeah. As long as I maintain that attitude.

Later Bob wrote about this attitude:

Two thoughts immediately pop into my mind about this core attitude. First, I *truly* want to know and understand my client. I believe that everything [client's name] said and did is pointing to her exquisite *meaning.* What is primary, i.e. focal, for me is to "catch" her meaning and give it back to her. Sometimes with a client I am very dramatic/ demonstrative (my style/way of being) in describing to her or encouraging her to describe for herself what *is* her meaning. Secondly, I do not pursue helping the person. Rather, I am more like a discoverer/explorer passionately pursuing hidden truths in the service of, and with, my client. A *by-product* of following the core attitude is that the person feels "helped." By attentively straining my senses to know and understand what the client means, what ensues is the awareness of being deeply and personally known and understood, and this is sensed as being significantly helpful.

A Client's Reactions

I found myself reluctant yet wanting to be the client today at the Client Centered Therapy Workshop. My problem, "anorexia," has been with me for a long time and not much light has been shed on it for a long time. But there were breakthroughs today. I didn't come to some new, clearer understanding of the problem. I certainly wasn't cured nor did I feel that I was partially cured. What I did feel was better. I felt better. Isn't that what therapy is all about? We want to feel better, be happier, live fuller.

Well, today after a session of client-centered therapy I realized I had never had that in *any* other of the therapies I've had. Other psychologists would give their possible explanation and I would entertain the notion for a while—trying to—even hoping that it was the answer, the reason— thus one closer step to being "cured," but I never felt better. Sometimes I felt worse; I wan't sure if it was right, and I wanted to know, how could I know.

Other counselors tried to give me advice on how to stop my anorexic behavior, thus ending the immediate problem with perhaps exploring reasons afterward. I tried to do what they suggested. I never felt better; in fact, I felt worse. My anorexia felt better, so I preferred it to their therapy and their suggestions. Others asked and asked and asked me questions, to which if I knew the answer I wouldn't have been there, aside from the fact that even for those I could answer it didn't make me feel better.

Well, I felt better today. I was able to talk about my problem and truly feel understood, cared for, empathized with. I perhaps saw some things I hadn't clearly seen or understood before but mainly I left changed. I didn't go home upset, confused, worried, frustrated, wondering. I left feeling a little lighter, a little clearer, a lot happier. *Better.*

It just has struck me now, this evening as I think about the experience, that therapy is really just that. We can't go looking for cures or remedies. The looking is the cure and I get a little medicine each time I get this kind of experience. It's not as if the doctor had to wait and search until he found out all the reasons for my broken leg or my cold or my brain tumor before giving me medicine or treatment or surgery. And this is just what many therapists or counselors do.

The client later said that this point marked a break in her writing. Later she was concerned that what she said was incomplete, and so she returned to add a less personal discussion of the following issue.

I understand as I'm writing this that it is very limited (just a part), but I think definitely one aspect of therapy. For example, one would hope that therapy would not *merely* be a means for helping a client feel better about all the things he or she does, whether bad or good (from a cultural or even legal point of view). . . . Eventually the long-range goal includes much more than this—perhaps a better understanding for the client, ease of feelings, or even some solution of a particular problem being found—and also importantly clients learning the tools or "senses" to help themselves outside the therapy session. But all these often are overplayed or rushed into—even concentrated on—to the point where the acceptance, warmth, empathy, and thus the client's "feeling better" are neglected or lost.

Observing David Martin—*The University of Manitoba, Winnipeg, Manitoba*

Introductory Comments

Three of the interviews in this chapter are from early sessions, so I wanted to give an example of therapy after the client and I had been working for a while. This is the eighth interview with a 30-year-old professional woman. This excerpt begins somewhere into the session, so you will need to read a few lines to get into the flow of what we are exploring together. I like the word *exploring* to describe the mutual search that the client and I are engaged in. I hope that is made clear by what I do as the therapist. Some students who have listened to this session commented that at times they didn't know where my responses were coming from, although the client generally picks up on them as though they were accurate. I suppose that this happens partly because she and I have a shared store of knowledge from past sessions. I think, too, that by this time she knows that my intentions are empathic, that I will not try to take over the control of therapy, so I can take more chances; she knows that what I say is tentative and can be rejected. Similarly, I notice that I say "Right" a lot, where others might say "I understand" or "Uh-huh." I'm pretty sure that my client knows how I mean this, but it is something that can be misunderstood as "That is correct." I promise to try to stop saying "Right" so much.

Something I haven't commented on so far in the book is the use of humor in therapy. You will notice that I use facetious humor a couple of times in this interview. That is partly just part of my personal style, and I am comfortable with it, as long as the client and I are sharing a little joke. I don't really plan it as a way to "provide relief" or "regulate the tension level" or anything like that. I must say, however, that the only thing I'm really unhappy with in this session is the place where I do a kind of "interpret the defenses" move and comment on how the client uses humor in the hour. I don't know why I did this, but it certainly broke the flow of therapy temporarily. This is the kind of simple-minded therapist "cleverness" I have been warning you against for seven chapters. Oh, well.

THE INTERVIEW

Therapist: . . . there is something distorted in here . . . Something's affecting your life that you don't understand . . .

Client: Yeah . . . like . . . well . . . It's certainly around this whole thing with [material omitted] . . . Is our time up yet? [laughs] . . . I don't like this . . . That's awful, isn't it? What a horrible feeling.

T: It's about ten to one . . . Time flies when you're having fun, doesn't it? [Mm-hm] Make you uncomfortable when I look at you? [Mh?] Does it make you uncomfortable?

C: Well, no . . . not really . . . I . . .

T: What makes you uncomfortable is . . . you're cornered, in a way.

C: Well, yeah . . . I feel very much like I'm cornered. 'Cause I think that I'm going to find out something about myself I don't like. Something I'm not facing. [right] Y'know, like I want to avoid a whole bunch of things, I think, around that . . . and what that says about me . . . something that isn't going to fit together very well, that I'm going to be some . . . I want . . . that I'm trying to be somebody that I'm not, or something . . .

T: Mm-hm . . . and that is frightening . . . yeah.

C: Like I keep feeling underneath all this that maybe this is . . . maybe I really want to be dependent on somebody . . . y'know like I am in a lot of ways . . . but I don't really . . . y'know like [right] . . . like I feel that maybe that's what's happening . . . some dependency that maybe feels all right but that I don't really want . . . uh . . . oh, I don't know what I'm saying.

T: That's pretty clear, I think [yeah . . . I . . .] . . . If I ask you what do you want, you say "I want to be an independent, successful, strong person. That's what I want." . . . And it's almost like part of you says "No, I want to be taken care of." [Mm-hm] "I really want to be taken care of."

C: It's all too much for me, y'know, like . . .

T: Uh-huh . . . just somebody to hold me and take . . .

C: . . . nurture me . . .

T: . . . and if that's true, that part of you you don't want to look at.

C: The part that wants to be taken care of [yeah] the part that wants to be dependent on somebody . . . yeah . . .

T: It's going to be a jolt to look at that part of yourself.

C: I guess . . . I know it exists, and I know intellectually that's fine because everybody has those parts, y'know.

T: But you don't accept it in yourself? . . . or at least . . .

C: I don't like it. I don't like to need . . . to need that or to have to let someone have that much power over me or to be that vulnerable to someone else . . .

T: And the you that you know well almost couldn't respect a person like that. Like the you that you know is the independent.

C: The "you" that I think I want to be [Uh-huh] . . . or like best about myself . . . and then . . . and then I think that I almost feel that I have to be dependent or let people control me to have people . . . to . . . there's that part there, y'know. I've got to do what he wants or they want or . . . a friend wants to be accepted and cared about and wanted, y'know . . . [Right] The conflict is really difficult. If there's any struggle, I'd give in to have the person, rather to have me, y'know?

T: Because you have to have the person. You . . . if . . . You're dependent. That means you have to let yourself be in trouble . . . 'cause you need the person so much.

C: Yeah. If the need to have that person . . . yeah . . . is that strong . . . then I would, eh? Like I . . .

T: Mhm. You wouldn't take the chance of losing him. You couldn't afford to take the chance of losing him.

C: I'd lose me.

T: So you'd lose something that you have to have . . . Pretty needy?

C: Am I? Well, I guess I must be . . .

T: Kind of hard to say this . . . [Mhm] . . . to say . . . You're almost saying . . . "I'm a dependent person."

C: And I need people always telling me, y'know, you're doing OK, and [Mm-hm] that this is right and that . . .

T: You can't just live on your own approval of yourself. You can't say, "I know I'm valuable and good." You need people to . . .

C: . . . need it to be said to me all the time.

T: . . . reassure you . . . I was just going to say to "feed" you . . . (mhm) . . . occurred to me after, that's a double entendre . . .

145

C: Mhm . . . so what's that say about me? . . . Too insecure?

T: Oh, I see what you mean . . . too insecure . . .

C: Like everybody needs people, but why do I do it to the point of losing myself? Y'know . . . what is it that makes me need them so much that I won't, uh, that I can't say no, or I can't, uh, . . . like even last night when [material omitted] I didn't want her to come, because I wanted it to be people that had worked with this guy in the same unit, and we've had a lot of fun together, and . . . but I said "Sure, you can come." I wanted to say "No, I'd rather it be just a unit thing." I needed her to be there and give me all this support, and I didn't say no.

T: And you needed her not to be angry at you . . . [material omitted] uh, . . . you would have been the same with the department wimp too. If . . . it would have been very hard for you to say, even with somebody very passive, [yeah] . . . they'd say "Can I come along?" . . . "Oh, all right."

C: Like that must affect me every day, eh? That must affect me all the time.

T: Sure does . . . I mean it must.

C: What do I think is going to happen?

T: Something awful. [Yeah, really] . . . really awful.

C: It's no wonder I'm always feeling irritable and pissed off . . . most things I really want to do, or . . . yeah . . . or rationalizing everything because I've got to do it to get, y'know, people to be involved with me . . . That's awful [Mhm] . . . but that's what I do.

T: [Inaudible] You sort of said something like this a couple times ago. Why can't I stand up for myself? Why can't I say no . . . take good care of myself. [Mm-hm] Now this makes it clearer, in some ways, because you're so scared . . . of losing a person, I guess . . . of the person being irritated at you.

C: Because that person is the only reflection of me that I've got. Like they, y'know [yeah].

T: I'm not quite sure how you mean that. I think it's like this . . . it's you don't have a "core."

C: I'm only OK if you say I'm OK.

T: Exactly . . . [Yeah] . . . you don't walk around knowing you're OK.

C: Yeah, I need someone to . . .

T: Autonomous [Yeah] . . . And the way they say that is by praising you or saying "I like you" or being nice to you.

C: Mm-hm. See, I have glimpses of I'm OK, um, without that, y'know, at times, but I think that it has to be a fairly obvious situation. If there's any degree of judgment, I'm the "un-OK" one in the whole thing, y'know.

T: The glimpses are like little tastes of "Oh, that's how I would like to feel all the time." Or to have that feeling—I'm a good person?

C: Yeah. Yeah. Well, it's things like, uh, at a meeting I had some ideas I had written down and I had expressed some of them but not all of them, and a person sitting a couple seats away expressed similar ones, and I thought "Oh, well, he's thinking the same way I'm thinking. I can't be that bad." Y'know, I need to make those kinds of judgments all the time . . .

T: Even then it was something external that told you you were OK. [Mm-hm] You're not stupid [Mm-hm], somebody else thought the same thing. [Mhm] I see . . . what you want is . . .

C: I want something internal . . .

T: . . . to know that, that's right . . . without the always getting confirmation from somebody else that you're OK. No wonder you can't take any chances . . . with people. My God, they might get mad at you . . . implicitly tell you you're not a very good person. [Bad . . . yeah] And a core . . . that is somehow . . . you . . . you are your judge . . . that's what you want [Yeah] . . . You're in terrible conflict then, between, by God, wanting to be independent . . . and wanting to be so dependent and taken care of . . . somebody confirming you.

C: Yeah, like I'm almost a nonbeing without all those people around me . . .

T: I guess you almost can't stand to look at that about yourself.

C: No. I don't like it. [Uh-huh] Then I sometimes think that I overcompensate, especially with [name omitted] . . . overreact. That part of me . . . you're not going to get it . . . you're not going to control it, y'know . . . maybe I try and go too far the other way.

T: Uh-huh, I understand . . . that, uh, even stupidly the other direction. Or stupidly with some people you give in and let yourself be controlled out of fear . . . sort of to assert yourself and make up for it.

C: Yeah. I talked about that before too. Well, no . . . well, not on the same terms.

T: So with him you do irrationally controlling things. It all averages out.

C: Yeah, and it's just a crock of shit, eh? [Yeah, right] . . . So how do I get to feel OK? Where do I . . . My God, I'm 30 years old. Where do I get a deficit like that . . . to begin with?

T: You mean where does it come from or [Yeah] where do you get it overcome?

C: Well, both . . . I mean [OK] . . . I'm just wondering how does that kind of thing develop that you have to always be . . .

T: Always be praised . . . and not able to love yourself . . . or . . . I don't know what the word . . . that's the wrong word. [Yeah] Something like that. Love yourself . . . accept yourself . . . feel worthwhile. I guess that's closer [Yeah] . . . feel your own worth without somebody else giving it. Do you really mean that as a question? . . . like, how you get there? Forget it . . . I'm going to cop out anyhow, so I might just as well cop out now . . . um . . . I'm going to half cop out. Well, I can't answer that question, but I really think the process that we're engaged in is the [inaudible] . . . both the why, if it's important to know the why, and where you go from here.

C: Because I really think that . . . that that's probably what's happened to me all my life when I felt depressed or . . . or . . . what's the word? Just really like, really frustrated all the time with everything, y'know [Mm-hm], like . . . and that's probably where it's all coming from.

T: Yeah. You said that . . . no wonder you're angry all the time. Sort of always giving in. [Yeah. Yeah] You never get what you want, but you also don't feel good about yourself. You feel unhappy and depressed . . . and frustrated . . . It really makes a lot of sense. [Mm-hm]

C: It's almost like I have some . . . something's going to happen to me, y'know, in those situations . . . I . . . like what? I'll be a nonperson? I will die? They will reject me?

T: You seem clearly to fear they'll reject you.

C: Mhhm. Because you know . . . I was talking about . . . last night about people leaving me and how I felt really devastated when people left, and um [material omitted in which the client says she told a friend "I've never forgiven you for leaving me" because the friend left their mutual place of employment], which is really significant I guess, you know [Mhm], and we were just talking about why I . . . you know . . . she was talking about the same kinds of . . . of feelings of rejection and stuff . . . just why . . . why is she just so much a part of me that when she leaves, like that's . . . the relationship didn't end, but something happened. It's not been the same.

T: And you felt it as a hurt [Yeah], as a . . . she did it to you.

C: Yeah, it was a personal affront. You know, she can't live her life. She has to live mine for me. She has to stay there. That whole . . .

T: Or something like that, but in any . . . or whatever, she rejected you. You were hurt that she left.

C: Yeah. Yeah. How can you leave me here and go away? [Yeah] And that happened with another girlfriend too that left there, who I was really emotionally close to y'know . . . almost like go through each day with them . . . and spend time with them . . .

T: Mm-hm. Hurt. Terribly hurt and, uh, depressed in a way that's like being rejected . . . [material omitted] and you feel awful about yourself. It's almost like you go through that a lot [Yeah] every time a friend leaves—so you're hurt and angry at them for doing it [Mhm] although I doubt you express the anger.

C: No, of course not—no, but that's what happens repeatedly with relationships, I mean the relationships don't end . . . I carry on with them. And I do think the only one I've never felt that with has been the one in [city name] . . . except . . . except when she was saying at one point, um, well, she's really into TA and uses that with her . . . in her own practice and stuff, and she said at one point "You know, there's a lot of things happening with you, and maybe you should go talk with somebody and get some help." And I thought "Oh, she doesn't want to talk to me anymore." You know, like she can't do it and . . . y'know . . . but, uh, and I *know* that, but I feel like it's, y'know . . .

T: Sure. Intellectually, you know she's . . .

C: . . . going to be there and . . .

T: . . . she's going to be there. She was saying "Get some extra help." [Yeah] And your first thought is "You don't want me anymore."

C: Yeah. That's awful. That's what I've always felt . . . just . . . even . . . we had a kid staying with us on one of these student exchange things in grade 11, and he was my brother's age, [material omitted] and he stayed for a week and . . . I was devastated for two days when he left. Just, y'know, I didn't feel hurt, but I just felt like "Oh, he's gone," and I . . .

T: You didn't feel like he had hurt you [no, but just the whole . . .], but you just felt like somebody had died. . .

C: Yeah. Like everybody's left.

149

T: Yeah. When people leave, you feel . . . you mourn. You feel . . . abandoned.

C: Yeah. I wonder if my mother left me when I was young [laughs].

T: That word hit home?

C: What?

T: Abandoned? . . . Did it feel like people . . .

C: Yeah . . . it's like—what I am I going to do? Like how can you leave me here? There's no plan for me, y'know? That . . .

T: Oh, I see. Who's going to take care of me now?

C: Yeah. That's it.

T: I need you . . .

C: Or I'll have to take care of me. Well, if that's the [inaudible] that I have felt . . . That's really awful . . . Because I know enough intellectually to know that I shouldn't be feeling this way, like I know [Yeah, I know what you're saying] . . . about relationships, and people don't dump people all the time and walk all over them and, y'know.

T: You should be able to trust that . . .

C: And it will continue, you know. They don't just all end, you know.

T: And you've had lots of experiences that haven't just ended.

C: Well, yeah. And good ones.

T: It seems like I should learn from those experiences. But you know what the book says—what you're supposed to be feeling—modern person . . .

C: But here I am. Like so wishy-washy and insecure that without all these people giving to me all the time, I can't survive. And I wonder how much I give back, if I need all this, am I really giving . . . Why are they sticking around? Y'know, what am I giving?

T: Mhm. Feel like you're just sucking all the time . . . taking, taking, taking [Yeah] . . . Um. Wait a minute . . . Up till this minute, you feel like you do give back—in a lot of relationships? Now are you saying "How could I possibly be giving back if I'm always so needy?"

C: Yeah. Well, I don't think I have been recently. I've been taking. But this last while is . . . but like, see, even the girlfriend in [city name]. It's reciprocal. She'll call me with the same kinds of problems, and she'll say "Gee, I feel great talking to you, and that's really helped," and like with the one I was talking to last night, she told me a lot of stuff that was going on in her life, and I listened and understood. Like it wasn't all focused on me.

T: That's what I'm wondering about, yeah.

C: Like, but yeah . . . very . . . so conscious of saying things about me all the time—my problems—and I—and my life—and not giving. I'm wondering how much I'm really giving.

T: I see, right. OK, sometimes you do give, but you may give a lot less than you thought . . .

C: . . . than I'm getting. Or than I'm getting.

T: . . . that you're getting. [In some ways] Because if you need that much, you must be taking a lot . . . or looking for a lot . . . or seeking a lot.

C: And draining people. That's why I don't have any friends. [laughs] But I do . . .

T: Yeah, you do . . . That's something else you don't want to be true about yourself—is that you drain people.

C: . . . that I'm so self-focused or something.

T: I'm almost waiting for you to say "I need so much."

C: . . . I was thinking about yesterday. I had fun. I laughed . . . I mean I have fun . . . even. We can even laugh about tragic things. I guess a survival thing, but . . .

T: You had fun . . .

C: . . . at work. Monday [inaudible] . . . that's pretty good, eh [facetiously]?

T: Oh, that's wonderful . . . You do that in here too. You laugh . . .

C: I know. Well I . . .

T: Funny . . . I go along with it too . . .

C: Aren't I supposed to laugh?

T: That's fine. That's good. I'm just saying that we both . . .

C: Humor's my big defense too. I use humor a lot. You know to sort of say what I mean. I think that's all right [Yeah] . . . Therapy can be fun.

T: As we know, it's not always, though. [inaudible]

C: . . . What were we talking about? Oh, draining people . . . It's almost recently, I have to consciously get talking about something other than me . . . Y'know . . . I have to make an effort at it. Which I guess is OK as long as I do it. I'm really not . . .

T: At one level it's OK. You wish it came more naturally [Yeah] because that's evidence to yourself almost that you are so needy . . . self-centered.

C: I have so much going on in me that I can't look at the other person and give to them . . . I just feel like this is all so, like, sort of overwhelming. You know? Like so much is going on in my head.

151

T: Today, you mean. [Yeah] Also, I was about to ask you . . . Oh, golly we're almost out of time. It really did fly by, the last part for me. [Yeah] A lot of this clearly is new for you . . . clearly . . .

C: The feeling isn't new but maybe the . . . thinking about it that way is.

T: That the perspective is different in a way [Yeah], and it's almost too much to handle . . . or assimilate or something.

C: Like it makes sense in terms of what I'm doing with my life and my interaction and my relationships. Yeah. It makes a lot of sense. But then I think, but, God, what do I do now? . . . You partially answered that . . .

T: Well, I did partially answer that before. Um, are you saying now "My God, do I have to wait till next Friday to get back into this?" and would like to come in sooner? . . . come in a couple times next week . . . Are you saying that?

C: Well . . . I don't know what I'm saying. I'm saying I'm feeling like, God, there's so much going on and . . . Like I guess I'm just feeling like this . . . will I ever . . . will that ever get better [OK] . . . it's just so . . .

T: Is there anything that can be done about this? [Yeah] That I can . . . I'll tell you my feeling. I feel good. I'm sorry about the pain you go through, but I feel good about what we're doing . . . feel good about . . .

C: That we got through some of the crap . . . yeah . . . I was avoiding, yeah . . .

T: And you feel—does something like this ever change at 30, for heaven sakes. If it doesn't, I'd get out of this business.

C: I guess the frustrating thing is . . . intellectually I have that information—or I should have it. I do have some of it, but . . . how do you . . .

T: . . . if we do what we did today . . . remember that . . . 20 minutes ago, when I . . . I didn't know what else to say . . . just sort of "Boy, something sure is goofed up." That's when it hit me how overwhelming and blocked up . . . and distorted—that's what it was—how distorted your understanding and knowledge of yourself is. Something's going on . . . that neither of us understands, but we'll get to it. I really believe in this process . . . I've really got to quit.

C: Do you . . . like with school being over, do you change your schedule at all, or will you be able to see me . . . for a while? [Oh, yeah] That's no problem?

T: That's no problem. I'll be around almost all summer. I'll go away for maybe ten days . . . but usually . . . I'm very flexible in the summer. I'll take a few days off here and there to go camping . . . whatever . . . so, sure, I'll be here.

C: Like I don't know if seeing you twice next week or something is going to . . .

T: You answered my question. That is not what you were saying. See you could have been saying "My God, I can't wait till Friday to deal with this." Or you could have been saying "Wow, is there any way out of this?"

C: OK . . . I . . . yeah . . . I can wait till Friday because I can avoid it for a few days . . .

T: Right. OK, we'll say Friday at 12:30 . . .

C: . . . [Heartfelt sigh]

Observing Bill Coulson—*College of Notre Dame, Belmont, California*

Introductory Comments by Bill
The Glazed Look

Trying to communicate with a foreign person is good discipline for a counselor who may have gotten sloppy.

The glazed look in my clients' eyes announces my sloppiness. It appears when I am talking. When *they* are talking, by and large my clients look alert and interested. When I speak (particularly when I speak at length) is when the glazed look appears.

In a way, the look is a sign of respect. My clients are not so rude as to say "Shut up, this is my hour, not yours." So they feign interest and comprehension. The glazed look gives away the deception. What it means is "I am trying to get what you're saying, but, really, I don't get it."

I saw the glazed look once too often in my private practice recently and realized I needed a tune up. I needed discipline. I needed to learn again to stay within my clients' frame of reference.

Fortunately, we had a number of Japanese people in town for a program of community building: long hours of daily nondirective encounter for two and a half weeks with a large international group.[1] I decided to take advantage of their presence by asking one of them

---

[1] This experience was part of The La Jolla Program.

to speak to me for an hour. I realized this might turn out to be difficult for us both, since she did not consider herself to speak good English at all. I would have to strain to catch her meaning, and that was the point.

It was a very good experience for me. When she returned to Japan, she wrote "I felt completely accepted and deeply understood by you." So I have reason to think it wasn't bad for her either (though I am aware of the Japanese reputation for politeness). She said the interview seemed to make the many disparate experiences of her weeks in La Jolla cohere. I was pleased, because what I look for in counseling is that a person might pull together loose ends, more nearly taking possession of his or her life.

In the interview itself, she chose not to ask for counsel so much as to tell me the story of her time in La Jolla, particularly about what she called her "language handicap." I had been prepared for this because of the experience of other Japanese in previous La Jolla programs. It was the reason I had asked her to talk and not an American. But it was important not to take her as a specimen of a language handicap or as a specimen of the Japanese people.

At the end of the taping session, she told me she wished she could have expressed herself better. I said the problem of expression wasn't hers alone. "Sometimes, when I want to understand what you are saying, I don't quite understand and say it wrong. Then that's my language barrier." The reason it was good discipline for me to try to catch her meaning (and what makes me want to start a Rent-a-Foreigner agency for other counselors) is that the glazed look was *immediate* when I didn't catch her. It didn't wait until I was three-quarters through a long speech. If I exceeded her framework even in choosing a particular word, I could see that I had lost her and that counseling was momentarily over.

I want to comment on a few specifics of the interview.

1. *Her laugh.* I think it is cultural: part of her native framework and therefore not to be questioned. Even if it were not cultural, I would try to resist highlighting or asking about it. In general I want to avoid distracting clients (or myself) by noting their manner. My goal is to see the world *through* their habits, just as they do.

An easy interpretation of an embarrassed laugh is that it discounts oneself. The counselor's own manner, however, is usually sufficient to set the tone for counseling to occur in spite of client embarrassment. The counselor takes everything the client says seriously. This is not to say the counselor is stodgy, but it means that counseling is quite different from conversation. The counselor bears down, is figuratively on the edge of his or her chair, trying always to catch the client's exact intention. I think you could define the uniqueness of counseling by the counselor's attitude: "I take myself seriously here, and I take *you* very seriously indeed." Such an occasion—signified by the singlemindedness of the counselor's devotion to the client's meanings—is fraught with a significance the client might never before have openly faced. In itself it is a giant step toward healing.

2. *Asking questions.* I learned in training that client-centered counselors don't ask questions. But when I don't understand, I like to ask—if asking doesn't impede the flow. There are points in the interview where I ask too clumsily and find that I have gotten in the way and other points when asking was a good thing because it forestalled having to *pretend* I understood. My goal is to stick with the client and not fall too far behind, though (of course) I don't like to be just curious. Waiting often pays off, too. There is no rule. It is a matter of judgment.

3. *Going for the feelings.* There is a point late in the segment when, in rehearing it now, it seems she might have been expressing a present sadness rather than talking about something past. I'm not sure. In either case, I am pleased I didn't exploit it. I used to count my clients' tears and wear them like medals. I don't seem to need to do this so much any more and am glad for the shift.

4. *Going too fast.* At the very end, she describes the situation in her marathon group (a 24-hour, non-stop encounter) when everything went too fast. Then she felt herself to be Japanese (that is, foreign). I think people come to counseling precisely because of such experiences. So much is happening in their lives that they can't keep track of it. Life comes into them but lodges in some secret place. They don't gain possession of their own experience.

Taking pause can be as good for the counselor as for the client. I know it was good for me to listen and speak to this client. Often being with people goes too fast for me, too. I neither catch their meaning nor say my own, and I don't stop to ask for help; it seems I *assume* I have understood, when, if I were more attentive, I would realize I haven't.

This conversation with a foreign person slowed me down. Going slower in itself helps me understand—and to know that I understand. I think it is similar for the client: because we are taking such small steps, she realizes her counselor is still with her. To believe (on good evidence) that your counselor knows you—and yet has no mind to condemn you—is one of the effects that make counseling worthwhile.

THE INTERVIEW

C: At first, I would like to say . . . yesterday I joined your group . . . yesterday afternoon . . .

T: Yes . . . on conviction . . .

C: I tried to listen to your lecture, but your English is . . . words . . .

T: . . . too fast . . .

C: Yes, and like music to me [laughs].

T: Not like words, but like . . . sounds [yeah] . . . like sounds, sure.

C: And sometimes words . . . some words . . . came into me. For example, *client-centered therapy* . . . *mother* . . . or something . . . and my imagination worked hard, but I had to give up.

T: Yes, I understand. Is it different when you listen in the groups—in the small groups—to people speaking in English of themselves and their feelings? Do you find that you hear more of what they mean than in a lecture? . . . Do you understand . . .

C: Yeah . . . easier . . .

T: Easier . . . yeah. And does . . . is it that your heart hears then . . . or how does it work . . . is it just your brain or what?

C: Ummm. Maybe heart.

T: I've heard that. Other Japanese have told me that they hear many feelings, but they don't understand the words, but they understand with their heart is what they . . .

C: Yeah, maybe. I experienced . . . in my first group and the second group . . .

T: That understanding what a person feels . . . is that what you're experiencing . . . ?

C: And I was very surprised—at me [Ahh] who could understand without words.

T: I see. You didn't expect that you could understand.

C: Um. Before I came here, I knew I had language handicap. So at first I didn't want too much from this program.

T: You didn't want . . . too much . . .

C: At first, I didn't want too much from this program. [OK] I didn't expect so much.

T: Uh-huh . . . because of the language handicap . . . yeah.

C: And, uh . . . astonished . . .

T: You were astonished?

C: Yeah. In the first group . . .

T: Astonished at how much you understood?

C: Yeah . . . of course, I couldn't understand the details . . . exactly . . . but I can imagine . . . I could imagine . . . what they are . . . what they were talking about there. And . . . I could feel the feelings . . .

T: Even without grasping every word, you could imagine their experience.

C: Of course, sometimes . . . a sentence, or some words came into me. [Yes] Of course they helped my imagination.

T: The words would help, yeah.

C: Of course. But, uh, in the first group, I always felt I was there—with them . . . [Mhm] So I was pretty comfortable with them. [Yes] . . . And at first, in the first group, a facilitator asked me about my language problem [Yes] and then I answered him . . . I couldn't understand the details, but . . . I would try to ask you when I could, and then, . . . since then they didn't worry me about my language handicap . . .

T: I see. They . . . they were able to relax and trust you to ask them if you didn't understand . . . yeah . . . and so they didn't have to worry about you . . .

C: [Laughs] Yeah, and that made me easier.

T: I see. You would have to worry about them worrying about you otherwise—yes, so when they said "Now we will not worry," then you could relax too.

C: In the third day . . . that's . . . I'm sorry. My English is some-times strange . . . In the third day . . .

T: Second day or third day?

C: Third day [third day] in my first group . . . they began to talk about our facilitator . . . and because our facilitator didn't move so much, and some people was angry with him . . . and, uh . . . and one of them got angry with him very strongly, and I couldn't understand why she was interested in him so much.

T: Puzzled you . . . her interest.

C: Yeah. Of course [inaudible].

T: But you didn't say that there . . .

C: And then I forgot my language handicap [Ahh], and I asked her "Have you ever experienced a facilitator in a small group?" I asked her. I forgot my language handicap.

T: I see. You just spoke to her . . . not . . . uh-huh . . .

C: And then suddenly she cried. I was very surprised. And then she began to tell us about her problem. [Oh] She identified her father with the facilitator [I see] because facilitator . . . were not interested in us and maybe for a while the meeting time . . . in the meeting time . . . for a while he ignored us . . .

T: Yes . . . I think I understand what you're saying. You're . . . right now you're puzzled about what you want to say . . . is that right? . . . that right now you are trying very hard to say what was happening in the group . . . or there is some . . . are you a little confused right now . . . that's what I wanted . . .

C: No. [No?] It's hard to—for me to explain . . .

T: In English. I see. OK. I think I understand. Now let me see . . . let me see if I understand. You tell me if I have this . . . if my understanding is correct, OK? That when she got angry with the facilitator, then, to your surprise, you spoke right to her, forgetting that you didn't speak English, and you spoke to her . . . and to your further surprise, she started to cry. You had touched something in her . . . and it turned out that the facilitator reminded her of her father [Yeah] that her father was like the facilitator. And that the way he was like—that they were like one another was that the facilitator seemed not to be attentive to the group . . . or not to care . . . is that what . . .

C: She felt . . .

T: Yes, that was her impression.

C: So . . . I could understand her . . .

T: Ahh, surely. You could understand from your own experience? Is that what you mean? You could understand why she was angry with the facilitator.

C: Yeah, yeah. [Uh-huh] And after group . . . after group meeting, I confirmed my imagination and my experience to . . . I asked one of members of my group [Yes] . . . and then she told me . . . my question was good . . . sharp [Sharp question] and then I was surprised.

T: That was more than you expected. [Yeah] It was . . . yes, it's um . . . you know the word *remarkable*? [Remarkable] . . . As I understand it, that you came here not . . . not expecting much because of your language handicap, and in that moment, you were

158

. . . you forgot about yourself, and you just spoke directly to her, and it was a very facilitative question. Your friend said afterward, it was a sharp question, and it seemed like you surprised yourself . . . yeah . . . that's a good feeling . . .

C: Highly exciting . . . experience . . . and, uh, in the second group, uh, our facilitator . . . the facilitator asked me about myself. He was interested in me . . . in my life in Japan. Then I could express myself.

T: You could be . . . unself-conscious then? [What?] Well, when he asked you about yourself, then you were free to speak up without thinking of yourself or your handicap—your language barrier? Or . . . I would like to understand what you . . . what you told me there.

C: Uh . . . If they are talking about themselves too fast, of course I try to listen to them, but sometimes I must give up. [Yes, you're tired] And sometimes I can't ask them, because I can't understand, because of too fast English, and I can't ask them. I can't say . . . I can say nothing. [Yeah, you can say. . .] But he is . . . he was interested in me, and he asked me, and I had opportunity to express myself [Ah, yes], and I could . . . I could.

T: Yes, you could tell your story. It was your story then, and that you could say.

C: And after that meeting, one of members told me I could express myself . . . I could express myself better than I think . . . I thought.

T: Did that surprise you? [Yeah] Yes . . . and did you have to agree? [Yeah] that you did better than you thought you would do . . . Did that . . . what the person said to you . . . that [client's name] you can express yourself better than you think. [Yeah] And then did you say "Yes I can" . . . or is that true . . . that you thought so then too?

C: Maybe. I said maybe.

T: Not so sure . . . I think you would like to express yourself even better. Is that correct? Did you wish that more people had asked you about yourself?

C: Yeah. I want to meet many people here. [Yes] At least . . .

T: At least here you would like to meet them?

C: I didn't want so much . . . I didn't expect so much because of the language problem, but at least I want to meet many people here. I know I can talk with some . . . with other people if they speak to me slowly [Yes] . . . I believe I can understand what they mean . . . so I know . . . I can understand them if I have time enough to talk.

T: Yes, I understand that. And were you . . . were you ever disappointed that more people did not give you time to talk and to understand?

C: Mmm, not . . . not so disappointed [OK].

T: Then did you . . . you did get to meet many people? [Yeah] Ahh . . . I'm glad.

C: I need much more time . . . to meet more people . . .

T: To stay longer.

C: I want to stay longer.

T: So that you have not been lonely while you have been here.

C: Yeah, but in . . . in the third group, I had a difficult time. In marathon group. Because maybe we were too tired. The members were too tired, and there were more people than in small group, and they were talking too fast, and . . . my imagination wasn't working. And I slept and maybe they were angry with me because I slept . . . very well.

T: And you slept very well, huh? [Laughter]

C: And in marathon group everything was too fast. We didn't have silence and . . . I felt they didn't try to accept a person . . . a member in marathon group, I felt so, it was very difficult for me to follow them or to catch their feelings.

T: They . . . you felt that they didn't accept a person . . . do you mean many persons or do you mean a certain person that they didn't accept? [Please, once more] OK, you said, if I understood you correctly, that there was not enough silence, and they talked too fast, and that they didn't accept a person. [Accept] Accept a person. [I felt . . .] Yes, you felt that they did not accept you either . . . is that correct? [Yeah] They did not accept one another, and they did not accept you . . . [Yeah, I felt . . .] Uh-huh . . . unaccepted.

C: So . . . and . . . and . . . they can express themselves . . . or their feelings . . . or their emotions . . . so strongly and so intensively . . . and I couldn't catch them. I wanted to escape.

T: You didn't want to be there with them when they were so heavy.

C: And then I felt I was a Japanese [Ahh]. I was different from them.

T: I see . . . that earlier, you had felt like a person . . . in your first group and your second group.

C: Yeah . . . yeah. I never felt I was a Japanese . . . in those two groups.

T: Uh-huh . . . but now, when they . . . then when they say too much too rapidly and do not take time to accept one another. Then you feel like a stranger . . . a foreign person.

C: In my case, I want . . . if a person . . . if a member . . . if a certain person . . . begins to talk about himself or herself, I want to taste her feelings . . . or her mind or her emotions, and I need enough silence . . . in the group . . .

T: . . . take it in and really taste what she says and feels.

C: Very big . . . I was about to cry.

T: It really did upset you that you couldn't feel what they said.

C: I couldn't catch . . .

T: . . . the person . . . and it hurt you. [Mhm?] It hurt you. [Mhm?] It hurt you? It made you feel like crying.

C: Yeah . . . I hurt sad.

T: Uh-huh, yeah, I understand.

Observing Joan Strachan—*Catholic Pastoral Center, Winnipeg, Manitoba*
Introductory Comments by Joan

About "M" in the therapy. When "M" first arrived at my office, she presented the image of defeat. Her large size, plain hairstyle, and bulky clothing made her difficult to define physically—and she sat with her hands concealed beneath her rolled-up coat. Her speech, faint and halting, seemed to convey that she was barely able to function, and her breathing was too shallow to lend any impetus to her words. Something in her had died.

Slowly, with encouragement, she began the painful story of her experience during and following a voluntary period in a mental hospital. While there, she had 39 shock treatments and the attention of three psychiatrists without, in her view, being given any understanding of what was "wrong" with her. Eventually, after leaving the hospital of her own volition and throwing away her pills, she tried to face the world again, only to find it less friendly to her than before. Confused and frightened, she retreated into a one-room apartment—her "box"—and stayed there, unable to work, to eat well, sleep well (she did not even own a bed), or finally to consider any real life outside her four walls.

Our contract became to experiment with movement—out and back into the box. "M" said she wanted me to help her find the courage to act. Yet, having come close to suicide, she could not face an expectation of consistent success. She needed to know she could "give up" in small doses and for short periods. Giving herself permission for forward movement *and* retreat, she began to reward herself for whatever she did, learning to measure movement in little steps and, finally, learning to celebrate the *self* that began to emerge. She took some charge of her therapy (which she had felt unable to do at the hospital)—bought a bed—had her hair styled—lost weight deliberately—exercised—reached out to others—began a project on recreation therapy—and started to feel *alive*.

About me in the therapy.   Before "M" could move, she had to deal with feeling stuck in her anger, hurt, and confusion. I saw my work beginning with listening to her story of what she experienced as betrayal at the hands of professional helpers. Since she felt the need to repeat this story like a broken record, to me and inside her head, I helped her gradually to add something new (from her) to the narrative, so that it began to sound different: for example, ". . . I did a smart thing for me and got out," and later ". . . I chose to leave, and I can keep on making choices."

I supported "M" in her choices, from the buying of the bed to an occasional move back into the box, which I reframed as "creative resting." The ideas came from her. If I got ahead of her (for example, using the word *celebrate* when it was too strong for her, or moving her to action too quickly), she began to put me straight in a positive way.

"M" is currently assuming more and more responsibility for her therapy—for her life. She is finding the courage to act.

About the Sessions

The tape includes brief segments from sessions 14 and 16. In session 14, she refers to her "project"—designing the kind of treatment program that might have helped her and sharing it with the professionals who might learn from her experience. She is planning a visit to one of the professionals at the hospital where she had had the experiences that seemed so destructive to her. She subsequently had this visit, and it went well. In session 16, she makes it clear to me that I had nearly sidetracked her in a previous session, by focusing on what was really my agenda—encouraging her to get a job. She, however, is going another direction, and I try to respond by staying with her and acknowledging that I had misheard her before—not by apologizing but by thoroughly understanding what she was saying to and about me.

INTERVIEW FOURTEEN

C: I had a good week. I didn't really do anything special. Just felt good during the week.

T: Am I right in thinking that's . . . that's new? It's new for me to hear you say that.

C: Yeah. It's new for me to say it. Before I would have just said . . . if you'd said "How are you?" I would have said "Fine." But it really was a good week. I don't know what made it good. Like I say, I didn't do anything different . . . differently than I did other weeks. I just enjoyed it.

T: Maybe you learned something about yourself: that you don't always have to be doing something different to feel good?

C: I think I knew that before. I think I knew that you didn't have to do something extra special, something fantastic, in order to feel well . . . just felt good. And when I was feeling good, it . . . maybe one thing I did differently was that I didn't get scared about feeling well . . . and turn it off and say "You don't deserve this."

T: You didn't sabotage it.

C: Yeah. I just . . . I felt good and was grateful for that, and so when the next day came and I kind of wondered whether the feeling would continue, and it did, and I was willing to just let it continue. And I didn't . . . I had a few bad moments, but nothing that was too overwhelming. Nothing that lasted long.

T: So not only are you telling me that you felt good, but you're telling me that you felt good about feeling good.

C: Yes.

T: Huh! . . . Last week you said no matter what you did to feel good, you were always carrying around those thoughts—these negative thoughts.

C: Well, they were still there. I didn't get rid of those . . . just didn't let them bother me. I don't think they took up quite as much time in my brain as they normally do, but they were still there. It . . . maybe one of the things that made me feel good was that, uh, the last couple of weeks you've kinda of drummed into me that I have changed, so I sat down one day with a pen and a pencil, and I . . . pen and paper . . . and wrote down what I was like before and what I'm like now. And you're right. I've changed. You see, before when I was thinking, "change" would be a job, and a nice place to live, and a completely different lifestyle. That's what I wanted in change. I wasn't willing to accept the little things

163

... like you said the first day I'd ever been here ... the little accomplishments.

T: It's not easy just to accept those where you have such a wide vision of what you want to change, and you think there's so much you've got to do. [Right] And yet when you take great big chunks like that of expectations, it's very hard to be able to digest all that, and so it's easy to give up ... You told me that you're going to see the one ally that you have at the mental hospital ... going to see him on Thursday? [Mhm] Having just talked to him ... you actually talked to him. [Mhm] Was that a good experience? Was that OK for you?

C: Yeah. That was fine. That never bothers me.

T: The making the phone call bothers you, but once you've got ...

C: And worrying, will he answer it? Do I leave my name and number or ... that worries me ... getting to talking.

T: Yeah, I was going to say, getting through that hurdle of picking up the phone and calling like that would be a major—a really significant thing for you. Whatever happened at the other end, I would think that, uh, that would make you feel good, to have gotten across that. Then when he answered, it was OK. You could breathe again.

C: Right.

T: You set up an appointment?

C: Thursday. Meeting down the road. I won't go to the clinic. He didn't seem to mind at all. I am not too sure what we're going to talk about.

T: You ... you sound like you need to be sure before you can ...

C: Well, there must be a purpose in my going down there, other than just to say hello. I ... I did that on the phone. I don't know what I'm going to say. I don't know what the topic of conversation is supposed to be. He wasn't too clear either, so we're going to be in a little bit of trouble. He said he didn't quite understand ... understand things.

T: That's like when you come here, and I put you in charge of the agenda, you feel kind of anxious about that.

C: I don't like it, no.

T: It would be easier if I knew exactly what I wanted from you, and how I was going to go about getting it out of you.

C: Right, and I would willingly participate.

T: I know.

C: But just don't ask me to start.

T: Now when you go on Thursday, he's going to ask you to start.

C: Right . . . but the way I see it is that I'm supposed to be going down there to talk about my project, I think. I think that's the main idea.

T: Is that your idea?

C: Well, I'm not really sure. Last week, when we were talking, and I said, for my project I didn't know the right way—the proper way to approach it—from which angle to approach it. I said that I didn't understand the philosophy behind the mental institution—what they were trying to do and the ways they went about doing it. And it was almost as if I had said the magic word, and you just sort of jumped, and you offered to call him, and you've never offered to do anything before for me, so I took you up on it. And I guess I'm going . . . that's the idea to go down, but I don't know the questions to ask yet. "Could you please tell me the philosophy of the place that you work at."

T: That's one possibility.

C: I think I should be a little more specific. [OK] I don't know . . . I don't quite know how.

T: Well, would you be willing to practice that a little bit here? To just kind of talk it out a little bit here?

C: Sure. I think I'd probably end up saying much the same I've already said to you . . . Give it a try. [Yeah] . . . You're waiting for me to start?

T: Maybe I could say something to you like your friend is likely to say, such as "It's good to see you again. It's really good to see you again." He'll probably say some other things too about what he, uh, notices about you. He may notice that you cut your hair. You could cut it again. Looks terrific.

T: Thank you.

C: He may notice that you're slimmer. He is bound to notice that you've made some moves just in your phone call and your agreement to meet him, and then he may say to you something like "I understand that you're doing a project and you need some information about this place."

C: I would probably say "Well, it's not really a project. It's just one of my fantasies." [OK] I'd explain to him what it is and why . . . and then . . . don't know . . . I'm lost from there on. See I think this week has been so good, I don't even know if I want to do this thing. Just another part of the problem.

T: Huh. So if you go down there, you might gather information to put in a file somewhere for a while in case you felt like doing it. Would that be fair?

C: Yeah. Yes. I still think it's a worthwhile way to spend my time.

T: Well, yeah.

C: I haven't really thought about it for two weeks now. Maybe that's what's making me feel real good, is not going back into what happened and thinking of ways to make it better.

T: Mm. Like, uh . . . let me see if I, if I'm getting with you. I feel OK right now. I feel better than I've felt in quite a while. Would that even be fair to say? [Yes] And if I get into this project . . .

C: I wouldn't . . .

T: I'm going to go back to the hospital, and I'm going to go through all that stuff again.

C: Right.

T: Do I really want to get into that crap?

C: Right. I think it's worthwhile. Maybe . . . Maybe they know. It was . . . On the phone I told him the . . . I told him why. I explained the project very briefly and what I thought the benefits would be. And I told him eventually I'd probably just get into an argument with him about how rotten their program is and how this fantasy program of mine would change things. And he said "That's OK." Said that was fine. He said "We know we failed with you."

T: Huh! Wow!

C: Kind of knocked me off the chair, and, uh, I think he used the . . . when he said "We know we failed." I think he meant to say "*He* knows they failed."

T: That makes a difference to you.

C: You see, I don't think he failed. I . . . I know he cared, and I feel that he tried. And you really can't ask for much more than that from anybody, but I don't feel that the others tried. I really don't feel that any of them put any sort of ingenuity or creativity into what they were doing.

INTERVIEW SIXTEEN

Note: this segment begins after the session has started.

C: I know that if I see something that upsets me or if I hear something or do something or something's done to me, I know

now that I can't dwell on it or I'm just putting myself . . . moving myself backwards. And I'm . . . I don't want to do that.

T: It feels bad to do that.

C: Yes.

T: You don't deserve all that punishment . . . when you come right down to it.

C: No.

T: So that's one of the things that's made your week kind of good: the fact that you didn't get stuck in that box or whatever.

C: Right. It's been about three weeks now that it's been pretty good. I just don't seem to . . . it doesn't seem to bother me as much.

T: I'm going to ask you a kind of a funny thing. How do you feel about the fact that you don't feel so bad? Do you know what I'm saying?

C: Yes. Like that book. You have to create anxieties. I think that's a large part of it . . . that I feel good about feeling good. Last week when I was sitting here and I was really feeling frustrated. I didn't . . . There was something wrong, and I didn't know what it was. And you'd say to me a couple of times "What are you thinking?" And I didn't know and I . . . I was walking back home; I thought about it and for the first time I really feel good about feeling good, and you were sitting here talking about going back to work. And here I am feeling so good, and the idea of working doesn't appeal to me in the least. And I wanted to celebrate.

T: You wanted to celebrate.

C: I wanted to celebrate, and I thought: this word *celebrate*. [inaudible] I wanted to do something that I haven't done, you know, for a long time. I just wanted to go away on a holiday or do something really interesting or exciting. Here we were sitting; you kept telling me . . . well, you kept saying "Maybe this week you can inquire about a job." I kept saying "I don't think so for this week." [Uh-huh] That's 'cause I . . . I still want to do something that's exciting and that's . . . I haven't done for a long time. Something that I'll enjoy.

T: You heard me say you should be applying for a job.

C: No. You didn't . . . you were just . . .

T: We were talking about some possibilities for . . .

C: Right. You said "Maybe this week you could call . . . call a certain place." You said "That's one of the possibilities for this week," and I said "Forget it. It's not even a possibility."

T: Uh-huh. That's right. You put me straight.

C: I wanted to do something that's, you know like go away on a holiday. Just do something that's really fun.

T: As I remember it, it was like you weren't in touch with that—what you wanted to do—until maybe after you got out of here, because I didn't . . . I didn't hear that celebrative tone in you . . .

C: I didn't know it either.

T: I thought you were all business, but you . . . you're saying now, no wonder you were frustrated, because you were trying to express yourself on that level—that business level—but inside there was a little itch to get out and have fun.

C: Right, but I didn't realize that until I sat down and figured out well, why . . . what was wrong. What was it that I really didn't want to do? I didn't want to go out and look for a job. And that was the reason. I'm no further ahead in figuring out what I'm going to do to celebrate. I'm . . .

T: But even getting in touch with the fact that that's what you wanted to do and using that word for the first time . . .

C: Oh, I know. When it hit me, I just laughed.

T: Well, it would be fun to use your creativity to figure out what *celebration* would mean. How it would translate for you.

C: I think I would like to go out to the mountains and go camping. I would really enjoy that. I think that would be an appropriate celebration.

T: You haven't been camping for how long?

C: Five years.

T: When you were away? You mean? When you were overseas?

C: I camped with someone when I came back. I came back in the spring, and then I went camping that summer. Haven't been since.

T: Would you go back to the place where you were that summer?

C: I was . . .

T: I don't know where that was.

C: No. That was like a regular camp. I would like to just go out with a backpack on my back and go out into the mountains and pitch a tent. And I would like to do it with somebody, and therein lies the problem. I need somebody to do it with. I think that's what I would like to do to celebrate. Because before I wouldn't . . . no matter how much fun it was, I wouldn't let myself have fun. I wouldn't let myself enjoy it. And now I can. I can just forget about not expecting a good . . . forget about everything that's happened and just go out for a week or so and just have fun.

T: Well, spin that out a little bit, you know? Spin it out. What's . . . look at how you might put a little flesh on your dream. Is that what you want to do now? This time? I've got to check that out this time, so I don't make a mistake. [Shared laugh]

Observing Morgan Henderson—*Full Circle Counseling, Inc., Staunton, Virginia*

Introductory Comments by Morgan

This is my second session with a single mother (never married) in her 30s. Her 3-year-old son died about six weeks ago. She was holding him in her arms in the ambulance, on their way to a better hospital. His last words to her were "No more machines, Mommy." She spent the last 68 days of his life sleeping at the hospital, there 24 hours a day. It appears from the autopsy that there was medical mismanagement, and the physician involved has had a number of children in his care die during this past year.

In our first session together, she spent much of the time expressing her pretty obvious rage at the doctor and the hospital and her desire to work in the field of death and dying, to do something to stop the needless death of children and to help grieving parents. In this session, there clearly are times when her statements include both anger and her struggle to survive and cope. I notice that I tend to respond more to the second part of the message; here I think I am doing this partly because of how intensely we dealt with her anger in the first session. I want her to know that I understand both her anger and her need. There were times in this interview, however, when it would have been more helpful to have articulated the anger a bit more than I did. In the session, she refers to Compassionate Friends, which is a support self-help group for parents of children who have died. As you will see, she is a very intelligent, sensitive, and gutsy woman. Her struggle to make it financially right now is taking any energy she might have left over from her grieving.

In our workshops and counseling on death and dying, we [Morgan and her husband, Steve] have been traveling full-time for the past four years. Thus, all of my counseling has been done on the run, and I get out of town by sunset. That is, it has been crisis-oriented and intensive—maybe every day for a week, and then I don't see the person again for a year, or we work by phone after that. That means that all my long-term clients, like this woman, are new, and the trust and relaxation are just being built up.

I do want to comment that starting to tape-record sessions has been a big step. Sometimes I have been conscious of watching myself, which of course interferes with *hearing* the client. I also think that I responded more frequently than I usually do. There are times when I could have let her do more of the work. I seem to be more affected by this than my client is, but I am feeling quite convinced that taping will be a big part of my own growth as a counselor.

THE INTERVIEW

T: I'm finally feeling back from the summer—summer off.

C: Yeah. You took the whole summer off?

T: More or less. I did some training workshops, one in Maine and one in California, but I more or less just vegetated. It was really nice.

C: I bet it was.

T: You didn't.

C: Huh-uh . . . I think, though, it was vegetating. [Yeah] . . . essentially it was that.

T: In the sense that it wasn't living. [Mm-hm] Is that what you mean?

C: Very definitely.

T: How are you doing now?

C: Um . . . I just . . . I don't know what to do. I don't feel like I'm in any way ready for a job, but I have to work . . .

T: Feeling pushed by the money?

C: Yeah. And it's hard to start moving and not know where you're going.

T: Kind of like you're not ready yet to move and . . .

C: And I'm not ready to stay there, but I can't . . . there's no way I can afford to keep the place. [The apartment?] Mhm . . . so . . . there's no choice in that.

T: She's gone up on the rent? . . . I'm not sure what . . .

C: Yeah, and uh . . . course it was in the subsidized housing also, and that will be shot . . . so . . .

T: Why will that be shot?

C: Well, (her son) qualified for subsidized.

T: Oh, I see. I see. Yeah . . . you . . . that's another loss . . . isn't it?

C: I don't . . . it's . . . how do you work when you just don't feel like you can do anything? And the only option is to go and live with my family, and that's not really an option.

T: So it means . . . neither choice is . . . They're both crummy choices right now and neither one is what you need to be doing.

C: Uh-huh. And I need to have a place to stay, in order to get, you know, to get a job. And I don't want to take a job that's too far away from what my ultimate goal is, and that's working with families of sick kids. Well, you know what that entails . . . back to school . . . more money. Blah . . .

T: Doesn't . . . it doesn't seem like there's any options right now . . . going to get you where you want to . . . where you want to go or what you need right now . . . I guess you must feel just kind of up against the wall. You've no choices that are good ones.

C: Really. Because . . . there's just . . . what can I do? [A male friend] really wants us to marry, and I love him . . . I'm not in love with him. But it seems so soon to take on the responsibility of loving someone again.

T: Yeah. You haven't finished . . . haven't finished this process, and it's . . . someone else is saying "Now I need you to love me, and . . ."

C: And I think you do . . . just sort of need to shut down for a while after death.

T: Not love anybody. Just not have that responsibility . . . just want to check that [tape recorder] . . . Last week we didn't get anything, so that's why . . . no problem . . . Yeah, and I guess what I . . . one of the things I heard you saying last time was . . . I need some time to just love myself . . . find out who that is and care for that person and . . .

C: Or find out if there's anything there to love. And that's a real kicker.

T: And if I . . . what if I take the time and there's nobody lovable there . . . it's really scary.

C: Oh, very . . . I don't know. I don't know, you know . . . people have a tendency to say, OK, you shouldn't do anything for a year . . . or no, you should make a clean break . . . or . . . and none of it seems right.

T: Their advice is so neat.

C: Mhm. And it, you know, you just wrap up everything . . .

171

oh, OK, a year from now then I'll do so and so. What do you do in that year?

T: Telling you what you shouldn't do, but nobody's saying here's how to survive it . . . here's how to . . . yeah.

C: It's like get rid of everything of [child's name]'s. His clothes, his toys . . .

T: And that doesn't fit . . . yeah.

C: Mm-hm. You know—what if I want another kid?—that's my argument.

T: What if you want to just keep [child's name]'s things . . . just because . . .

C: And if . . . you don't . . . how do you give a whole life to Goodwill?

T: Just throw it away . . . just sort of . . . as if that would get rid of [child's name], or . . . sounds like you need to hold on to him and those things [Mm-hm] . . . in a good way.

C: It's not as painful as it was to see his things . . . um . . . but I can't just discard them either.

T: That would be like discarding him, I guess.

C: And I have to wonder if it's selfish . . . I'm just keeping them . . . what is it C. L. [*sic*] Lewis says—that incredible selfishness or laziness of grief.

T: You mean it's sort of . . . does this mean I'm hanging on to my grief and not willing to go on . . .

C: But I . . . I don't know . . . all I know is that I can't seem to get rid of the things.

T: Mm-hm . . . just doesn't feel right yet . . . yeah . . . hasn't been very long.

C: And his death itself I think I'm . . . you know . . . I think I'm accepting his death. What I can't accept is the medical information after the glaring lack of it and misdiagnosis and wondering why . . . in the hell has this happened.

T: The medical information is . . . is wrong?

C: Apparently the kid was misdiagnosed.

T: He didn't have renal failure.

C: Mm-hm. And the medications interfered with the renal functions so much for so long . . .

T: Ch- . . . it's like now you have to look at—did he have to die? Was it a medical mistake, or was there really an illness that was killing him?

C: Right . . . And that has really . . . it's better than not knowing.

T: Yeah . . . even the worst . . . even the worst is better than not knowing.

C: But processing the information is just impossible.

T: What do you do with that? What do you do with all that stuff [Yeah] that you've been . . .

C: To whom do you go . . . what, to his doctor and say "What's happened here?" You're not going to get . . . why should I get any information now? I never got any when he was sick.

T: It's like going back to the same source that screwed it up.

C: So how do you find out? And it's never going to be resolved . . . not with the complications that . . . and it's really difficult for me to accept the lack of resolve there.

T: It's like no end . . . there's no end. How do I ever let this go. How do I get rid of it? And I guess I hear you saying that your friends are giving you these real neat solutions after a year, and you're saying—am I going to live with this uncertainty and this helplessness in the face of this injustice? How do I deal with that?

C: Yeah, because you're not . . . you not only have the whole psychic energy that's drained, but, you know . . . practical matters . . . I can't really even make a decision about practical matters . . .

T: Yeah . . . just the day-to-day garbage . . . moving and . . .

C: To where? I don't know. My things are in [town name], but I'm not there.

T: You don't even have a place right now . . . to hide out in to do this kind of work that you want to do.

C: It's a lot of pressure to get . . . I understand the need for people to see what they think is positive for their own sake—and I need positive things too—but I don't know how to find them.

T: They're not coming from those statements and platitudes, are they? Guess it's that feeling of—so where do I turn and find . . . positive . . . find the good?

C: Right. I can accept his death, and that's positive. I'm beginning to accept his absence. But, Lord, I can't take what's happened.

T: Why it happened and the way it happened . . . not right.

C: Mm-hm. Isn't anybody responsible? And they are but shifting responsibility or naming responsibility doesn't stop the whole process of this kind of horror.

T: That's like . . . you have this helplessness of—am I the only one watching this horror and . . . everybody's busy shifting it around, and still children are dying.

C: Yeah, and you know the kind of credibility you get if you walk . . . if a layman walks in and says "Hey. Look at this. You made a misdiagnosis." Oh, sure. That's really credible.

T: Just seems like some mother comes in . . . that makes you even feel more powerless, I guess.

C: And that only leaves the legal profession, and what is it to them?

T: They only . . . they see the black-and-white stuff, but they don't see the pain and . . . that you're carrying and what's happened to you.

C: Do they see the necessity to make it stop happening to kids or to anyone . . . and who does? Except the victims . . . who does?

T: When it happens to you then . . . you know in a way you can never know if you're just a lawyer or . . . so who do you find to be on your side?

C: Right.

PART THREE

Beyond the Basic Skills

Direct Interventions

The first eight chapters have described a therapy that gives the client control, trust, and independence to find his or her own solutions. I think it would be naive, though, to say that evocatively empathic therapy, done within an accepting relationship, is the answer to all human problems. There are times when other approaches are more appropriate, depending on the circumstances and the nature of the problems. I will try to specify some of those times in this chapter.

BEHAVIOR MODIFICATION

It may or may not surprise you to hear that I see great explanatory power in learning theory, especially in more cognitively oriented versions of it. I think that thinking and feeling are behaviors that occur inside the skin, follow the same general principles as do overt behaviors, and are the most important behaviors to understand if we want to understand human behavior in all its complexity.

I find that I operate at two very different levels. In doing therapy, I seldom think in terms of learning principles; I am trying to be with my client, to understand deeply, to let the client know all that I hear, and to let her struggle toward becoming the unique person that she is. Outside the therapy session, if someone asks how and why therapy works, however, I completely shift gears and use learning principles for explanation. You will see this somewhat jarring shift in perspective when you read Part 4 of this book, "Theory and Evidence."

Some of what I have to say in this chapter and in Chapter 10 would make more sense if you first read the chapters on theory, but putting those chapters here would break the flow of the practical orientation of the book. You can decide whether to read them first or not.

Powerful Principles—Different Applications

Although I believe that the principles by which evocatively empathic therapy works are the same as those underlying behavior therapy, proponents of the two approaches usually view each other harshly. I once was on a panel at a behaviorally oriented convention, to discuss "the relationship" as an important part of behavioral interventions, and was introduced as a clinical psychologist. Before I said anything, someone shouted from the audience "Don't reinforce that bullshit!" Checking the location of the nearest exit, I said I thought there was value in living like a humanist and thinking like a learning theorist. They did not find me charming. One panelist sarcastically referred to empathy as "some kind of essence" (I insisted it was behavior), and another totally ignored me, using his time to give a summary of other papers at the convention. On the other side, I have heard more traditional therapists refer to behavior therapists as rigid, compulsive mechanists who have no appreciation for human experience.

I think that the principles are the same; the *application* of the principles is different in evocatively empathic therapy and behavior therapy. I will try to integrate the two and specify some of the times when each is appropriate.

Behavioral Methods

This book is not a manual on behavior therapy techniques. Other books present that material (for example, Goldfried & Davison, 1975; Wilson & O'Leary, 1980), and I think that a well-trained therapist should have a good grasp of these techniques. In general, the techniques can be divided into three approaches: (1) desensitization methods designed to reduce undesirable emotional reactions, such as fear and anxiety, through extinction (exposure to the feared stimulus with no aversive consequences) and/or counterconditioning (exposure to the feared stimulus along with positive consequences and responses that are incompatible with fear); (2) operant or positive reinforcement methods, which use reward to establish desirable behavior; and (3) aversive conditioning, which uses punishment to eliminate undesirable behaviors.

It seems to me that there is good evidence that the first two approaches are effective in the treatment of clearly definable behavioral problems but that aversive methods are effective only as a part of treatment that includes much positive reinforcement and that

177

aversive methods sometimes make problems worse (Rachman & Teasdale, 1969; Gomes-Schwartz, Hadley, & Strupp, 1978).

Within these three broad categories, it is difficult to specify a short list of particular techniques. Rather, the emphasis is on principles of learning, and specific techniques are limited only by the imaginative application of the principles to the complexities of individual cases.

When Behavior Modification Is Effective

Using this broad definition, one student argued that I was a behavior modifier, which, in a sense, is true, since I explain what I do in learning terms. Evocatively empathic therapy can be seen as a form of graduated counterconditioning or even systematic desensitization. What the client fears is his own thoughts and feelings—internal experiences (or covert behaviors, to use that language). Thus, the client doesn't think clearly—doesn't know himself accurately. The therapist helps the client face those feared thoughts and feelings, and the fear extinguishes and is counterconditioned (by the therapist's acceptance). The principles are the same; the applications are different. In its common usage, however, *behavior therapy* does not include evocatively empathic therapy. What I hope to lead you toward is an eclectic appreciation that the distinctions between psychotherapy and behavior modification are artificial.

There are several circumstances in which I think that explicitly behavioral treatment approaches are most appropriate. I will discuss a few of them. *Directly conditioned fears* result from experiences of pain in the presence of particular cues. If a person feared water as a result of nearly drowning, or long dark hallways after being trapped in a mine cave-in, or dogs after being bitten and scratched, or automobiles after being in an accident, direct reconditioning of the fear would probably be the most appropriate treatment. Much of this kind of "treatment" goes on in everyday life. We are often advised to face the things we fear (in small doses) and "face down the fear." There is a lot of experimental evidence that this explicit desensitization approach is effective with mild fears, such as fears of snakes and spiders. Mathews (1978), however, cautions that it is misleading to generalize from these analogue studies to the treatment of clinical phobias. As we will see in Chapter 15, the development of clinical phobias is vastly more complex than that of directly conditioned fears.

A large area that is commonly called *behavioral deficits* can be appropriate for explicitly behavioral approaches, although boundary lines between treatment and teaching become hard to establish. If the client lacks particular information or has missed the opportunity to learn particular skills, giving that information and teaching the skills can have an important beneficial effect.

The problem here is in distinguishing a lack of information from an inability to use information which is available to the client but which the client is unable to use for anxiety-based reasons. The temptation to teach can be very strong in therapists, and so there is a real danger that giving advice and solutions can masquerade as simply giving information and teaching the client skills. Both the therapist and the client may be fooled into thinking that the therapist has not taken over control of the process. So teach. But be sensitive that your teaching be limited to giving information that is not available to the client.

Clearly defined, limited goals often can best be achieved with behavioral approaches. Most surveys (Klein, Dittmann, Parloff, & Gill, 1969) and practicing therapists (for example, Kramer, 1970) report that very few clients who find their way to therapy have well-defined problems that fit the phobia or specific-symptom pattern. The vast majority are deeply unhappy or can't understand why they can't stay in an intimate relationship or have unpredictable anxiety attacks or report other such complex and ambiguous problems. The process of evocatively empathic therapy both discovers the real complexities involved and relieves the problem. In those cases, however, with clearly specifiable problems and goals, a behavioral program can be helpful, and can be helpful in a relatively short time.

There is a real risk here, though. One client came to me with a fear of water and the information that he had almost drowned in a pond as a child. He wanted to pass a swimming test but panicked each time he got into the deep end. Piece of cake, I prematurely thought, cleverly planning a desensitization program in my head. Fortunately, I followed my usual procedure of doing a fair amount of empathic therapy and simply offering the behavioral approach to him as a tool for him to use. The more I listened, the clearer it became that I had better open up my ears (to say nothing of my mind). After the first session, virtually nothing was said about water, as we discussed a complex situation in which he desperately feared the independence that he seemed so actively to be seeking. About six weeks later he said "Oh, I forgot to tell you I passed my swimming test a couple weeks ago." Therapy went on for some time after that; the water fear had quite clearly been a side issue.

A year after this client terminated therapy, he phoned to say that he had had some recurrence of the water fear at a lake. We talked again, and when he asked me about the relevant learning principles, I explained about graduated extinction and step by step exposure to feared things. He took this principle, designed a behavioral program for himself, and phoned a week later to report that it had worked well. I tell this story to illustrate another area of useful application of explicitly behavioral methods, *self-defeating habits based on former conflicts*. Conceivably a self-defeating behavior pattern might develop because it helped avoid some complex internal anxiety. It would be rewarded so often and so strongly that it might become a strong habit. Even if the terrible anxiety were relieved by therapy, the behavior might persist as a habit. If it no longer served as a way to avoid anxiety, directly changing it should work well. The risk, obviously, is again that it is difficult to know that the real anxiety problem is relieved.

COMBINING APPROACHES

In Chapter 1 I said that evocative empathy is the fundamental skill you need to learn. Behavioral methods are clearly among the other skills a well-trained therapist has available. The flexible therapist should be attentive to the fact that behavioral approaches might be appropriate in therapy, under much the same conditions as those for the therapist filling the role of teacher. Many of the dangers of the teacher role also apply to the role of the therapist as behavior modifier, since much depends on the accuracy of the judgment that a particular problem is not based on internalized conflicts—that is, on fear of one's own internal experiencing. It is also possible that the therapist will take on the role of the expert healer rather than contributing to the client's ability to solve his or her own problems.

With these cautions in mind, a therapist might well incorporate behavioral techniques into interview therapy, without losing the perspective that the client is the problem solver.

A Philosophical Conflict

In practice, the differences between empathy-oriented and behaviorally oriented therapists seem to center on the role of the therapist. The basic principle of evocatively empathic therapy is that the client is the problem solver who can be trusted to guide the course of therapy content. Behavior therapy traditionally casts the therapist as an expert who generally assumes that it is his or her responsibility to plan and direct the course of therapy, which should not be "left to the vagaries of clients" but should be "carefully regulated by psychotherapists" (Bandura, 1969, p. 484). In Chapter 16 I will argue that it is perfectly respectable to be an empathic learning theorist and that a complex learning-based view of neurotic problems indicates that clients' direction of therapy is not based on "vagaries" at all—that clients will try to talk about what they need to talk about.

Offering Tools

The resolution of this who-is-the-expert philosophical conflict that I find most helpful is to treat behavioral methods as information— as tools about which I know something and which I offer to the client to use or not, as he or she decides. As you know from the previous eight chapters, I want to facilitate the client's own thinking, feeling, and taking action. If we therapists make ourselves the experts, we deprive clients of the experience of solving the problems independently, and we will inevitably make errors in choices of goals. We are experts on processes, not on individual persons. There is no reason, however, not to share our expertise on processes and principles with the client, as long as we honestly offer them as tools and not as (subtle?) manipulation.

A Growing Rapprochement

As early as 1970, Naar reported the "peaceful coexistence" of empathy-based therapy and behavior therapy and presented an illustrative case study. D'Alessio (1968) described his attempts to combine behavior modification techniques with a general psychoanalytic approach, and Strupp (1979) wrote an article called "A Psychodynamicist Looks at Modern Behavior Therapy," in which he found many commonalities. Egan (1982) and others oriented toward empathy-based therapy have explicitly incorporated learning principles into their thinking.

I want to repeat, with vigor and some new optimism, something I said elsewhere (Martin, 1972).

"Polemics and hostility between more traditional psychotherapists and behavior modifiers have been elicited and emitted by both sides, and the resultant split has hampered communication among therapists. Both groups have distorted the other's positions, and we must hope that we will move toward integration and winnowing of ideas, rather than toward the kind of rigidification of "schools" that has marked psychotherapy in the past [p. 136].

I really do think that boundaries are slowly dissolving and therapists are basing their practice more on general principles that span different traditional theories.

DIRECT ENVIRONMENTAL INTERVENTIONS

It is clearly inconsistent with evocatively empathic therapy to view the therapist's role as taking direct action in changing the client's life circumstances as a therapeutic tool. There are social roles in which this is considered appropriate, but therapy is generally not one of them. Even highly directive therapists usually exert their influence through the client's action on the environment, as prescribed by the therapist.

Emergencies

Life-threatening circumstances sometimes demand intervention by a therapist; short of this obvious situation, however, there are occasional situations that will call for very difficult decisions about your role in a client's life—decisions that will trouble you no matter which way you decide to act. These situations will be ones in which your client will be about to take action, or fail to take action, with serious long-term consequences.

Judgment Calls and the Price You Pay

There will be no clear guidelines on which to base your decision to intervene directly by giving advice, admonitions, and taking some action that affects your client's life. Once the evocatively empathic therapist decides to intervene directly, the price she or he pays is that the direction of therapy changes hands—to the extent that the therapist took over direction. This is a high price to pay, but sometimes it is worth it. Sometimes the therapist needs to intervene. A client once phoned me on the weekend, somewhat drunk, and said "Dave, I'm gonna take my babies out into the bush. They're never going to take them away from me." He went on like this for some time. I knew reasonably well that nobody was really going to take his children from him and thought that he was distorting the situation. I also was afraid that if he did run off into the wilderness with the children, someone might consider *that* reason to take the children away. I listened and responded and hoped he would "come down" if we talked long enough. Eventually I felt I had to try to persuade him to change his plan. I did, and I'm glad, but a couple of weeks later I mentioned that he could call me about a particular situation if he needed to, and he said "No, I don't think I will; you talk me out of things too much." I paid the price, but I think I would do the same thing again.

Other incidents trouble me. In Chapter 6 I told you of advising a client to move out of his apartment to escape a destructive roommate. The next week he said "You didn't trust me," and he was right. I had made an incorrect judgment that intervention was called for. Similarly, a colleague told me he had phoned a university dean because a client had said he definitely was going to beat up his roommate. This therapist felt he needed to prevent the fight and made a judgment that seemed to me to be both a clearly unwarranted intervention in therapy and a betrayal of the client's confidence. My colleague disagreed. What if the client had quite convincingly threatened to kill someone? Even here, though, the issue isn't all that clear. Of course, a therapist would prevent a killing, but many clients talk about wanting to kill someone. In most settings it is seldom obvious that a therapist must intervene.

Many therapists would have made judgment calls different than mine; these gray areas are very difficult to work in. The most helpful approach is to find your therapist/friend for a consultation in these fortunately rare situations, but that's not always practical. I couldn't very well hang up on my client so that I could consult somebody. Experience will teach you a lot, and it will help to share experiences with other therapists. The more of this preparatory work you do, the readier you will be to make your judgment calls under fire.

Potential Suicides

Nearly all therapists with whom I have discussed suicide find it one of the most difficult issues they have to deal with. The end of life is so overwhelming in its finality; chances for change end; and it is very common to feel guilt over the death of someone close. When the therapist has been involved in the very issues of emotional distress that contribute to suicide, thoughts over what might have been done that wasn't are very difficult to resolve. I suspect, too, that a client's suicide feels like a failure as no other therapeutic

failure, including psychotic breaks, can. Therapists' trouble in dealing with suicide makes this a special area of deafness in hearing
clients. Intuitively, it often seems to the therapist that talking about
suicide might make the risk greater, and so clues are missed or
intentionally avoided. The client might say "I'm not sure it's all
worth it—but at least I know there's one way to find peace." Since
this statement may or may not refer to suicide, you don't want to
suggest that in a way that might be frightening to the client who was
talking about moving away or getting drunk or even coming to therapy. You can't ignore the possibility that he or she *is* talking about
suicide, either, and so you could firmly but gently get ahead of the
client without using the word *suicide*. "I'm not sure of all you mean
there, but sometimes you'd like to give up—to stop this pain by
escaping it somehow—how? . . . just by stopping everything?" The
therapist is trying to be forthright—not at all timid about grasping
the issue and staying with it—but not scaring the client off.

　　C: Yeah, stopping everything is right . . . everything.
　　T: When you say it that way, it sounds like you mean dying.
　　C: "Mm-hm."
　　T: So suicide feels attractive, even peaceful, at those times when
you feel like giving up.

As soon as the therapist was sure of what the client was hinting
at, he or she used the explicit words to give the client freedom to
discuss the real issue. It is frightening to talk so openly about suicide, but you really have no choice. Ignoring the issue won't make
suicide not seem peaceful. It is very unlikely that you can argue or
persuade the person out of the feelings. You can explore the feelings
together. In the process of this exploring, you might express some
of your own feelings and reactions, saying something like "You probably know this, but I want to say that it matters to me that you live."
If done sensitively, this would be only an expression of concern and
caring, not a judgmental guilt message that the client shouldn't feel
the way he or she does.

Suicide talk should always be taken seriously and dealt with openly.
It is sometimes used manipulatively by clients, especially when
dependency is a central issue, and so you will have to walk the
narrow line between refusing to deal with the issue and being upset
and overly responsive to the implicit threat that if you don't give
more, you'll have the client's life on your conscience. It is more
obvious here than anywhere that you must be as clear as you can

be about what the limits of therapy are. You are not the solution to the person's problems. Will you accept calls in the middle of the night and subsequent long talks? How often? I would say to my clients that I am available for such emergency calls, but only occasionally and within the limits of real emergencies. Beyond these limits, there are agencies and hospitals designed to handle emergency needs. I can't serve that function regularly and live my own life.

If a client calls in a suicidal crisis, the therapist must take it seriously and do what is necessary to see that care is provided without making the incident an integral part of the therapy relationship. Depending on circumstances, you might suggest that the client phone an emergency service (whose number you should memorize) or even phone the police for help getting to a hospital. In the process of talking with the client, you might make the judgment that the effects of an overdose are too advanced for the client to take such action and call such an agency yourself. You might even take the action of transporting the client to the hospital yourself, but this has a lot of consequences, and you should have a colleague accompany you—both to protect yourself and to make it clear that the quality of your involvement is very different from your involvement in therapy.

CHAPTER TEN

Assessment

The two extreme positions on the role of assessment in therapy are, on one hand, that assessment is totally inappropriate, misleading, and detrimental to therapy and, on the other, that we need to diagnose and categorize clients in order to plan their treatment more carefully. In this chapter I will take a middle line, leaning somewhat toward the first position. The two functions that assessment is used to serve are (1) the selection of particular clients to be assigned to particular kinds of treatments and (2) the ongoing planning and execution of treatment as a function of ongoing assessment.

Personally, I use formally identified assessment with clients only rarely and reluctantly, primarily because it so heavily places the therapist in the expert role, implying that the therapist diagnoses and fixes people, once he or she has gathered enough information. It often means to clients that the therapist has secret methods for getting things out of the client and making judgments based on this information.

These implications would be difficult enough if we had reliable and valid assessment methods and diagnostic systems. Extensive reliability data are not yet available for the *Diagnostic and Statistical Manual,* third edition (DSM III) (American Psychiatric Association, 1980), but previous evidence on the reliability of diagnostic methods should make us extremely cautious (Beck, Ward, Mendelson, Mock, & Erbaugh, 1962). Temerlin (1970) reports a distressing study in which psychiatrists, psychologists, graduate students in psychology, law students, and undergraduates listened to a taped interview with a man who said he had read a book on psychotherapy and wanted to discuss it. He was actually an actor who played an essentially healthy person—happily married, confident without being arrogant, and generally reporting none of the traditional "symptoms" of emotional disturbance. Professionals who were told ahead of time that this was an employment interview or who were told nothing rated the man as mentally healthy in most cases, although about one-third called him neurotic. If there had been a prior suggestion that the man was emotionally healthy, all the professionals rated him as healthy. The shocking results came among those raters who heard a respected person say "I know the man being interviewed today. He's a very interesting man because he looks neurotic but actually is quite psychotic." Fifteen psychiatrists called the man psychotic, ten said he was neurotic, and none said he was mentally healthy. Among the other groups, the bulk said neurotic, a few said psychotic, and a few said healthy.

There is some evidence (Helzer, Clayton, Pambakian, Reich, Woodruff, & Reveley, 1977) that diagnostic judgments can be made fairly reliably within large groupings, such as anxiety neurosis, schizophrenia, and antisocial personality. The validity of such judgments is difficult to establish, however, since most criterion measures also involve diagnostic judgments. These observations lead into a discussion of the first application of assessment to the practice of therapy—can we assign different clients to different treatments?

WHAT TREATMENT FOR WHOM?

Kiesler (1966) discussed "the uniformity myth" in psychotherapy. He argued that it is misleading to speak of "clients" who receive "therapy" as though such terms told us anything about who receives what. Because there are many kinds of therapy and many kinds of clients and problems, questions like "Does psychotherapy work?" are nearly meaningless. Many others have echoed this idea (Paul, 1967; Strupp & Bergin, 1969; Ford & Urban, 1967). Kiesler (1969) later proposed a "grid model" in which a three-dimensional matching system might be used to assign particular kinds of clients to particular kinds of therapists who would use particular treatment methods. Beutler (1979) proposes a similar model in which symptom complexity, client defensive style, and reactance (tendency to resist external influence) are used to assign clients to behavioral/noninsight therapy, cognitive modification, or insight therapy. Beutler is careful to call his model "speculative" and to limit it to guiding therapy research.

The notion of specifying treatments for disorders is a popular idea that seems sensible in principle. In application, however, it seems clear to me that such a practice would require us to make diagnostic judgments that we are not equipped to make. The evidence seems to be that we can only make moderately reliable judgments of the three major groupings, neurotic, psychotic, and antisocial personality.

As I understand these three kinds of problems at present, I am willing to say only that evocatively empathic therapy works with anxiety-based disorders. I suspect that it would make some kinds of antisocial behavior worse (from society's perspective) by lowering anxiety in persons who already have few feelings of remorse for such acts as hurting others. The psychological treatment of psychosis is a puzzle to me (and to most other therapists I know). It seems clear that medication is often called for as part of treatment. Some evidence suggests that therapy adds nothing to the effects of medication (May, Tuma, Yale, Potepan, & Dixon, 1976; Grinspoon, Dwalt, & Shader, 1968), while Karon and Vanden Bos (1972) reported suggestive evidence that two very experienced therapists were more effective than medications in treating patients with schizophrenia. Those who advocate psychotherapy for schizophrenia stress the issue of trust and that of focusing on reality rather than on inner conflicts.

These last observations make it clear that I think that some assessment decisions need to be made in the practice of psychotherapy. My purpose here is not to detail assessment methods; I assume you will either learn such methods elsewhere or seek consultation about them when decisions are needed. I will discuss some of the practical implications of assessment decisions for therapists.

Anxiety-Based Problems

Unless you work in a hospital, the bulk of the clients you will see will have anxiety-based problems in living. (The term *neurosis* is dying a slow but well-deserved death.) These are the problems which I think I understand and for which evocatively empathic therapy is effective. In Chapters 15 and 16 I will give a detailed description and explanation of such problems.

In practice, I nearly always start therapy being as empathic and accepting as I can, assuming that external assessment is not going to be needed. If I become concerned about possible antisocial or psychotic problems, I slow down (become more intellectually structured and less evocative—less leadingly empathic).

In a very important sense, I do match treatment to particular anxiety-based problems. I will follow the same general principles, but each client's content of therapy and solutions are unique to that client. I am objecting to the contention that evocatively empathic therapy treats everybody the same way; it treats everybody differently because there is no prescribed personality pattern and no best solutions that grow out of a particular theory.

Antisocial Behavior

The older terms *psychopathic* and *sociopathic* are being dropped in favor of *antisocial personality* in DSM III. These labels describe behavior that seems relatively devoid of feelings for others, of appreciation for future consequences, and of the ability to enter into interpersonal relationships—behavior that centers on immediate gratification. Just as no one is "a neurotic," no one is "a psychopath." These problems in living are on a continuum with "normal," and there are no sharp dividing lines between them. Some people, however, do seem to be in trouble a lot and do seem not to respond well to the experiences that guide most people to appreciate the interpersonal consequences of what they do.

Attempts to treat such problems with relationship-based therapy have been notoriously unsuccessful, and devoting your career to such therapy will probably trigger a very early midlife crisis for you. Templeman and Wollersheim (1979) report a system of cognitive modification that is based not on a therapeutic relationship but on appeals to "socialized hedonism," but no evidence has been gathered on the effectiveness of such an approach.

I don't think I should be treating such "sociopathic" problems. I am not comfortable with the powerfully controlling role that seems required, and what I am comfortable doing seems to make some people behave more destructively. The enormous difficulty comes in validly deciding whether a particular person's antisocial behavior results from impulsive immediate gratification or from anxiety-based problems. In addition, some antisocial behavior is not even a treatment issue; it's a cultural issue. If everyone you know fights a lot, and you have always been rewarded for what other groups call criminal, in a sense it's normal to act antisocially. This last source of antisocial behavior is seldom an issue in therapy, however.

The real problem is knowing whether your client's acting out is somehow related to anxiety. Perhaps the client seeks continual stimulation as a distraction from internal conflicts; maybe there is a partly conscious guilt that is relieved only by being punished, and acting out brings the punishment; possibly fears of sexual inadequacy can be avoided only by being so harsh and violent that no one will become intimate with the person. The possibilities are endless. The principle is that if the anxiety were relieved, the person would no longer behave so destructively, and so evocatively empathic therapy is entirely appropriate.

Because I do feel obliged to be careful that I not contribute to "sociopathic" antisocial behavior, I am sometimes caught in the bind of making internal judgments about the occasional client who displays this behavior. Such thoughts are destructive to the therapy process with a person with anxiety-based problems, and so we have a very real problem. In practice, this dilemma makes me go slowly in therapy at first, knowing that I am being judgmental in a sense, but trying to make up my mind as soon as possible on whether I should continue seeing the person. I want either to commit myself to therapy or to refer the person as soon as I can.

This particular judgment will face you only rarely unless you work primarily in the correctional system or receive many forced referrals, in which clients come to you under some kind of external pressure. In fact, the path by which the client comes to therapy is one sign that alerts me to think about this issue. You should be familiar with the description of antisocial personality in DSM-III and with Cleckley's (1976) classic list of characteristics of "sociopaths." The Minnesota Multiphasic Personality Inventory (MMPI) can also be used as a source of data for making a decision about antisocial personality, but I would use such a formal assessment procedure reluctantly because of the effect it has on the therapy process.

Psychotic Problems

It also makes me cautious in therapy when the client frequently makes very loose associations that seem to reflect grossly illogical thinking. Again, this book is not able to teach you details of recognizing different kinds of problems; this is just a general alerting you to issues. If you have any concerns along these lines, you should either be well trained in psychopathology or freely consult with someone who is.

No one really knows what the effects of evocatively empathic therapy are with people who have trouble with psychotic thinking. My experience and the writing of people like Fromm-Reichmann (1950) and Sullivan (1962)—both rare therapists with reputations for success treating schizophrenia—suggest that reality-based structuring and focusing are needed rather than evocative arousal and facing of internal conflicts. In a sense, defenses need to be strengthened, rather than faced and got through. If I am concerned about grossly illogical thinking, I still respond empathically but more cautiously.

Again, the difficulty is telling what is loose association that results from a thought disorder and what is metaphorical and meaningful experiencing. The latter can be an important part of evocatively empathic therapy.

The Intake Interview

Many counseling and therapy jobs require the professional to do intake interviews to decide whether the potential client is appropriate to the agency and to guide assignment to a particular therapist or treatment format. This interview is serving two purposes that sometimes conflict. First, information has to be gathered on which to base a decision. Second, however, it is important that the client have a positive experience in his or her first contact with the agency and with therapy. A difficulty is that the intake interviewer often does not become the person's therapist, so that it would be inappropriate to begin therapy, but if the intake interview is done in the Perry Mason style of evidence gathering and judgment making, a powerful set can be created in which the client expects therapy to be a question-and-answer session, with the expert therapist treating the client.

A useful approach is often to start the intake interview with a brief description of its purpose and with the information that the interviewer likely won't be the person's therapist. If the interviewer then responds empathically, helping the client feel comfortable and understood, it is probable that far more information will be offered than if the interviewer starts digging for it. The interviewer might ask minor questions to fill in the client's story, and near the end of the interview he or she will have some idea of information still missing that is necessary for the decisions that have to be made. Asking for it now will be less jarring, and both purposes of the intake can be served.

ASSESSMENT WITHIN THERAPY

A large difference exists between therapists who see external formal assessment as essential to treatment and those who see therapy as a process of mutual search in which the client is the problem solver.

As you know, I think that our assessment methods and our diagnostic schemes are so crude and unreliable that they can't possibly form the basis for treatment planning. More important, they are not needed for effective treatment because well-done evocatively empathic therapy helps the therapist and client discover together the unique nuances of the client's problems and solutions.

Therapy as Continuing Mutual Assessment

One student suggested that I call this book *How to Get Your Client to Tell You What's Wrong with Him*. He had a strong commitment to behavioral treatment but was willing to grant some validity to evocative empathy if the problem was difficult to specify. Another title he suggested was *Evocative Empathy: A Behavioral Approach to Nonspecific Anxiety Disorders*. A section of Chapter 5 was called "The Hierarchy Emerges," making the point that the client's problems are complex and, to some extent, unknown to both the client and the therapist, but you can trust the process. In therapy, steadily more accurate understanding emerges as the client becomes more able to think fully thoughts that previously were so anxiety-arousing that they were avoided.

In this sense, therapy is a process of continuous assessment—but not assessment imposed by the expert therapist. The assessment is an integral part of therapy, carried out as a mutual search. The goal is for the client to discover the essential information and to use it to solve problems effectively.

Tests

I have already mentioned the use of tests to make decisions about the appropriateness of evocatively empathic therapy and have said that the implications of doing this are deleterious to the kind of therapy I have been discussing. Tests, however, can have a useful function in therapy if they are offered as tools for the client and therapist to use together. Vocational interest tests can form the basis for helpful discussions; intelligence tests can help the client know his or her own strengths and limitations; responses to projective test stimuli can form the basis of discussions, much as you might discuss dreams in therapy. Two important principles to remember are that all the tests we are of limited validity and must be interpreted cautiously and that, to be useful, the tests should be used nonjudgmentally. I assume that you will not use tests unless you are well trained with them and know their limitations, and therefore the first principle is not of great concern. The second principle is more difficult to follow because tests traditionally carry a strong implication of judgment. If their use clearly grows out of the client's interest and if the therapist is very candid about the limitations of the tests and about the uses to which he or she will put them, they can help.

Behavioral Assessment

The principle that makes tests useful is that they be used as a shared tool. The same principle applies to explicit methods of behavioral assessment. I am talking, of course, of the use of behavioral assessment as a part of treatment and not of its other uses, such as in research and in making judgments about people in the more traditional sense of *assessment*. I think that behavioral assessment, like most assessment procedures, is traditionally seen as imposed by the professional on the client. This is clearly not essential to its use, and like so many other skills and tools the therapist has, it can be offered as one more way available to the client and therapist for mutual problem solving.

CHAPTER ELEVEN

Ethical Issues

As a practicing counselor or therapist, you will almost certainly be associated with an organization with an established set of ethical standards, such as the American Psychological Association or the American Personnel and Guidance Association. These guidelines cover many aspects of professional activity; although I will only touch on some principles that apply to your treatment of clients, it is your clear responsibility to be familiar with all the standards. I assume that your training program includes formal exposure to ethical issues and an opportunity to examine and discuss the complexities of actual incidents. You would also find interesting articles that describe the adjudication of actual cases (Sanders, 1979; Sanders & Keith-Spiegel, 1980).

In Chapter 6 I discussed several examples of ethical dilemmas that can arise in the therapeutic relationship. This chapter will center on more general issues.

IN WHOSE BEST INTEREST?

It is easy enough to state the general principle that therapy is designed to serve the best interests of the client. In nearly all instances of conflict of interest, thinking of this principle will resolve the issue. Occasionally, though, you will face difficult decisions that make it obvious that therapy does not occur in glorious isolation from the rest of the world, all of whose members claim that their best interests count for something too.

Therapist Needs and Client Needs

First we can say that, within therapy, the therapist's needs are secondary. One of the functions of putting limits on therapy is to enable the therapist to set aside his or her best interests for a limited period of time. In therapy, whether or not the therapist expresses feelings or talks or is accepting is determined by what is best for the client. It is a very real problem that some therapists and counselors use the therapy hour for their own gratification—perhaps by eliciting admiration from the client; perhaps by inducing the client to continue therapy needlessly for the therapist's financial gain.

Outside the limits of therapy, different principles apply. Clearly the therapist cannot make his or her own interests secondary to the client's, although there still is the obligation to do everything possible to be helpful to the client, within the limits that the therapist is willing to accept.

Social Needs and Individual Needs

The issue becomes more clouded when the client's best interests are weighed against the needs of others in the society. Here we face some of those difficult judgment calls discussed in Chapter 9. Then we were concerned with the client's doing something that would be severely damaging to his or her own best interests. Occasions also arise in which your client will talk about doing things harmful to others. In most cases your responsibility will still be to your client, with intervention called for only in extreme circumstances. If, because of his emotional conflicts, your client is yelling at his wife a lot in ways that seem to you to be doing her emotional damage, it would almost certainly be useless and would damage therapy for you to intervene in some direct way. Your most effective intervention is to do the powerful things you can do to facilitate his resolving his emotional conflicts. It is possible that you might express the distress you feel, but it is likely that whatever restraining effect that would have on him would be offset by his withdrawal from the therapy process. But, to move along the continuum, what if he said he felt like cheating his wife by transferring their savings and then leaving her? What if he said he felt like killing her? What if he said he was going to kill her? Clearly somewhere along this continuum we passed the point at which direct intervention was called for— or did we? What if you don't think he really means what he says because he has said it many times before?

The APA ethical principles say that psychologists reveal information obtained from a client "only with the consent of the person or the person's legal representative, except in those unusual circumstances in which not to do so would result in clear danger to the person or to others" (American Psychological Association, 1981,

p. 636). The general guideline this offers is that society's interests must be considered, but it is a rare instance in which they take precedence over the client's. The principles go on to say that information from counseling or therapy is "discussed only for professional purposes and only with persons clearly concerned with the case" (p. 636). I frequently advise you to seek consultation with another professional; I hope this doesn't sound like an evasion that lets me escape dealing with difficult issues here. It is the best and most responsible advice I can give you about these gray area decisions.

ROLE CONFLICTS

So far, our discussion has assumed that you will be operating in a setting such as private practice, in which you have only one fairly well defined and understood role. You may, however, have conflicting roles, especially if you work for an agency. I frequently teach counseling skills to probation and parole workers, to school counselors, to therapists in large hospitals, to counselors hired by firms to help their employees, and to those in settings in which their administrative superiors are insistent on meeting agency needs.

Whose Agent?

It is most comfortable to be able to say that you are the client's agent, with only the rare problem arising over the fact that you also have some responsibility to society. Conflicts of interest are nearly inevitable in some settings, however, and they nearly always have a dampening effect on therapy. It will be necessary to be honest with yourself and with your client about the limits these role conflicts place on therapy. Your evocatively empathic skills will still be useful, and your client can gain meaningful help from your counseling, but the process will be different.

The two biggest problems are making judgments and confidentiality. The power of the therapy relationship lies in its being nonjudgmental. Many counseling and therapy roles ask you both to give counseling and to make a judgment about the person; the two are incompatible because in one instance the client's best interests are served by being open about weaknesses, and in the other they are not. Some schools, for example, require that counselors report any drug use or use of contraceptives that students discuss. Such a requirement would, in my opinion, make therapy nearly impossible. If I were under a constraint like this, I would tell the client exactly what the limits of the relationship were and say that he or she was free to withhold any information, but we would do what we could within those limits.

As it is, I do tell clients that I don't have privileged communication and can be subpoenaed by a court, so that they should consider that in what they say. Even trying to maintain clear guidelines, however, can fail. Once a parole service asked me to see a potential parolee and his wife, apparently at the man's request (it turned out later that it had been implied to him that counseling was a condition for his receiving parole). I went to great lengths to make it clear to the clients and the agency that I couldn't operate as a therapist if I was ever to be called on to make judgments, that it would then serve the clients not to be honest with me. Everyone agreed that this was wise, but several months later both the parole service and the clients said that if I would only give my approval, the man could get a day parole to be with his family. The day parole did seem like a good idea; the couple practically pleaded with me; and the parole service said they were sorry, but they felt I was the only person in a position to make such a judgment, and so they would not grant the parole unless I said so. I still don't know whether I did the right thing. I wrote a letter approving the parole, but in retrospect that clearly changed therapy. Now I was useful to the couple in manipulating the environment, and so they needed to hide some things from me. A colleague once consulted me on whether he should act as a counselor for a friend's family that was breaking up, since he might be called on to testify at a child custody trial. The answer was clearly no, although that was not clear to the counselor—I suspect because of his personal involvement in the case. (He clearly did the right thing in seeking consultation over his uncertainty.) First, one definitely does not attempt therapy with clients with whom one has other relationships—exactly because of the personal involvement. The more subtle issue here, though, is one you will probably face numerous times in your career. If the family involved saw the counselor with the knowledge that he might soon be testifying about each of the parents' competence to care for the children, there are many things that neither the mother nor the father would honestly say in counseling.

Judgmental roles conflict with therapeutic roles. Therapists and counselors almost inevitably face this conflict at times, and so you must clearly think through your position in each such case. When possible, I try to be as absolutely clear with the client as I can about such conflicts. Sometimes I have told clients about whom I might have to testify, for example, that this probably means there are things they shouldn't tell me. Usually, after the need for my other role disappears, therapy changes toward a more complete and useful process, although the prior sessions were not wasted. They might even have been quite productive, within the limits demanded by my role conflict.

Involuntary Clients

I usually avoid seeing clients who have been forced into therapy. Many people and agencies act as though psychotherapy were a kind of magical treatment that could be imposed on people, but it is just a human relationship with certain special structures and limitations. The client enters therapy to improve his or her life by making personal changes; the motivation to do this comes most effectively out of the person's dissatisfaction with the way he or she is living life. Therapy done for other motives may not be impossible, but it surely is difficult.

If I do see an involuntary client, perhaps an adolescent whose "parents said I should come," I acknowledge the reluctance, respond as empathically as I can, say what the limits of our relationship are, and suggest that we talk "at least this one time, since you're here, to see if there's any way I might help you be happier or figure things out or whatever you decide you want." In a sense, now my goal is to make the process attractive enough that the person will want to continue out of his or her own desire. If the person decides not to continue, I certainly accept that decision.

CONFIDENTIALITY

An issue implicit in all of our discussion of role conflicts is confidentiality. The APA standards say "Psychologists have a primary obligation to respect the confidentiality of information obtained from persons in the course of their work as psychologists" (American Psychological Association, 1981, pp. 635–636). The promise of confidentiality is fundamental to counseling and therapy. It frees the client to face thoughts and feelings that she couldn't otherwise face, because she comes to trust the therapist's acceptance; she doesn't have to worry about who else might hear these things and judge them.

Probably the most indefensible violation of this principle occurs when counselors and therapists use confidential information in a gossipy way, even when discussing therapy with another counselor. By this I mean discussing clients with the implication of "Boy, have I got something interesting to tell you!"

Confidentiality does have limits. Professional considerations will require you to consult with another therapist about the course of therapy or about concerns you have at times. In training you will be discussing therapy with your supervisor and perhaps a few other trainees. The "clear danger" rule will apply in very rare instances. The law limits your confidentiality, and the structure of your job may have the role conflicts discussed earlier. The legitimate limits of confidentiality will be different for each counselor, and you should be very clear what those limits are.

Having Clear Ground Rules

One reason that you must be clear about the limits of confidentiality is that you will need to make those limits absolutely clear to your client. Most clients assume that therapy is confidential and are not highly concerned with confidentiality (some are, of course), and so I usually look for an opening early in therapy—a time when I will not interrupt the therapy process—to state my view of confidentiality. I say that confidentiality is total except that I can be subpoenaed, that I sometimes consult with one or two other therapists about my sessions, mostly to help me stay clear about what I am doing, and that any other sharing of information will be done only with the client's permission. You may need to say something different, but it is essential that you be explicit and clear.

Legal Testimony

The legal requirement that therapists testify under oath if subpoenaed is, in my experience, a formidable-looking but rarely encountered limit on confidentiality. It does create a conflict over the completeness of records it is wise to keep. Ethical standards require record keeping about client contacts, but detailed reports can be subpoenaed and are easily misunderstood. The condensed notes that you might write for your own reminders can mean quite different things if read in court or by some other agency. A compromise solution is to keep only brief records with one- or two-word reminders to trigger your memory.

Parents and Young Clients

An awkward confidentiality problem often arises when parents want to know what their child or adolescent is talking about in therapy. The parent has legal responsibility for the child and can remove the child from treatment, but if you can't promise the child confidentiality, therapy will be difficult or impossible. More subtly, and probably more likely to happen to you, the parent can phone and say "Don't tell John that I've called because it would hurt him, but there is something that you just have to know to be able to help him, and I don't think he'll tell you." Even more insidiously, the parent might say there is something that even John doesn't know but that you should know to understand him.

You might be quite clear that you are not going to betray the client's confidences but be caught very off balance by this intrusion. As soon as you enter into this secret agreement with the parent, however, you are compromised and in danger of losing the client's trust. Now the parent is in a position to destroy that trust by revealing to the client, maybe weeks later, that he or she talked with you. There is no perfect way to handle such a situation, but you might say to the parent, as soon as you realize what the drift of the phone call is, "Can I stop you for a minute? It's important that I explain something to you about the way I work. I'm sure you can understand that it's important that John be able to trust me for therapy to help. What I always say to a person who talks to me about someone I'm seeing is that I have to be able to share with my client anything that is said to me. I know that makes it difficult for something like what you want to talk about, but I find that I can't work otherwise." Now you are free to share with your client whatever is said. If the parent insists, you could say that you would rather work without the information but be just as insistent about your ground rule.

THERAPIST COMPETENCE

Finally, you are required to work within the limits of your competence.

Psychologists recognize the boundaries of their competence and the limitations of their techniques. They only provide services and only use techniques for which they are qualified by training and experience. In those areas in which recognized standards do not yet exist, psychologists take whatever precautions are necessary to protect the welfare of their clients. They maintain knowledge of current scientific and professional information related to the services they render [American Psychological Association, 1981, p. 634].

You might be registered or licensed as a school psychologist or clinical psychologist or psychiatric social worker or psychiatrist someday and be permitted by law to perform a wide range of services for a wide range of clients. Operating within the letter of the law, however, will not necessarily meet ethical standards. Well-trained professionals know that there are procedures with which they have too little experience to offer independently to clients. There will be clients whose problems personally bother you intensely or feel beyond your depth. In such cases it is important either to refer to another therapist or to seek consultation. If experienced therapists have to seek consultation and further training, it is obvious that therapists in training must be sure that they don't get in over their heads, that they be closely supervised, and that they not try to operate as independent therapists "on the side."

CHAPTER TWELVE

Beginning and Ending

It's been a long time, but I still remember my first real therapy interview as a practicum student—not the interview actually, but the nervous waiting before, half hoping (maybe three-fourths) that the client wouldn't show up, wishing that I had a better idea of how to start the session, and being afraid I would get stuck with nothing to say to a client with nothing to say. I muddled through, but I hope you will do better; I hope this book might help you have some confidence that there are skills you will take into your sessions.

ARRANGEMENTS

Many details of physical arrangements and setting appointments will depend on the setting in which you work. I can share with you some of my experiences.

Making Appointments

When working in an agency, the therapist typically does not make the first contact with a client. A receptionist might explain something of agency procedure and schedule an intake interview. Subsequently, the client is assigned to a therapist, who then contacts the client to arrange an appointment. During this contact, the client will be forming some impression of the therapist, and so it helps to be friendly and quietly confident on the phone but to limit the conversation to arranging the time. Clients will usually be uneasy about discussing any aspect of their problem in such a contact, but if one does start talking about the problem it is a good idea to gently suggest that you wait until the first appointment to get into those things. If the client's desire to talk seems to grow out of an urgent distress, you might ask whether it would help to have the appointment be earlier than scheduled and to try to accommodate that. In the rare instance that the client persists in talking, it is important to him or her that you listen and respond supportively and move toward making an early appointment as soon as the client is comfortable.

In private practice, the therapist typically does make the first contact with the client. It will take some skill to assess quickly whether an appointment with you is appropriate, whether you should refer the person elsewhere, or whether he or she just wants information. Again, the potential client is being affected by this first contact with you and your manner and in this case will not have had the buffer of an intake interview. Clients seldom want to say much in such a conversation, and so I usually get some feel for the general area of the problem and how they have come to call me and suggest that we "get together for an hour to see if I'm the right person to help you." This phrase permits both me and the client to treat the first interview as a trial session, without a commitment to longer therapy. You would give practical information about the location of therapy, fees, and length of sessions at this time too.

During this first phone contact, it is important to be sensitive to the intensity of the person's distress. When I suggest a time for us to meet, I listen carefully to the quality of the response. If I sense any dismay, I ask "How does that feel, waiting that long to talk?" This gives the client an opportunity to express any felt urgency, which leads me to try to work in an earlier appointment. If the client seems to want the earlier appointment but refuses so as not to impose, you can leave the door open by saying "OK, we'll leave it for Tuesday at 3, and if something comes up that you want to talk sooner, give me a call."

Physical Environment

The most comfortable room arrangement is to have two or three (for seeing couples) chairs of about equal size and comfort arranged facing each other, perhaps with a low coffee table between them or off to the side to hold a box of tissues and an ashtray. This arrangement implies that therapy is a face-to-face mutual process and avoids the intial awkwardness of who gets the big chair or the most comfortable chair. Some offices imply that the therapist is the aloof expert, mainly by putting a desk between client and counselor, an arrangement that I have always suspected is designed to protect the therapist somehow. A friend of mine got a good deal on a matched set of chairs for his office, but it turned out that one was slightly higher and better padded than the other—apparently the "daddy chair." He kept the chairs, but a lot of people comment on the difference, and clients, especially couples, often stumble for a moment deciding who is going to sit where.

Recording and Notetaking

Most training settings require that sessions be recorded or videotaped for supervision, and I have repeatedly said that listening to yourself on tape is one of the most effective ways to improve as a therapist. Even if you take extensive notes immediately after a session, you will filter and distort what happened in the session when you consult with a colleague or supervisor. The tape is a faithful record. It also can be used for research and teaching, if informed consent has been obtained from the client.

The presence of a tape recorder does seem to have an inhibiting effect on some clients but not all. It is a good idea, if you tape sessions, to present it to the client as standard procedure with assurances of confidentiality and to place the recorder in an unobtrusive but not hidden location. Read the client's reactions sensitively so that if there is hesitation you can say "Well, let's try it, and if you find it interferes too much, let me know. I use the tape only for my own growth as a therapist, so I can listen to myself and occasionally to consult with the one or two other therapists that I told you about here at the clinic." Another helpful phrasing can be "I much prefer to tape because it helps me improve as a therapist and be sure I'm hearing you accurately, but if we cover some material that you want erased, just tell me, and I'll erase it right away." This takes away some of the threat, since the client has control of the tape after the fact.

Taping is also threatening to the therapist. Trainees sometimes say they feel as though someone were watching them. I still feel that way sometimes, unless I tape all my sessions. If I tape only a few, I can feel myself sometimes trying to "work harder" and do therapy "by the book" in those sessions, which distorts what I do by making me "techniquey." It's probably better just to get used to taping and do it regularly. One problem I have with this is that I am reluctant to tape private clients, who are paying fairly substantial amounts for therapy. In a training or free clinic, the client (and therapist) may perceive taping as a price the client "pays" for service. My experience has been that few therapists in private practice do much taping, and so others may share this reluctance.

Notetaking is a different matter; it directly interferes with the process between the therapist and client, since it is nearly impossible to write notes at the same time that you are engaged in an intense listening and responding to the client. Notetaking also strongly implies that therapy is an evidence-gathering process rather than a mutual search. Any notes that you need can be written in a few minutes immediately after your session. In fact, many therapists schedule clients for the traditional 50-minute hour so that they have a few minutes to record some notes while the session is still fresh in memory. If you do keep notes, be clear about the purpose they are to serve. A therapist who is seeing many clients will probably need some reminders of details to keep things straight. Therapy, however, is an ever-changing process that goes in unpredictable directions, and so notes probably won't be useful to "pick up where we left off last week," because the client is nowhere near where he was last week.

Money and Time

In a clinic setting, the issue of fees will probably be out of the therapist's hands and is less likely to enter therapy as an issue, since the client will tend to perceive the fees as imposed by the agency. Most clinics charge on some kind of sliding scale according to ability to pay, so that the client ends up paying some amount that is a real cost but not a debilitating one.

In private practice, the issue is more salient because it is the therapist who is personally charging the fee, although this can be complicated by insurance coverage. There is a lot of discussion of whether paying a fee makes clients work harder in therapy and appreciate it more or whether fees distort therapy by inducing clients to work toward short term goals or whether charging fees keeps clients from inappropriately extending therapy. No one knows the answers to these questions. Whatever the effect on therapy, the main function of fees is that the therapist must be compensated for his or her time. Fees are not based on benefit received; they are based on time devoted, and so ultimately they will be set according to the level of compensation that sufficiently rewards therapists for doing therapy.

From the client's perspective, fees introduce considerations of trade-offs into therapy. Is the benefit received—the relief of problems in living—worth the financial sacrifice? To some clients, $5 a session is as personally costly as $50 or $80 would be to some other clients. Considerations of simple justice would suggest that all clients should be seen on a sliding scale, but then many therapists would be unable to afford to continue working. Most therapists I know work out some kind of compromise in which they do some work through an agency where therapy is subsidized and in their private work charge a standard fee consistent with general professional fees in their community, occasionally reducing a fee if it is burdensome. Be prepared, though, for fee setting to be an issue to be discussed as a relationship problem.

Most therapists see clients for slightly less than an hour, once a week, leaving a small break between appointments. Occasionally a client will be seen twice a week, especially at particularly stressful times, but more frequent sessions than this seem to suffer from diminishing returns. The client has to live life in between sessions too. Some clients seem to use a longer session more productively, but it is best to anticipate this with an individual by scheduling a one-and-a-half or two-hour session ahead of time. Setting flexible ending times for sessions can create problems, even if you can tolerate the uncertainty and unused therapy time. The ending time of a session is not absolute and inviolate, but you're asking for trouble if, near the end of a session, you are always deciding whether a continuation of the hour is justified. It can happen that the client has to "earn" a time extension by saving the painful material till the end, or stopping at an hour could mean that you didn't think the session was all that good.

I find it helpful to say, as I sense the end of the hour, "I'm going to have to stop in a few minutes." This gives the client time to bring the session to some closure, makes it clear that your time is limited and you do have other things that you want to and have to do, but does not have the abrupt and uncaring feeling of "Time's up." I break all these rules at times, of course, but try to be clear about why.

THE INITIAL INTERVIEW

So your client really has shown up for the first appointment. If this is your first appointment, you're pretty uneasy and are hoping that the client won't recoil and say "But you're so young!" or "Are you sure there's no mistake?"

Introductions

Using the client's name as you approach expresses your interest and involvement. I prefer to use his or her first name and to introduce myself by first and last name in most cases. This helps create an atmosphere of mutuality and diminish the doctor/patient nature of therapy. I said "in most cases" because there are awkward instances, particularly with clients much older than myself, when using the client's first name feels overly familiar. This is all related to cultural training, of course, and so you should follow your impulses, keeping in mind the principle that you are trying to establish a mutual-exploring set. I must also admit that when I was an intern, I frequently wished I had finished the dissertation, so I could be "Dr. Martin" and impress my clients. That way they would have known they were getting good therapy, see?

Openers

Your client will probably sit down with a what-do-we-do-now look, and you can get therapy started with "Let me tell you everything I know about you, and we can go from there." Some therapists want extensive background on a client before the first session, but I feel quite strongly that this creates powerful and inaccurate expectations about the client. The background material can be useful, but much of it will emerge in the session, and you will be getting it straight from the client's perspective. Any information you receive ahead of time is already well filtered through the selective perception and memory of the person who provides the information. It will inevitably include distortions. I much prefer to know very little about the client in the first session, both to avoid these expectations that will cloud my perceptions and to be able to say to the client words that imply "I don't have the drop on you here. I don't work that way. I can quite openly tell you everything I know about you. What really matters to me is your problem solving and experiencing."

After saying something like "So I know that something's got you pretty unhappy and scared," I would help the client start talking with an open-ended "Why not just tell me what's on your mind and let me get to know you?" If I don't know anything about a client, I might start with a phrase like this or "How can I help you?" or "What brings you in?"

Creating a Mutual-Exploration Set

Once the client starts talking, you should be very attentive, listen very hard, and start responding to what the client is implying. Your client has come in with some expectations and a lot of apprehension about therapy, and so these first minutes are showing him what therapy is. He will probably fear not having anything to say and will expect you to ask a lot of questions. If, however, you respond evocatively empathically, he will keep getting the feeling of being understood and will find it easier and easier to talk. You will be teaching by example that mutual exploration is the nature of therapy.

Teaching about Therapy

In Chapter 5 I discussed ways to teach the process of therapy, and so I'll only briefly mention the principle again here. Usually, the process will just get going if you respond empathically. Occasionally, the client will ask "What should I do?" or "How is it going to help just to talk about it?" The principle is that you are an expert on a process but not on this particular client. You can teach the process, using some of the phrases from Chapter 5.

Starting Subsequent Sessions

Since the client is in charge of the process, the best way to start most sessions is simply by remaining silent until the client starts or by making some general opening invitation like "Hi" or "How are you?" or "What's on your mind?" For the therapist, there is a continuity between the last session and the current one, and so it is sometimes tempting to try to start up "where we left off last time." So much has happened in the client's experiencing since last time, however, that this will almost inevitably distort the exploration process. The client is at a much different place from the ending of the previous interview. Sometimes there will be issues that the therapist needs to deal with or hopes the client will deal with, and sometimes this is legitimate. It is more helpful to hold these issues back and wait for an opening. This opening can take the form of the client's trying to talk about the issue, and the therapist's having waited will have helpfully left control in the client's hands. There is a risk that the therapist will "hear" the client deal with the therapist's issues when he or she really isn't doing so, and it is therefore important to be careful not to fulfill your own prophecies. If the client doesn't bring up something that you need to discuss, it will be more honest just to create an opening by waiting for a pause in the client's process and saying "There's something I need for us to talk about. . . ."

TERMINATION

One of the most gratifying and most difficult aspects of counseling and therapy is ending a relationship, particularly a long one. Successful therapy is obviously rewarding to the client, but the therapist also gains satisfaction at having contributed to another person's emotional growth. Unsatisfying terminations can feel like personal failures to the counselor, in addition to the concern they cause about the client. Knowing when and how to terminate a therapy relationship takes sensitivity and skill.

A Mutual Decision (Who Is the Problem Solver?)

My experience has been that the most common route to termination is also the most satisfying one. When the client has made progress toward relief of the problems that brought her to therapy and feels stronger, she starts feeling less need for therapy. There will be hints and implications of this in many things the client says, and, as with any issue, the therapist's job is to hear these tentative approaches to the idea of quitting therapy. The therapist can articulate what he or she thinks the client is implying, being tentative and leaving control in the client's hands. There is some risk that if the therapist says "When you talk about how well things are going, I wonder if part of what you mean is you're thinking about trying it without therapy," the client might hear this as the therapist's urging termination—if this isn't what the client was implying. This therapist statement is tentative enough, though, that the client probably wouldn't take that meaning. It is a message that clients often fear, and so you should be sensitive to hearing it.

When the evocatively empathic therapist makes the client the problem solver, part of the control that is given to the client is that of deciding when treatment is over. There is some cost to the client of being in therapy, and there are meaningful advantages to being independent once he is strong enough, so that usually the client will want to terminate therapy at a time that is good for him.

I always try to make it clear, long before termination is an issue, that deciding to quit therapy is not an all-or-none decision. Virtually any format—tapering off; quitting and then starting up; or stopping with the understanding that the client can call to resume therapy if he or she chooses—is acceptable to me. This knowledge makes it easier for the client to consider termination because it is not such a momentous decision.

When Just the Client Wants to Terminate

Termination as a mutual decision is the most common ending to evocatively empathic therapy, but it would be naive not to think about the less satisfactory ways it happens. One of these is when the client wants to terminate, but the therapist feels that there is much work yet to be done or that the client's decision is impulsive and unwise. The temptation is to argue the client out of his or her decision, but this strategy is almost doomed to be useless. To win the argument is to take over the course of therapy and treat a reluctant client who may well feel betrayed by your insistence. To argue and to lose anyway will make it very difficult for the client to return to therapy later because of the loss of face.

It would be within the spirit of therapy to say "That surprises me some, and I'm not completely comfortable stopping now. But I really believe that ultimately you're the one who knows best for you. What I would like to say very clearly is that my door is open, and if you'd like to talk again, I'd certainly see you. It could turn out that a break right now would be helpful or that it really is time for you to do without therapy." I would try to hear, too, whether the client wanted to continue therapy with another therapist, to be as accepting of this as I could, and to help find that other therapist.

I know that I would seek out my therapist/friend to explore my discomfort (which might well just be my problem) and possible reasons for the early termination.

When Just the Therapist Wants to Terminate

An even rarer (fortunately, because it's also more complicated) problem is when a client wants to continue, but the therapist wants to terminate. Legitimate reasons may be that the client has achieved reasonable goals and just comes in to chat, using the therapist in a friend role, or that other demands and limits on the therapist make it very difficult for him or her to continue. It may also be, however, that the therapist is responding to countertransference needs. The therapist may be bored or discouraged or threatened by what the client is dealing with. Most insidiously, the therapist may be threatened by a client's growing dependency and attachment. Without being aware of what's happening, the therapist might run from therapy, rationalizing that termination is somehow in the client's best interest. This could contribute to the client's problems by rejecting him or her in the middle of the kind of dependency problem the client may need to deal with. Thus, the therapist's independent decision to terminate has to be taken very carefully and certainly with consultation.

When the therapist does terminate the sessions, the reasons must be specified to the client and effort made to remove implications of personal rejection. The process can be accomplished more gently with an "open door" statement like "I know you're not comfortable with stopping now, but it seems important to me because . . . [whatever the reasons are]. How about trying it for a while, like a break, and then you call me in a couple of months if you want to get together to talk about how things are going." There is no getting around that this violates the perspective that the client is the problem solver, but it may be necessary at rare times.

Forced Terminations

Because many training settings operate on the school year, it looks as if clients all get well in May and June. These artificial limits certainly often interfere with the most productive course that therapy might take, but they can be handled in a nondestructive way. Several months before circumstances require the therapist to leave (or even go on vacation, by the way), it should be made absolutely clear to the client that this will occur. The information should be repeated a few times, and effort should be made to read the client's reactions to and understanding of what this means. The advantage is that termination is imposed from the outside and does not reflect rejection from the therapist. Similarly, when the client's life circumstances force a termination, therapy can be productive and not end unsatisfactorily. In fact, the impending time limit can sometimes accelerate progress in therapy. An interesting study reported by Shlien, Mosak, and Dreikurs (1962) showed that clients reported as much improvement in self-esteem in 20 sessions of time-limited therapy (client-centered and Adlerian therapy) as did clients in unlimited therapy after an average of 37 sessions. I was in a practicum with Shlien at that time, though, and he mentioned the impression of therapists in the study that clients felt some rejection at the therapist-imposed time limit—rejection that did not seem to occur when similar time limits were forced by outside circumstances.

CHAPTER THIRTEEN

Other Formats—Building on the Foundation

This book focuses on individual therapy, but the skills I have been discussing are also the foundation of what you will need for many kinds of therapy. Evocative empathy is far from the only thing a therapist does and often is not the most appropriate thing to do in therapy. For all these other things to work, though, you first need to make your client feel understood. You have no coercive power over clients; your constructive influence exists because it is rewarding to your clients to be influenced by you. This chapter will extend your skills to formats in which there is more than one client. I told you therapy was hard work in which you have to scramble. Group, family, and couple therapy are even harder work because there are so many permutations of relationships.

RESPONDING TO SEVERAL PEOPLE AT ONCE

Making two persons feel understood at the same time is not easy, especially if they strongly disagree with each other. What saves you is that empathy is not agreement or sympathy but simply understanding. You can say "As I hear it, John, when she comes home late, you feel worried—in two ways, I guess—worried she might be hurt and worried she might be with someone else. But, Mary, to you that's hard to understand because you feel you've clearly said you wouldn't do that—but that you need some freedom." I think both persons will feel understood and will be facing not only what they said but also what the other person said. This skill will be useful when doing group therapy, as well as couple and family therapy.

It is beyond the scope of this book to give you an adequate introduction to group, couple, and family therapy. Each of them is an area of study in itself. I will mention a few ways that evocatively empathic therapy applies and can be adapted to them.

GROUPS

The most typical format for group therapy seems to be that one therapist meets with about six to ten clients for at least an hour and a half, once a week. There are significant advantages to having two therapists working with a group, but this arrangement usually occurs in training settings or in agencies where the economics of having two therapists aren't so restricting. Group therapy is sometimes thought of as a cheap substitute for individual therapy, but each format has benefits and limitations that the other doesn't. A discussion of these advantages and disadvantages will make more sense if we first look at what Yalom (1975) has called the "curative factors" in group therapy. Yalom's book, by the way, is one of the best introductions to group therapy.

Curative Factors in Groups

Yalom says:

> From my viewpoint, natural lines of cleavage divide the curative factors into eleven primary categories:
>
> 1. Instillation of hope
> 2. Universality
> 3. Imparting of information
> 4. Altruism
> 5. The corrective recapitulation of the primary family group
> 6. Development of socializing techniques
> 7. Imitative behavior
> 8. Interpersonal learning
> 9. Group cohesiveness
> 10. Catharsis
> 11. Existential factors [1975, pp. 3–4].

Some of these factors are available in both group and individual therapy, but some of them require group membership to occur. The instillation of hope can come solely from the therapist's confidence and acceptance, but only in a group can the client see others make progress and hear them tell of gains made in problems similar to the client's. *Universality* refers to the discovery that one is not unique in having threatening thoughts and debilitating problems, a discovery that is more likely to be made in a group. *Imparting of information* simply refers to teaching about coping techniques, the dynamics of emotional adjustment, and the like. It can be part of the teaching aspect of either individual or group therapy, although in a group, other clients probably can add information not available to the therapist. Altruism is an experience that the group member can have through helping another client grapple with problems. In a good group, the members learn to become therapeutic toward each other, often giving empathy, caring, and honesty in a much more powerful way than the therapist can. Such things are often seen as part of the therapist's job but as based only on a desire to help when given by another client.

Only a group offers the possibility of a reliving of the complex kinds of relationships that exist in families, and Yalom feels that this reliving is often an important part of group therapy. Clients are often assigned to group therapy after an intake procedure if a lack of social skills is an important part of their problems. The group offers a chance to learn to talk to several other persons and to be in a more reciprocal relationship than individual therapy usually is. Imitative learning is extremely powerful and occurs in both group and individual therapy. In a group, though, the client has several persons to imitate and, probably more important, has the opportunity to see and learn from the therapist's interactions with other clients. It has been my experience that clients steadily become more empathic with each other as group therapy progresses. The first few sessions are usually filled with advice giving, since each member is sure that the others could solve their problems if they would just try some fairly simple solutions. Later, however, clients come to show an appreciation for and communicated understanding of the other clients. I would hope that they are learning to be therapeutic, partly by imitation.

Interpersonal learning and relating can take place more in a group than in individual therapy, whose limits usually make it a one-way relationship. *Group cohesiveness* refers to a remarkable experience that develops in a successful group—a feeling of belonging to a group that is really important and trusting. This feeling is qualitatively different from having a good relationship with a therapist. They are both powerful but in different ways. "Our group" often becomes a very important part of the person's life. Yalom uses *catharsis* to refer to the emotional relief that follows talking out painful material, a process that also happens in individual therapy. Finally, "existential factors" are mentioned as "almost an afterthought" (p. 84) that centers on realizing and accepting personal responsibility.

Advantages and Disadvantages

With this long list of advantages available in group therapy, you might wonder why one would do individual therapy at all, but there are clear advantages to individual therapy too. In fact, my personal preference is to do individual (and couple) therapy, both because the logistics of organizing and running a group are very difficult and because some therapeutic processes seem more likely to occur in individual therapy. Acceptance and understanding from six persons are surely more powerful than from one, but they are also less likely to occur. One problem with groups is that trust is very difficult to build in even one other person, so that clients frequently hold back in group material they would have talked about in individual therapy—often for good reasons. Some therapists do damage, primarily those who are "open and honest" in an attacking way (Lambert, Bergin, & Collins, 1977; Yalom & Lieberman, 1971), and the group therapist often has to deal with similar interactions between group members. In individual therapy, if the client perceives the therapist as empathic, accepting, and honest, a successful outcome is much more likely (Gurman, 1977). But Gurman says that what little evidence exists for group therapy suggests that this finding is much weaker in this treatment format. He speculates that group members' perceptions of each other as empathic, accepting, and honest will, if we ever have the data, turn out to be more important.

A format that many clients find helpful, when it is feasible, is to combine individual therapy with group therapy. This gives the opportunity for group interaction and to deal with material too sensitive for the group. The obvious disadvantage, especially when another therapist does the individual work, is that the individual therapy becomes the "real therapy" at the expense of full involvement in the group. It also can be very destructive to the group process when the group therapist sees some of the group members in individual therapy, because of the secrets and implications of special status that result.

Changes in the Therapist's Role

In group therapy the therapist has a special role but still is only one of several persons with whom the clients interact. The relationships are much more complex; the clients can be together against the therapist; one or some clients may curry favor with the therapist against other clients; the therapist often is a member of the group in a more personally involving way than in individual therapy. In addition, a group process is occurring at all times, and the therapist's job is often to comment on and intervene in this process. The clients are still the primary problem solvers. The therapist (and group members) still needs to be evocatively empathic, accepting, and honest. But much more is involved.

COUPLES AND FAMILIES

One dissatisfaction that is often voiced with individual therapy is that it is removed from the person's life, especially when he or she is involved in significant relationships—that the person can't really change except in relation to those significant others. The most obvious instance of this is in married and cohabiting couples and in families, but even "network therapy" is sometimes tried, in which many people in a client's life are brought together as a group. It's not unheard of to see a client, spouse, and lover together, although skills in addition to evocative empathy, acceptance, and genuineness might be handy to have.

You're Dealing with a System

The fundamental principle that guides and justifies family and couple therapy is that these persons who live together are an interacting system, and changes in one part of a system cannot occur without changes in another part. Bell (1963) tells of his having to switch from the perspective that the client was a problem to the insight that "the family is the problem!" (p. 3). From this basic principle, family therapists argue that treatment should occur within the context of the entire family—within the system that maintains the problem. Okun and Rappaport (1980) present an overview of theory and technique in family therapy.

The Relationship Is the Client

A common risk in couple and family therapy is that one person will become singled out as the *identified patient*. Usually, the initial contact made for therapy does center on the problems of one person, and so one task of the therapist is to take the perspective, and help the clients take the perspective, that no one is the patient; the relationship is the focus of treatment. Often one spouse will be "willing to come in if it will help" the other spouse. Sometimes therapists let a statement like this pass, as a means of engaging the reluctant family member, but the perspective should be shifted to the relationship as soon as possible without driving anyone from therapy.

Make Them Feel Understood

This won't come as a big surprise, but your first and most fundamental task is to make each member of the family feel understood— both because that will facilitate his or her problem solving as it does in individual therapy and because you have no coercive power to make a person engage in what is inevitably a difficult process. One family therapist I know talks about various techniques and interventions she uses but says that she does none of these things until she has "won the family."

More Direction of the Process

Family therapy is communication-based, and its effectiveness comes primarily from changing destructive patterns of communication between the members of the couple or family. As with group therapy, the therapist's job is often to comment on the nature of the process and to directly change it. With a couple, I often empathically respond to one person and turn to the other to ask "How did you hear that?" Or sometimes I will simply ask one of them to tell me what the other has said. You will often be startled at how helpless this leaves the person, who, it turns out, wasn't listening to a thing. Usually I don't let the person stew and get threatened (like all rules, this one gets broken sometimes) too long before I say what I thought I heard the other person say. Gradually, the clients start to be able to articulate what the others are saying, although they may do so grudgingly. In a sense, I am forcing empathic listening between the individuals.

Fading Out as a Communication Channel

The goal is that the couple or family be each others' therapists, in the sense that they are understanding and accepting of each other. You can think of the therapist as one point of a triangle with a couple (or as the hub of a wheel with a family). At first, the communication flows from each individual through the therapist, who is listening to everybody. Later in therapy, the goal is that the communication occur between the clients, as the therapist gradually fades out and becomes unnecessary. You won't be able to force this change simply by ordering it. The clients will start listening to each other and risking communication with each other only as it becomes safe and rewarding to do so. You teach by your example of listening and by keeping the process going in positive ways.

Goals—Explicit and Implicit

Setting goals in individual therapy is a complex enough process. In couple and family therapy, several individuals' best interests are involved, and these interests often conflict. Even the format in which clients are seen implies certain goals. Ideally, I say to all involved that my goal is that they all find the most satisfying solutions they can. But even before therapy starts, there is sometimes a decision about whether a separated couple should be seen together or each separately or whether only one person will be seen in therapy. Seeing them together carries more implication that reconciliation is a goal than seeing them separately. How will you make this decision? If a couple with children ask for help with their marriage, will you include the children in the sessions? One person in a couple might be quite decided that the relationship is over but afraid to tell the other person, who is still quite hopeful that they can work things out. This situation would probably call for couple sessions to clarify the situation but could quickly change to individual sessions. The point is that family and couple therapy nearly always involves complex and different specific goals. As with individual therapy, goals will emerge and change in the process of therapy, but it is an issue to which you will have to be very alert.

Cotherapy

In doing sex therapy, Masters and Johnson (1970) recommend the use of male/female therapist teams so that each client will have a "friend in court" to facilitate the feeling of being understood. This often is an advantage of cotherapy. Another advantage is that, especially with families, the interpersonal dynamics are so complex and so often involve the therapist that it is easy to lose perspective on the process and feel overwhelmed. Having a partner often permits one therapist to hang back, less involved, and bring a different perspective to the process. In addition, it is often a rewarding shared experience for the cotherapists to be working together. Particularly with families, having a cotherapist helps, whether the therapists are of different genders or not. The biggest problem seems to be economics. In private practice, few families or couples can afford two therapists at once, and the caseloads of many agencies are so large that cotherapy is not practical. This is an unfortunate reality, and so if you have a chance to do cotherapy in training, grab it.

Combining Multiple-Client and Individual Sessions

One serious problem with couple and family therapy is that, for all the advantages of seeing people together, there are a lot of things people just won't say in the presence of other family members, especially early in treatment. There are issues of mistrust and unwillingness to become vulnerable by giving the other person ammunition. There is no easy solution to this problem, and my experience has been that the most productive approach is different for couples than for families. With families, as with group therapy, there are so many permutations of relationships that individual sessions with one person (or some persons) in the family help make that person the "identified patient" and set up a special status that breeds mistrust of the therapist in other members of the family. The therapist could try to see each family member equally in individual sessions, but that is seldom practical, and so it is usually best to settle for a role in concentrating on changing family processes.

With couples it is a more manageable (but still complicated) matter to say that the main work of therapy is in couple sessions, that the relationship is the client, and that the goal is that they establish solutions as a couple but also to say that occasionally you will see each of them individually. If there are cotherapists, it is important that each therapist see each client, so that neither therapist becomes identified as "on the side" of one person. Masters and Johnson (1970) report considerable success with this format, but the ground rules are tricky and therefore must be made absolutely clear. I usually say "The purpose of these sessions is that sometimes there are things that are hard to say in front of the other person, especially at first. If either of you wants things kept private from the individual sessions, you can say so, and I will respect that. Whether we deal with those things eventually in couple sessions will be up to you." This requires a good memory in the therapist and carries some clear risks, but my experience has been that such sessions are especially helpful early in therapy and that they actually facilitate the couple's dealing with threatening issues more quickly. The issues often would never come up just in couple sessions, but trying them out in individual sessions helps make them more manageable.

Individual versus Couple or Family Therapy

Proponents of family therapy sometimes seem to be saying that a person in a relationship should always be treated with the others involved in that relationship. In my opinion, this is clearly an overstatement. Individual therapy is often called for with individuals in families and couples, but it is also often destructive to the extent that it ignores the effect it has on other relationships. There is a place for both approaches, but deciding when each is appropriate is difficult.

The ideal principle is that problems that result mainly from internal conflicts (see Chapter 15) are best suited to individual therapy and those that result from poor communication patterns to multiple-client approaches. In practice, though, there are elements of both in nearly all problems. You will need to be flexible enough to feel free to consider both general approaches, depending on the demands of particular circumstances. To do this you will need training in family and couple therapy. Maslow is often quoted as saying, in another context, "I suppose it is tempting, if the only tool you have is a hammer, to treat everything as if it were a nail" (1966, pp. 15–16). Try to have as many tools as possible.

PART FOUR

Theory and Evidence

Why Theory and Evidence?

You may skip these next four chapters if you accept everything I've said so far. Three of these chapters will try to make some sense out of why evocative empathy works, in theoretical terms, and Chapter 17 will briefly review research evidence that generally supports the effectiveness of evocative empathy. Throughout the previous chapters, I have made brief reference to explanations of why a particular part of therapy would be effective at that point, but now it is time to organize these explanations into an internally consistent theoretical position.

Our concern so far has been with being helpful to another human being, and we have focused on integrating experiencing and thinking. Now we shift gears from the personal and subjective to the structured and intellectual. I have been beating on you to stop intellectualizing, and you have done so well that your reward is four chapters of pedantry.

THE SEAT OF YOUR PANTS OFF THE TOP OF YOUR HEAD ISN'T ENOUGH

My personal dilemma in writing these chapters is that I don't think any theory can possibly be entirely correct at this stage of our knowledge of psychology, but it seems irresponsible and even dangerous for therapists to be saying that they reject theory and go with what feels right at the moment. There is good evidence (Bergin, 1963; Lambert, et al., 1977) that some therapists do damage, and I talked about destructive "genuineness" in Chapter 6. Doing what "feels right at the moment" depends enormously on the therapist's own freedom from distortions and destructive personal needs.

Thus, we need to make as much sense as we can of how therapy works, remembering that our thinking is only a successive approximation of the truth. Getting as close as we can to an accurate understanding, however, can serve us well if we humbly let it guide our practice.

The field of psychotherapy is full of "schools" of theory, each with adamant, quasi-religious commitment. This commitment may contribute to the effectiveness of therapy at times, when our knowledge is so scarce and therapy depends so on the client's hope and the therapist's confidence. It also, however, has made therapists rigidly dismiss others' ideas with scorn—usually because they distort the other theories. Strupp and Bergin (1969) said "The barriers separating the major schools of psychotherapy are gradually being eroded, and the predominant direction of research is toward a nonschool approach" (p. 24). We can hope that they were right. It is distressing to hear therapists ask each other what schools they belong to, because as soon as they have labels for each other, misunderstanding begins. The alternative to school labels is probably to say what one does in therapy.

At the risk, then, of being misunderstood, I'll say that what follows is an attempt to explain how evocatively empathic therapy works, from a general cognitive learning-theory perspective, with elements of information processing and some focus on unconscious processes such as repression. There! Now let's see you put me in a category.

What follows makes sense to me; you may or may not find it helpful. The evidence in Chapter 17, however, suggests that even if you can't accept the theory, you can comfortably do evocatively empathic therapy, because it is effective with anxiety-based problems. It is possible to argue that all theorizing is premature, but I suspect that theory, evidence, and experience continuously interact to develop new knowledge and techniques. We need to keep rebuilding our systems, drawing from established therapies, restating different ideas that may only seem different, and integrating ideas in the light of new knowledge. The practicing therapist must be open to change—and even seek it—but at the same time trust what she or he does enough to honestly offer services to clients. The therapist must be a loyal revisionist believer, firmly committed to a tentative position.

223

The Functions of Theory

Theory is needed mainly in areas in which knowledge is incomplete, because established fact carries its own organization. A theory brings organization to thinking by serving at least four major purposes.

1. *Forming testable concepts.* One practice that has led to misunderstanding and disagreement in the psychotherapy literature has been the imprecise use of words and a failure to define words adequately, especially when describing behavior. To be most useful, a theory must use explicitly defined words, and it must describe behavior in a way that permits others to observe it.
2. *Incorporating previous knowledge.* A major function of theory is to clarify the future; a theory is useless, however, if it does not incorporate all relevant present knowledge in an internally consistent way.
3. *Generating predictions.* A theory forces the organization of present knowledge in such a way that relationships that were not seen before become apparent. These relationships then provide the basis for making predictions about behavior that can be verified through research.
4. *Guiding future practice.* The functions of a theoretical model for therapy are obviously not all scientific; we are also interested in improving the practice of psychotherapy. If a theoretical model helps to organize our knowledge and to make differential predictions about different kinds of therapist behavior, it provides the basis for modifying the practice of psychotherapy and for modifying the way people are taught to be psychotherapists [Martin, 1972, pp. 5–6].[1]

THE KEY QUESTION—
WHY CAN YOU TRUST THE CLIENT?

These chapters will try to answer many questions about how therapy works, but the most important one is the question that implies that evocatively empathic therapy is naive. In Chapter 5 I argued strongly that the basic principle is that the client is the problem solver, but the critic can answer "That sounds very nice, but the client has come to therapy confused and unable to solve problems, distorting the truth and not sophisticated in psychological matters. The therapist knows more about behavior and, we hope, has a clearer perception of reality. It is irresponsible to let the client wallow around, not knowing where to go, when you could give helpful direction.

[1]From *Learning Based Client Centered Therapy*, by D. G. Martin. © 1972 by Wadsworth Publishing Company, Inc. Reprinted by permission of the publisher, Brooks/Cole Publishing Company, Monterey, California.

Empathy is very nice and supportive[2] and probably even a necessary precondition for therapy, but it is not enough. *How do you know the client will talk about the things he or she needs to talk about?"*

A Personal Note

A brief personal digression will help clarify how some of the ideas in this book developed. My graduate training in therapy was taken at the University of Chicago, where I developed a commitment to client-centered theory and therapy. My internship year was spent in Chicago at the Institute for Juvenile Research, which at that time had a primarily psychoanalytic orientation. My experiences and reading of the research literature, however, kept me moving toward empathy-based therapy. My first job was at the University of Iowa, one of the most firmly learning-theory-oriented psychology departments in North America. Although I was gaining confidence as a practicing therapist, I got ripped to shreds theoretically at Iowa. People kept asking "But how does it work?" Through long and sometimes painful theoretical discussions, it became clear to me that a number of the theoretical foundations of humanistic theory were difficult to defend.

My dilemma was that research evidence and my own experience supported empathy-oriented therapy, but I couldn't make sense out of it, as I began to see considerable merit in learning theory (although many aspects of it seem oversimplified). I vividly remember arguing in my office one day with two graduate students, neither of whom was aware how much he was contributing to my thinking. We were talking about approach-avoidance conflict, and they asked me "How do you know the client will try to talk about what he needs to talk about?" The answer to that question hit me then and follows, in Chapter 16. But first I have to lay some groundwork.

It is an interesting sidelight that developing a theoretical model helped me see that I misunderstood empathy as fairly passive and forced me to change my therapeutic style to a more leadingly empathic one. It also became clear that many therapists seem to be doing similar things but are describing their actions in different words. A lot of the disagreement among therapists of different "schools" is unnecessary misunderstanding.

[2]I hear this a lot, and it upsets me so much I have to admit I get defensive about it. Empathy is supportive, in a way, but it is also confrontative and active and arousing and evocative, and many people don't understand this.

This is not the place for a detailed analysis of various theories of therapy, but an overall perspective of the theory to follow will be clarified by some brief comments about different attempts to answer the "How does it work?" question.[3]

HUMANISTIC THEORY

Empathic therapy grew out of the humanistic beliefs of Rogers (1959), Maslow (1954), and others who say that humans are innately self-actualizing—fundamentally motivated to grow in positive directions emotionally. Thus, people develop problems because their self-actualizing tendency has been blocked. The function of therapy is to create the facilitative atmosphere within which self-actualization can take place. The humanist's answer to the question "How can you trust the client?" is based on the client's inborn self-actualizing tendency.

Phenomenology

These theories are phenomenological—it is not reality that matters in understanding behavior; it is the person's perception of that reality that guides behavior. The humanist gives the person dignity and what sounds very much like free will—the responsibility to choose and the freedom to choose. Our lives are not driven by the past, say the humanists, but by our perceptions of the future. We choose the best alternatives for our lives, as we perceive the alternatives. If a person chooses unwisely, it is because he or she has misperceived the alternatives because of blocking and distortion of the self-actualizing tendency.

Problems with Logic and Evidence

There is a serious logical problem with this phenomenological position. The critic can say "OK, behavior is based on the future and not on the past because perceptions guide people's choices. But"—and here comes the fateful question—"why do people perceive the alternatives the way they do?" The answer must be either that perceptions of the future are somehow inborn (a position nobody seems to take) or that they are based on past experience. The critic then can say that phenomenology is a learning position that just fails to take the final step in its logic.

[3]In trying to be eclectic, I think I see strengths and weaknesses in each of the major theoretical perspectives. I will briefly describe those strengths and weaknesses. More complete discussions can be found elsewhere (Corey, 1982; Lichtenstein, 1980; Martin, 1971).

This general logical problem also applies to the self-actualization process: how, other than through learning experiences, can the person know what experiences are growth-producing? Through what process can the person innately be self-actualizing? Rogers (1959) proposes the "organismic valuing process" but still doesn't elaborate how it works, leaving us with simply another name for self-actualization.

A second problem with self-actualization as innate is that of evidence. The evidence cited by Rogers is based mainly on his clinical experience (he also has cited the general tendency toward growth and differentiation of functioning observed in the general process of physical development). He says "It has been my experience that persons have a basically positive direction. In my deepest contact with individuals in therapy, even those whose troubles are most disturbing, whose behavior has been most antisocial, whose feelings are most abnormal, I find this to be true" (1961, p. 26).

The critic can simply respond "*My* clinical experience is that Rogers is wrong." Menninger has said:

> Carl Rogers is only half right when he urges his students to recognize that in most if not "all individuals there exist growth forces, tendencies toward self-actualization, which may act as the sole motivation for therapy." . . . Sick individuals differ in the strength and effectiveness of their "drive toward health" [1963, pp. 397–398].

Cofer and Appley (1964) conclude that "self actualization . . . suffers, in our opinion, from the vagueness of its concepts, the looseness of its language, and the inadequacy of the evidence related to its major contentions" (p. 692).

AN EMPATHIC LEARNING THEORIST?

Various forms of learning theory still seem to be the most powerful influences among North American university psychology departments, although cognitive theorists might dispute this statement. One indication of this influence is the popularity of behavior modification as an approach to treatment. Another is the enormous research literature that is dominated by learning-oriented workers.

Powerful Principles

The one principle that has probably had more influence than any other is that of the power of reinforcement over behavior. To say that people do what they are reinforced for doing sounds, on one hand, so obvious that it is simple-minded, but on the other, it is a powerful bit of knowledge whose full implications few see. Clear understanding of it is leading, I think and hope, to more positive ways of dealing with people and a movement away from punitive relationships and organizations, for example.

The principles of conditioning contribute enormously to our understanding of emotions and of how to change emotions. To get rid of a fear, you must feel that fear in small steps, the evidence tells us, and that has sweeping implications for how we do therapy. The power of learning principles must be acknowledged.

Simplistic Applications

The problem is that learning theorists have tended to apply the principles in oversimplified ways. Messer and Winokur (1980) say that behavior therapy philosophically resembles the "comic view of reality," not in the sense of being "funny" or "nonserious" but in "following the typical structure of dramatic comedy."

> [The comic vision] emphasizes the familiar, controllable, and predictable aspects of situations and people. Conflict is viewed as centered in situations, and it can be eliminated by effective manipulative action or via the power of positive thinking. Endings are happy ones free from guilt and anxiety. . . . Early deficits and traumas are not usually seen as placing a ceiling on possible change. Behavior therapists tend to assume that it is possible to achieve more total change through relearning. They de-emphasize the centrality of conflict and fixation and replace them with faulty learning or the absence of appropriate skills [p. 823].

Messer and Winokur's point is that it is the behavior therapists who are naive about the simplicity of human problems. They draw a parallel with a North American belief in technical solutions. Most important for our discussion, they point to the behavior therapist's focus on factors external to the person.

I told a friend I might call this book *The Empathic Behaviorist*, and she politely told me there were better ways to make a fool of myself and offend people. That title would have misled everyone for several reasons, the most obvious being that the word *behavior* means, to most people, "overt behavior." The whole point of this theoretical chapter is to say that thinking and feeling are also behavior and, for our purposes as therapists, they may be the most important behaviors. The covert behaviors we call thoughts and feelings occur inside the skin but are still behaviors.

I will be arguing that a perfectly respectable learning theorist can talk about internal conflict, anxiety, unconscious influences, repression, and cognition. Above all, he or she can be evocatively empathic and understand that the client's goal is to take responsibility for his or her own life.

The basic principle is that the application of learning principles becomes incredibly complex once we see that it is the behavior going on inside the skin that is most important in therapy.

PSYCHOANALYTIC CONTRIBUTIONS

Psychoanalysis has influenced nearly all therapists and has made many of its ideas integral parts of our culture. It is hard for us to imagine that at the beginning of this century most people saw children as small adults and didn't appreciate that childhood experiences molded adult personality; the notion that human behavior follows laws grew partly out of Freud's influence, and the importance of sexuality in personality development was at first adamantly rejected. The idea of a "talking cure" was popularized by Freud, and most therapists recognize the influence of distortions their clients make without awareness—unconscious influences.

Observations versus Explanations

It is possible to accurately observe a phenomenon and then to give an incorrect explanation for it. Previous sections made just this point about humanists, who may describe an effective therapy technique but explain it in indefensible terms. It seems likely that Freud observed some very important phenomena but explained them in terms such as *psychic energy* and *the topography of the mind* that can no longer be defended. Other theorists, especially some learning-oriented ones, have rejected "clinical" notions like repression with statements such as Eysenck's "Learning theory does not postulate any such 'unconscious' causes, but regards neurotic symptoms as simply learned habits" (Eysenck & Rachman, 1965, p. 10) and Wolpe's "It does not appear that the repression as such plays any part in the maintenance of neurosis" (1958, p. 94). These "Freudian" phenomena, however, can be reformulated within learning theory terms, and it is an overreaction to reject everything that smacks of Freud.

Marmor says it well in *Modern Psychoanalysis* (1968).[4]

> At this point in history . . . the value of [Freud's] psychoanalytic *method* of investigating "unconscious" mental processes remains unquestioned. . . . However, . . . classical psychoanalysis as a *theory* of human

[4]From: *Modern Psychoanalysis: New Directions and Perspectives* edited by Judd Marmor. © 1968 by Basic Books. By permission of Basic Books, Inc., Publishers, New York.

behavior has not equally withstood the test of time; but this statement requires qualification. I do not wish to imply that all of Freud's views have been valueless. Certain of his basic constructs, such as those of conflict, repression, transference, and the "unconscious," still constitute an extremely effective foundation for an understanding of human behavior and psychopathology *despite the fact that the data upon which they were based can be dealt with just as effectively within other frames of reference such as those of communication theory or learning theory.* What has become obsolete has been the cumbersome metapsychological superstructure that Freud erected upon these fundamental concepts— notably his theory of instincts, of libido, of the tripartite structure of the psyche, and of psychic energy. This "mythology of psychoanalysis," as Freud once called his theory of instincts, has been rendered untenable by newer developments and findings in the behavioral sciences [pp. 5–6].

Unconscious Influences

For our purposes, the most important of these "Freudian" notions is that of unconscious influences on behavior. I noted some behaviorists who rejected it, and many cognitive theorists (see below) seem to ignore it as an issue. Scientific psychology seems to have dismissed unconscious influence as somehow mystical until the last few years, when there has been a resurgence in interest in it. One Skinnerian friend of mine says that he doesn't believe in repression except in his own case. Zajonc (1980, 1981) has summarized evidence that emotional reactions and cognitive processes can and do operate independently of each other, and Shevrin and Dickman (1980) marshal a wide range of evidence that unconscious processes are a necessary assumption of all psychological theory.

It seems clear that unconscious influences do operate on behavior. Finding a defensible way to explain how they operate will be our problem in Chapter 15.

INFORMATION PROCESSING AND COGNITIVE THEORY

Finally, the most visible current trend in personality theory seems to be toward "cognitive-learning" models (Mahoney, 1977), which have moved the emphasis of thinking about human functioning more toward "inner" variables. In some ways, this trend resembles phenomenological theories with such principles as that perceptions and cognitions control behavior. There is a strong emphasis in these theories on the overriding influence of (by implication conscious) thinking and a tendency to avoid mention of unconscious influences (Seligman & Johnston, 1973; Forgus & Shulman, 1979). This focus is strongly present in Ellis's (1962) rational-emotive theory of therapy, which is founded on the principle that thinking and reason determine emotions, so that changing thinking and reason is the way to change emotion.

But Thinking Is Behavior

Two problems with current writing in cognitive theory seem most important for our discussion. The first one, I think, is only an apparent problem, as I read the theorists involved. Cognitive theorists have reacted against their understanding of behavioral positions as almost exclusively focused on external variables, such as reinforcers and conditioned stimuli in the environment. In fact, many learning theorists have acknowledged the importance of "covert behavior," although they often seem to ignore it in the application of their ideas. However, behaviorists reject cognitive theorists for seeming to believe that cognitions are *things* that exist in the "mind," when in fact most cognitive theorists don't really say this.

If we conceptualize thinking and feeling as behavior that goes on inside the skin, we can embrace Mahoney's proposal that "we adopt a broad conceptualization of 'learning principles' . . . and entertain the possibility that these principles are directly relevant to the modification of cognition" (1977, p. 11).

The second problem is more serious, since other positions would argue that "cognition" is only part of the most significant internal behaviors that affect overt behavior. Enormously complex processes occur in the brain, and as Posner and Boies (1971, p. 407) conclude, "Conscious awareness is itself rather late in the sequence of mental processing." Recent evidence on information processing supports Duncan's (1980) calling awareness a "limited-capacity system" (p. 272), and McCauley, Parmelee, Sperber, and Carr (1980) report evidence showing "that extracting the meaning from a picture and consciously identifying it may be separate processes" (p. 265). Cognitive theories need to include some kind of unconscious processing or processing with diminished awareness.

This issue is greatly complicated because different theorists define *cognition* differently. I am using it to mean something roughly synonymous to *thinking*, but Lazarus (1982) says "The cognitive activity in appraisal does not imply anything about deliberate reflection, rationality, or awareness" (p. 1022). He then argues that influences without awareness are quite possible but that they involve cognition. Quite clearly, he and I are in essential agreement about the role of influences without awareness, but many readers would assume we disagree because of our different definitions of *cognition*.

The cognitive-learning trend has contributed a great deal to making learning theory more complex and useful, but we need to remember that cognition and perception are themselves behaviors and that they are only part of the story in understanding human behavior. Yes, cognitions do influence emotions, but emotions also influence cognitions. They seem to be at least partly different systems that interact with each other.

BEING ECLECTIC

My theoretical understanding is different than it was ten years ago and, I hope, different than it will be ten years from now. Yours will be different from any of these, of course, but our problem is to find enough internally consistent structure to guide our thinking, practice, and development of new ideas, while we stay open to new ideas. We all want to be "eclectic," of course, but this could mean just about anything.

I hope that my own current "eclectic" view is apparent from this chapter. My practice has been influenced most strongly by some humanists, but my understanding of inner conflict draws from learning theory, particularly when internal behaviors are considered. This understanding has affected my practice of therapy and helped me understand and appreciate some phenomena associated with psychoanalytic theory.

I used to say I wanted to "live like a humanist and think like a learning theorist," but even that led to misunderstanding. For a while everybody thought that humanists spent their time naked in large groups in swimming pools, and everybody has a different idea of what a learning theorist believes. I don't like being misunderstood, and so I try to avoid being labeled and wish the same for you.

CHAPTER FIFTEEN

The Nature of Anxiety-Based Problems

Understanding how therapy works requires an understanding of the causes of the problems we are trying to treat. Essentially, these are problems caused by (1) painful emotions, such as anxiety, guilt, and depression; (2) distortions of thinking and feeling caused by these painful emotions; and (3) self-defeating behaviors that help the person avoid the painful emotions, but at great cost—in other words, anxiety-based problems in living (Szasz, 1960). The older term for these problems, *neurosis*, is falling into disuse, largely because it was so misleading. It implied that these problems were some kind of illness, rather than the same kinds of problems that we all have. The term *neurotic/normal continuum* refers to this principle. We all have problems that would be called neurotic if they caused enough trouble for us and/or those around us. The point at which "enough trouble" begins is arbitrary and is based on individual circumstances and even cultural norms. In this chapter I will use the terms *neurosis* and even *symptom* occasionally but will do so on the understanding that they refer to problems in living, not to illnesses.

PRINCIPLES OF FEAR

Before discussing complex problems like anxiety, I need to review a few of the simple principles of fear. I hope this review doesn't put you off with its simple-mindedness or with its seeming irrelevance to therapy. Trust me; things will get more complicated very soon. If you are not familiar with these principles, I'd suggest you read a basic learning principles text.

The baby is born fearing nothing that is not physically discomforting. Through conditioning experiences based on the pairing of physical discomfort (pain, usually) with objects or even his or her

233

own behaviors that were originally emotionally neutral, the baby develops fears of those objects or behaviors. Once the child learns the powerful lesson of imitation, fears can also be acquired vicariously from the fearful reactions of significant others; although the process here is more complex than with simple fears, the principles are still the same. Fears are fundamentally learned from association with pain.

Complex Fears

These simple principles can directly account for only the most obviously acquired fears, however, and most adult fears and anxieties do not easily fit the model of directly conditioned fear based on painful experiences. You will treat a lot of people for fear of elevators before you find one who has been hurt or trapped in an elevator to a degree that would logically explain the fear. Understanding these complexities is the purpose of this chapter.

To Lose a Fear You Must Feel It

One implication of the observation that all fears are learned is that, in principle, they can all be unlearned. The basic principle here is that the only way to get rid of a conditioned response is to perform the response in the absence of reinforcement—in other words, to extinguish it. (Or you could perform the response in the presence of reinforcement incompatible with the response, which would both extinguish and countercondition the response.) With regard to fear, this means that the person *must* feel the fear to get rid of it. In slightly less mechanical terms, one must face fear and experience painful experiences to change them. To be most effective, this should occur in steps small enough that the fear response aroused is not strong enough to produce secondary conditioning of fear of the new situation or to cause the person to escape the situation before extinction can start. The terms *graduated extinction* and *graduated counterconditioning* describe this process.

The Persistence of Fears

There are at least four factors that make fears last so long. Time, they say, heals all wounds, but that is not true of painful conditioned responses. The only way to get rid of a fear is to face it, feel the fear, and have nothing bad happen. Unfortunately (or probably fortunately for survival of the species), fears just extinguish more slowly than other conditioned responses. A second, related factor is that humans quite understandably avoid the things they fear, and this prevents extinction from taking place. In fact, avoidance behavior is often strongly established and under conscious control, while the emotional reactions themselves take a few seconds to get started. Thus, we can avoid feared situations so quickly and efficiently that our fears never extinguish unless circumstances force us into contact with the sources of our fears. The third factor is that avoidance behavior becomes extremely strong because every time we avoid something feared, we feel better. Fear reduction is a very powerful reinforcer, and the avoidance behavior becomes difficult to change. Fourth, the experiences that cause fear are usually unpredictable. This kind of partial reinforcement results in reactions that are very resistant to extinction. The unpredictability comes both from the inconsistency of the persons doing the punishing and because we occasionally fail to avoid the real source of the fear—the unconditioned source of pain that is so punishing. These occasional failures to avoid are unpredictable and establish the fear and the avoidance behavior even more strongly.

Fearing Your Own Thoughts and Feelings

An important principle for understanding anxiety is that your own acts can become cues for fear. If one is severely punished for each head scratch, the *act* of scratching the head will subsequently arouse fear. Similarly, if a person is punished each time she thinks a particular thought, the act of thinking that thought can become a cue for fear.

I suspect that you have had the experience of being alone, thinking some particular thought or memory, and feeling awful or embarrassed or frightened. You *must* have been aroused by your own "painful thought." Any internal process, such as a feeling or thought, can become frightening, given the right learning experiences.

Punishment Works Through Inhibition

One last simple principle is that punishment works, in general, by suppressing the punished behavior, not by eliminating it. The punished behavior *seems* to disappear, but in fact what has happened is that a new behavior has been learned—that of stopping the punished behavior. In the words of Campbell and Church, "Punishment puts down a response by force and tends to conceal it from public view" (1969, p. 111). This goes against our intuitions, but it is important for our understanding of anxiety-based problems. The punished behavior is not weakened in strength at all, and so if the inhibiting behavior is somehow lessened, the punished behavior

235

that seemed to disappear will reappear in the same strength as if it had never been punished (Walters & Grusec, 1977).

CONFLICT AND ANXIETY

But we're not all that interested in simple behaviors. The experience we want to understand is the haunting, helpless feeling of apprehension or even dread that comes with anxiety. If someone asks "What are you so afraid of?," the person answers "I don't know. I don't know, but it's awful, and it just sneaks up on me and without warning. I'm so scared I have to run, but I can't run, and I can't think . . . it has to stop!" Or maybe it's quieter than this, with the person saying "I do things that just don't make sense, but I don't really care anyway because you can't trust people who say they like you and then leave you." The person's confusion and anxiety touch us, and we want to help. After some time in which we are evocatively empathic, the person says "I'm amazed, really, how much I felt trapped by my relationship with him and how angry I am at the way he puts me down . . . I don't know why I couldn't see that before, but now I see what I have to do." With a quiet sense of discovery, the person might say "I really do care, and I'm so lonely. People have hurt me a lot, but I see now that sometimes it was me almost wanting them to hurt me so I didn't have to love them." Or perhaps the person has an "aha" insight experience with "Of course! I just remembered how it was . . . she *didn't* love and support me all those times. She *said* she did, but now I can remember how fierce she looked and how worried she was about what the neighbors would think every time I did anything," although these smashing insights are relatively rare in therapy.

This is a remarkable process. Something hidden from awareness was still having a dramatic effect on the person, and a certain kind of talking made the person aware of it and somehow lessened its effect. Our problem is understanding this process without using indefensible concepts like "the unconscious mind" or "blocking and displacement of psychic energy"—to understand it in general cognitive-learning terms.

To do this, we must first understand conflict.[1]

---

[1] The ideas in this chapter are condensed and updated from more complete presentations (Martin, 1972, 1976, 1980). I am leaving out a lot of detail and corroborative references that might interest you in these other sources. Also see Dollard and Miller (1950).

Principles of Conflict

Phillips has gone so far as to say that "there is no psychopathology without conflict" (1956, p. 127). This is probably an overstatement, but it seems safe to say that without conflict there would be no anxiety-based problems. In general, conflict is *the tendency to perform two or more incompatible responses at the same time.* Dollard and Miller (1950) described four kinds of conflict, arguing that "an intense emotional conflict is the necessary basis for neurotic behavior" (p. 129).

Approach-approach conflict is the situation in which the person wants two things, but getting one means losing the other. You might want an intimate relationship but have two equally attractive persons to choose from in circumstances in which you can't have both without risking total exhaustion. In *avoidance-avoidance conflict* you fear and want to avoid two things, but avoiding one means that you must approach the other. You are late filing your income tax return and face punitive action when you do file it, but if you wait, the punishment will be greater. The immediate aversiveness of filing now feels just as awful as the worse consequences in the distant future.

Both of these situations are painful, but they usually get resolved because something tips the balance one way or the other or you escape the situation. But *approach-avoidance conflict* is devastating. Some people find this counterintuitive, but it is our nature that we can both want and fear something at the same time. A young man might desperately want to be involved with a woman but at the same time desperately fear her, fear intimacy, and fear sex. He wants her too much to say "Forget it, who needs her?" He can't just get involved, because he's too scared. What does he do? He suffers.

The fourth kind of conflict, *double approach-avoidance conflict*, is just an elaboration of approach-avoidance conflict in which there are two or more goals that are both desired and feared. Approaching one of the desired (and feared) goals means sacrificing the other desired (and feared) goal. In real life, conflicts are very complicated. Someone might want to graduate from the university but not want to because of the uncertainty of being alone, but if he doesn't graduate, parents will be hurt, and the person will feel guilty but also satisfied at hurting the parents, whom he both loves and hates, and so on.

Conflict is essential to an understanding of anxiety because simple fears are not much problem for the person. As Ohman and Ursin say, "Once [avoidance] behavior is established, the fear is quite efficiently coped with, and there is little need for further worry. It is only when the coping strategy is undermined by some approach contingencies that maladaptivity results" (1979, p. 180). Only when there is conflict does the person suffer, because otherwise feared things will simply be avoided, so you know that if a person is suffering, he or she is in conflict.

Figure 15-1 illustrates some interesting things about the way approach-avoidance conflict works, and four principles will help us understand anxiety later (Dollard & Miller, 1950). First, the line labeled "approach gradient" illustrates that as you get closer to something you want, your desire for it—your tendency to approach it—gets stronger. Second, the "avoidance gradient" illustrates that as you get closer to something you fear, the more you fear it—the stronger is your tendency to avoid it. Notice that "get closer" can mean get closer in actual physical distance, in time, or through a dimension of similarity (for example, if you fear a red light, you will also fear dark pink, but less than red, and light pink, but less than dark pink).

Figure 15-1 illustrates an approach-avoidance conflict because the person has both approach and avoidance tendencies toward the "feared goal," and the gradients illustrate the third principle—as the person approaches something both feared and desired, both the fear and the desire are increasing, but the fear is increasing faster. This means that if the person is far from the feared goal in this conflict situation, the approach tendency is stronger than the avoidance tendency, and so he or she will move toward the feared goal. Our young man is sitting in his room lonely and wanting to phone a particular woman. "I'm going to do it! I really want to talk to her, and there is just no reason I can't just go phone her right now." But he also fears her, and so as he walks toward the phone, his desire to talk to her is increasing (he's getting closer psychologically), but so is his fear, and the fear is increasing faster. He dials the phone as his mouth dries out and his heart starts to pound—the fear, the tendency to avoid, has almost caught up with the approach tendency. She answers in her warm and friendly voice, and now he is so close that his fear is stronger than his desire. He breathes heavily into the phone in panic and hangs up. She thinks she got an obscene phone call, and he returns to his room, mad at himself because now he wants her again. He is trapped in the "conflict region," in which his behavior will vacillate.

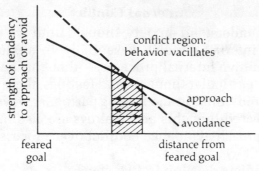

Figure 15-1 Diagram of approach-avoidance conflict show-ing the conflict area, in which behavior will vacillate between approach and avoidance. (From *Personality and Psycho-therapy: An Analysis in Terms of Learning, Thinking and Culture*, by J. Dollard and N. E. Miller. Copyright © 1950 by McGraw-Hill, Inc. Reprinted by permission.)

Using a fourth principle, there are four ways we can resolve his conflict. The principle is that the approach and avoidance tendencies can be strengthened or weakened, thus raising or lowering the gradients of approach and avoidance. We can weaken or strengthen his fear, or we can weaken or strengthen his desire. If he has some positive experiences with women or somehow lessens his fear, his desire for the woman will be the same as before, but the avoidance gradient might be lowered so that it never quite catches up with the approach gradient; although he may get nervous, he will carry through with his approach and not be in conflict. Or, second, he could try to phone her again, and before he can hang up, she screams into the phone "Is that you, Charlie, you disgusting creep!" Now he will become a monk. If his fear of women is strong enough, it may at all times be higher than his desire, and so he won't be in conflict. He will simply avoid women and not suffer and vacillate. If something could decrease or increase his desire for her, the conflict could also be resolved because the gradients would never be in balance with each other.

Of these four ways to resolve conflict, decreasing the fear is the one that is most within the power of therapists to effect.[2]

---

[2]There are some exceptions to these general principles of conflict, but the principles are firmly enough established for our application of them to understanding anxiety. A good summary of the research on conflict has been written by Crowne (1979).

Internal Conflict

We still don't understand anxiety, though, until we apply all these principles to internal conflict. Essentially, in anxiety, the person fears his or her own internal processes—thoughts and feelings. But if you just fear particular thoughts and feelings, there is no problem; you simply avoid thinking and feeling particular ways. The problem arises when feared thoughts and feelings are also motivated. Now you are in approach-avoidance conflict over processes inside your skin.

Internal conflicts develop in two steps:

1. Thoughts and feelings become fear cues because they have been punished. "Punished" can mean obvious physical punishment such as spanking a child for masturbating; the overt behavior is being punished, but so are the concomitant thoughts and feelings. "Punished" more likely means subtler processes such as guilt inducement and love withdrawal. The child might have been rejected and called evil and sinful whenever she expressed anger at a parent. Now, feeling anger is frightening—an internal process has become a cue for fear.

2. If the thoughts and feelings are somehow motivated, a conflict will develop. This motivation can be either biological or as a result of learning experiences. The child who is punished for masturbating likely will seem to lose interest in sex at about 8 years of age— and not be in conflict about it until puberty starts and the strength of the approach, the desire, increases so much that it is about equal to the fear of sexual feelings. He will suffer—guilt or anxiety or some other painful emotions, as he strongly needs to feel sexual feelings and strongly needs to avoid them at the same time. The child who is punished for anger will be in conflict if she has reason to have feelings of aggression toward the parents—if she learns to feel aggressively, as seems nearly inevitable. Another example of internal conflict might involve dependency feelings, which are strongly rewarded, especially through early childhood, and at other times strongly punished, especially among males. It is very likely that an individual might feel dependent and at the same time be "ashamed" of feeling this way. In our theoretical terms, he or she is being aversively aroused by his or her own strongly learned impulse. The most likely explanation of what has been called free-floating anxiety is that the feelings are cued by many different things, so that the cues are frequently encountered or, more likely, cued by

internal processes that are always potentially with the victim. The anxious person fears his or her own thoughts and feelings.

The person in conflict is constantly and painfully vacillating. He must think and feel the motivated thoughts and feelings, and he must avoid them. He suffers.

The Power of Anxiety

It is difficult to find words strong enough now to make the jump from these simple principles of conflict and anxiety to what the human experience of anxiety is really like. It can vary in strength, and we all experience it to some degree, but anxiety can be a helpless, sick feeling of guilt; a frantic, desperate shaking with no way to grasp the demons that seem to threaten; a confusion that prevents thinking about even simple things; or any of hundreds of experiences. The principles are simple; the actual experience is powerfully painful and complex. It is so powerful that it underlies one of the most important principles for understanding self-defeating behavior. *Anxiety reduction is an extremely powerful reinforcer.* This principle will help us understand behavior (including internal behavior) in ourselves and others that otherwise would make no sense.

REPRESSION AND COGNITIVE DISTORTIONS

Before we see how anxiety can cause people to do such self-defeating and odd-seeming things, though, we need to understand how one can fear something without awareness—or, more accurately, with partial awareness. I have mentioned unconscious influences; we all do fear things without being able to name them, but explaining this process is remarkably difficult. We say things like "I was lying to myself about that," but we can't really mean we are two persons, one of whom, "I," lies (consciously?) to "myself." The basic process underlying these cognitive distortions is *repression*, the unintentional forgetting of well-learned aversive memories. Repression is usually associated with Freudian ideas like "pushing thoughts into the unconscious mind," but we will try to understand the process in learning terms that assume only that we are dealing with brain processes, not a mind with different "places" in it.

Defining Awareness

A talk I like to give is called, "Can a Learning Theorist Have Consciousness?" Learning theorists have tended to avoid anything to do with terms like *consciousness* and *awareness*, wanting to reject their almost mystical-seeming meanings, but it is pretty obvious to most of us that ignoring a phenomenon that feels so important to virtually everybody will not make it go away. It is possible, though, to understand awareness in terms that don't imply mystical mental energy. The basic principle is that there is an enormous amount going on inside the brain, and only some of these processes include symbolic expression. These symbolic processes include the use of words, gestures, pictures—anything that stands for something else—and we learn to call these particular brain processes "awareness."

Only some of what goes on in the brain qualifies as thinking. When driving a new car one frequently tries to put the key in the ignition where it was in the old car "without thinking." Hebb has pointed out that it is possible to read out loud for some time (perhaps to a child) and then to realize that "I . . . have no notion at all of what the heroine had been up to" (1972, p. 31). Obviously, much complex brain behavior was involved "without thinking."

It would be difficult to imagine, however, that reading out loud does not involve some of what we call "awareness," and this points to a second critical aspect of our definition. *Awareness is on a continuum.* One can be partly aware, to the extent that one could symbolize if called on to do so. Thus, it is inaccurate to speak of a person as *either* aware or unaware. Hebb was partly aware of more than one thing at a time. There is no difficulty with understanding that a person can be aware of several things at once, if awareness is simply symbolizing brain processes that can occur at many different degrees of completeness.

Now the groundwork is laid for understanding anxiety; you can be frightened by thoughts (brain processes) that are fear-arousing but are only partly conscious—partly symbolized. You avoid them quickly to reduce the anxiety, but this prevents facing the painful thoughts—prevents your getting over the fear. We are getting ahead of the story, but therapy helps the person face those thoughts by articulating them more completely.

A Learning View of Repression

Repression is one primary way we avoid those painful thoughts,[3] and the spooky thing is that it happens "automatically," without our

---

[3]The term *suppression* is used to refer to conscious strategies to avoid painful thoughts. The person can intentionally think of other things or engage in distracting activities. It may be that habitually suppressing painful thoughts also inhibits them, with the same consequences as repression.

knowledge or plan. Remember that punishment works by inhibition and that thinking is symbolizing brain behavior. If a particular thought is punished, the act of thinking that thought will become punishing. The inhibiting behavior of stopping that thought will be rewarded by escape from the discomfort it arouses. Thus, repression is an instance of inhibition.

If thoughts are behaviors, they operate by the same principles as any other behaviors. If you punish me for scratching my head, that behavior will be inhibited. Now, where are all my unused head scratches? That's silly, of course; we all know they're in my unconscious hand. Actually, they're not anywhere. Head scratches are events, not things that can go somewhere. My arm and nervous system are still capable of performing head scratches and are still trying to do so, but the opposing behavior of stopping that is more powerful. Thoughts, similarly, don't go somewhere; they are symbolizing behavior that gets inhibited to some degree in repression.

Thoughts that have become fear cues will be followed by emotional pain when they occur and thus are likely to be inhibited. The degree to which they will be inhibited will depend on the balance of forces among (1) the strength of the punishment, (2) the strength of the motivation of the thoughts, and (3) the strength of environmental cues that are reminders of the particular thoughts. Remember that the punished and inhibited behaviors (thoughts in this case) are not weakened in strength in the least. They are only inhibited.

This description of repression is a general explanation for the phenomenon of the failure to think accurately because of selective inhibition of aversive brain processes. The general phenomenon could also include self-deception, denial, and the other traditional defense mechanisms.

Freud and even Rogers (1959) readily accept some version of repression, but learning and cognitive theorists have tended to reject it (Holmes, 1974). Recently, though, as we noted in Chapter 14, unconscious influences have been recognized more, and there is good laboratory evidence for this view of repression (Glucksberg & King, 1967; Weiner & Higgins, 1969; Glucksberg & Ornstein, 1969; Martin, Hawryluk, Berish, & Dushenko, 1981; Martin, 1980) that you may want to examine for yourself.

When Repression Is Costly

Repression is a normal process that serves an important adaptive function. If you constantly remembered all the disgusting things you've ever done or thought, you would be a mess. Up to a point, repression is adaptive. There are at least two general ways, though, that repression can cause trouble.

First, the person can fail to learn from experience, remembering events inaccurately. Second, and more painfully, repression is often only partial, since awareness is on a continuum and repression may inhibit only parts of thoughts. The thoughts (and other internal processes, such as feelings) can still be active enough to arouse anxiety without being complete enough for the person to be able to symbolize them. This, clearly, is the general explanation of anxiety, the remarkable process in which we are frightened of things we can't name.

Anxiety Cues That Have Never Been Articulated

Repression involves the inhibition of brain processes that were conscious at one time. Our understanding of anxiety as cued by partially symbolized internal processes is incomplete, however, if we consider only repression. We often see the effects of repression being relieved when a client says "It's amazing that I didn't remember those awful things. They've obviously been bothering me for a long time." But it is at least as common to hear something like "No wonder I'm always yelling at my wife. It never occurred to me that I was trying to prove to her that I'm strong. That's obviously ridiculous. I never thought of it this way."[4] Here the client was being affected by threatening thoughts and feelings that were only incompletely symbolized, not because of repression but because they were never fully symbolized. This is an example of what is often called "learning without awareness." Of course, it would be more accurate to call it "learning with partial awareness." We are most interested in the fears that are learned without full awareness, but the process also applies to other kinds of experiences, including joy, liking, and the whole range of human experience. I want to be clear that I am not saying awareness doesn't count for much; it obviously is very important. In fact, a major goal of therapy is to enhance awareness to help the person get over fears and gain control of life. The point is that there is a lot of experiencing that occurs without awareness, and it is this experiencing that is often the important focus of therapy. As Posner and Boies (1971) conclude from their review of selective attention, "Conscious awareness is itself rather late in the sequence of mental processing" (p. 407).

---

[4]Bill Coulson (personal communication) likes to call this the INTOT phenomenon in therapy: "I Never Thought Of That."

Skinner's (1969) analysis of awareness is especially useful here. He argues for two kinds of learning—contingency learning and rule learning. Thinking, feeling, and overt behavior are consistently affected by various contingencies (reinforcement and punishment, as examples), and only sometimes does the person formulate (become aware of) the rules governing these contingencies. "Learning without awareness is simply a special case of behaving without awareness, and the latter is common" (Skinner, 1969, p. 246).

Evidence for this contingency learning without awareness can be found in studies of self-deception (Sackeim & Gur, 1978; Gur & Sackeim, 1979), selective inattention to anxiety-linked stimuli (Blum & Barbour, 1979), subliminal stimulation (Dixon, 1971; Erdelyi, 1980; Martin, Hawryluk, & Guse, 1974; Stambrook & Martin, in press), operant learning without awareness (Hefferline & Keenan, 1963), binocular rivalry (Walker, 1978), emotional preference without awareness (Zajonc, 1980), target identification without awareness (Duncan, 1980; McCauley, Parmelee, Sperber, & Carr, 1980), and conditioning without awareness (Corteen & Wood, 1974; Forster & Govier, 1978; Von Wright, Anderson, & Stenman, 1975; Martin, Stambrook, Tataryn, & Beihl, 1982).

As a sidelight, it is also possible that anxiety results from fears of objects and situations in the environment of which the person is only partially aware. Likely both fear of external and internal cues are involved, but fundamental to both is understanding partial awareness. It is also interesting that both repression and fears learned with incomplete awareness have parallels in Freudian theory. Freud's "neurotic anxiety" can be fear of both repressed material and of "id impulses" that have never been conscious. A learning explanation of these phenomena is very different, of course, but we may be trying to explain the same human experiences.

Forming "Schemes"

None of us perceives reality accurately; in fact, the term *perception* means the interpretation of the direct sensations of our senses. We develop organized expectations of our world, and to some extent we perceive what we expect to perceive—what fits these "templates" to which we fit reality. The language of information processing theory can be applied to understanding therapy for anxiety-based problems (Rice, 1974): People develop "schemes" to facilitate the processing of new information. Elaborate and organized sets of information help us organize and select new information more effectively than if we had to start from scratch making sense out of each new situation. In addition to this useful function, however, "schemes" can prevent the accurate processing of novel experiences that don't fit our expectations. The person can encounter a situation, quickly fit it to a familiar "scheme," and stop processing novel information prematurely, distorting the experience. Information theorists would generally say that this process does not require such notions as repression, but the two views are not incompatible; they are just different ways that distortions enter thinking. Habit may stop the thinking process too early, without anxiety being an important factor, and anxiety can also inhibit aversive thoughts from being accurately thought. It is even possible that information that violates our "schemes" is threatening just because it's unexpected and is therefore inhibited.

In any case, the implications for therapy are the same—the person must be helped to "stay with" experiences to process them in new ways.

Impaired Problem Solving

The second characteristic of anxiety-based problems mentioned at the beginning of this chapter was "distortions of thinking and feeling" caused by painful emotions. Anxiety makes people unwise. Dollard and Miller (1950) coined the phrase *neurotic stupidity* to describe some of the foolish binds that people get themselves into, when the rest of us can see so clearly what "should be obvious" to the other person. Of course we do the same thing, to different degrees, forgetting or failing to consider threatening aspects of situations. Sometimes we later think "How could I not have seen that? Of course I can just [whatever the "obvious" solution is]."

One goal of therapy is to reduce these distortions—to help the person experience more accurately—in two ways. First, therapy reduces anxiety about particular issues, and second, the person becomes an independent thinker who tends to consider issues more completely.

MALADAPTIVE BEHAVIOR ("SYMPTOM") DEVELOPMENT

An interesting term is *the neurotic paradox*. If people do what they are reinforced for doing, why do some of them constantly lie and alienate people when they are desperate for friends; obsessively think about the death of a child in a way that brings great distress;

scratch their arms until they bleed, for no apparent reason; fail to study until just before the exam, or do any of the thousands of self-defeating things that people do? These behaviors are often called "neurotic symptoms," but this older term implies that neurosis is an illness. It is more accurate to think of them as *self-defeating behaviors that are usually established and maintained by anxiety reduction*. Anxiety reduction is an extremely powerful reinforcer, especially when the anxiety reduction comes immediately and the negative consequences of the reinforced behavior are delayed.

The Basic Process

The way in which anxiety-avoiding behaviors develop is complicated. The basic principle is that through trial-and-error learning some behaviors become effective in reducing anxiety and avoiding conflicts. Remember that "behaviors" includes internal processes, and a lot of this learning goes on with incomplete awareness. Accordingly, any behavior that is followed by anxiety reduction is strongly reinforced and therefore potentially a "symptom." It will be called a neurotic symptom only if it seems self-defeating.

Anything Can Be a "Symptom"

Trying to decide what *self-defeating* means, however, is a swamp of complex issues. Some anxiety-reducing behaviors are absolutely necessary for effective living, of course. When I feel anxious, I sometimes talk to my wife, who listens until I figure out what's wrong, face the painful thoughts, and feel better. This is anxiety-reducing behavior; is it neurotic? "How sweet," you say; "of course it's not neurotic." What if I add that I do this about five hours a day, following her around talking about my anxiety? Now it's neurotic, right? It is exactly the same behavior, but now you tell me that it's "too much," meaning that it has become self-defeating. I will ask you at what point talking to my wife became "too much"—four hours, two hours, one hour and 12 minutes? I may be perfectly happy with the five-hour arrangement, but she may be miserable. Is my behavior self-defeating? That depends partly on what she does, of course.

The whole point is that the calling a particular behavior a "neurotic symptom" is an arbitrary judgment based on social norms, personal wishes, others' demands and needs, and even shifting historical trends. A few years ago, if you asked another person not to smoke in public, you were considered weird. Now you might just be thought rude, but it is possible that in a few years smoking will be thought of as neurotic and smoking in public will be thought of the way spitting on the floor is now. The answer to "What's neurotic?" must always be "That depends. . . ."

If any behavior can, under the right circumstances, be considered a "neurotic symptom," it may seem foolish to try to discuss specific "symptom syndromes," but some patterns of anxiety-avoiding behaviors have attracted special attention and are worth considering as illustrations of the basic process.

Phobias

Phobias have recently received a great deal of attention, but they are widely misunderstood. A phobia is a morbid dread of something or a fear disproportionate to the actual threat represented by an object or situation. A useful distinction can be made, however, between strong directly conditioned fears and fears that develop as a result of other anxiety problems (what we might call "true phobias").

If a man were trapped in a mine explosion that nearly smothered him and then had a fear of long, dimly lit hallways, we would call his fear disproportionate to the actual threat involved,[5] but we could understand the cause of the fear. This would illustrate a strong directly conditioned fear. However, some people fear long, dimly lit hallways even though they have never had any traumatic experiences associated with them.

The general principle is that some fears, although they may cause real emotional pain, help the person avoid a much worse pain of anxiety. Remember that anxiety results from incredibly complex internal processes and intense fears of one's own thoughts and feelings. I can think of dozens of ways a person could develop a fear of hallways. Perhaps a 28-year-old teacher has strong feelings of responsibility for her aging parents, who she fears will die of accidental injuries if left alone but toward whom she also feels intense resentment for the guilt-based limits they have put on her life. She has some desire to be rid of them but would be sick with guilt if she fully thought such ideas. I could go on for some time complicating her situation, but even this oversimplified picture of internal

---

[5]Even here, though, the word *disproportionate* is as difficult to define as *self-defeating*. It ends up being defined as "disproportionate compared with other people." So many people in our culture refuse to stay on the 13th floor that hotels use numbers like 12B or just skip 13 in numbering floors. This refusal is clearly grossly irrational, but it's not defined as "phobic" because so many people in our culture act this way.

conflicts helps us understand how she might one day enter her school, feel panic and fear for no apparent reason, and return home, unable to face the "fear of the long hallway" that she felt. She doesn't know what causes her fear, but she does know that the panic swept over her as she entered the hallway. Other circumstances could have led to an anxiety attack in her car, in a restaurant, or in any other place related to her absence from home, leading her to attribute it to something other than hallways. Fear is a response, and the enormous relief she felt as she returned home strongly reinforced that fear. As long as she is afraid of hallways, she has to stay home, where her thoughts of the accident in her absence don't plague her. Her phobia is an anxiety-reducing fear, although that sounds paradoxical if you don't understand the principles. What she really fears is her own thoughts and feelings.

This is not to diminish the importance of directly conditioned fears. They do occur and sometimes need treatment, but at least with adult clients, the more complex fears are vastly more common.

Physical Symptoms

Hysteria is the classic term for physical symptoms with no physiological basis, and such symptoms were the basis of Freud's earliest work. Physical symptoms, although truly painful and debilitating, can develop through anxiety reduction without the victim's awareness. Pain is a response, and our teacher could have developed a headache, had to stay home and experienced anxiety reduction, strongly reinforcing the pain. Here the "underlying causes" are exactly the same, but the "symptom" is entirely different from the phobia, illustrating the difference between an illness model of symptoms and a learning model.

Acting Out

In Chapter 10 I said that some antisocial behavior cannot be effectively treated with evocative empathy—namely, antisocial behavior that is usually called "sociopathic" and is marked by impulsive immediate gratification without apparent remorse for the sometimes horrible consequences to self and others. To repeat, however, antisocial behavior can look very much like sociopathic behavior but really be an anxiety-based problem. I once had a client who repeatedly got involved with a woman, moved in with her, and eventually beat her, ending the relationship. He then went through the same pattern with another woman and then another. This could have resulted from thoughtless impulse gratification, seeking a sexual relationship and then hitting the woman just because he felt like it at a particular time whenever he was angry. Picture for a moment, however, the graph illustrating approach-avoidance conflict and imagine the behavior of a man who (to oversimplify) both wants and strongly fears intimacy, needs to prove his virility to himself by impregnating a woman (which has never happened in spite of his never using contraception), and feels both great longing and great anger and hurt over the death of his mother. All these factors combine to make him deeply ambivalent over being close to a woman. When he is not in a relationship, his desire is strong. As he becomes more and more involved with an individual woman, his conflicts will intensify until he can go no further, but he is not aware of what is happening to him. All he knows is that he is miserable. Many things could happen to relieve his conflicts, but one of them, the one that developed for him, was to hit the woman and end the relationship. Once therapy reduced his conflicts, however, he was able to enter a marriage that was satisfying. Had his behavior been based on impulse gratification and not on anxiety reduction, therapy quite possibly would have just made him more comfortable with his violent behavior.

It is often a difficult decision whether to treat a person with anti-social behavior, an issue we discussed as an assessment problem in Chapter 10.

Obsessions and Compulsions

Intuitively, one of the most difficult problems to understand is obsessive thinking, because the victim suffers so intensely that it is hard to see how the obsessive thoughts could be anxiety-reducing. We might imagine a father who constantly worried and brooded over the possible death of a child, to the point where he couldn't function normally. The principles are the same as with other problems, however. It is quite possible that the father feels some hostility toward the baby, a fairly common feeling that most parents find totally unacceptable in themselves, and may even want to be rid of it—as well as loving and wanting it. Like our teacher's wishing her parents would die (as well as loving them and wanting them to live), these thoughts are so horrifying that when they are even thought in very incomplete form, the person suffers intense anxiety that must be reduced somehow. Frantically caring for the baby every moment is not only unconscious proof against the unacceptable feelings, it is also so very distracting that the real anxiety can be avoided. Painful as the obsessive thoughts are, they are preferable to the internal conflicts they help avoid. Instead of developing a hall phobia or headaches, the teacher could have spent all her time worrying about her parents, protecting herself from her other thoughts.

Compulsive behavior can serve the same anxiety-reducing functions. Constant handwashing, elaborate rituals, and extreme orderliness can be both "proof" of correct behavior and a strong distractor from other, terribly painful thoughts.

PROBLEMS IN LIVING

These examples of "neurotic" problems are offered only to illustrate the general principles involved in anxiety-based problems. All of us obsess too much sometimes and have some unreasonable fears and lie sometimes because we're scared and even have physical symptoms that avoid anxiety. These are all problems in living that can be understood according to the learning principles that affect all of us. When they become extreme enough, the help we call therapy is needed, but it also operates according to the principles through which we all deal with life problems.

The Vicious Circle of Avoidance

Most of us are solving most of our problems most of the time. We face thoughts and situations that we fear, often because circumstances force us to, and we get over our fears and correct many of our distortions. We talk with friends, and that helps sometimes. Sometimes, however, the fears are strong enough or the circumstances are wrong enough that we get trapped so quickly and thoroughly in the vicious circle of avoiding the situations, things, and thoughts that bother us that the problems don't get solved. Then a special kind of structure is needed to help us face what we can't name but which must be faced, and we call that special structure psychotherapy.

Human Complexity

I need to say very strongly that the principles outlined in this chapter are grossly oversimplified. As far as they go, I think they are accurate and helpful, but the human problems they try to explain

251

are incredibly complex—so much so that if you lose sight of the unique complexity of each of your clients, you will categorize and distort their experiences to fit your "schemes." Remember that I've never had a client who didn't surprise me, and I think the same has to be true for you, if you are open to your clients' complexity.

CHAPTER SIXTEEN

A Theoretical Understanding of Therapy

This chapter assumes that you have a good grasp of what an evocatively empathic therapist does, including an understanding not only of evocative empathy but also of concreteness and specificity of language, of relationship issues, of the self-confrontative nature of therapy, and of all the other issues discussed in the first six chapters. I will now use your theoretical understanding of anxiety-based problems to explain, in theory, how this approach to therapy seems to work.

TRUSTING YOUR CLIENT

The fundamental theoretical question that must be answered is "Why, if you don't think self-actualization is innate, do you trust your clients to talk about the things they need to talk about?" In answering this question I will be using theoretical language, but remember that my ultimate goal is to explain why I really do trust my clients to solve their own problems, to take responsibility for their lives, and to leave therapy as autonomous, self-accepting, open-to-experience, caring persons.

There are a lot of general reasons that people are problem solvers; there is evidence that humans are naturally stimulus-seeking (Butler & Rice, 1963, apply this to empathic therapy); they have the capacity to learn and are constantly being rewarded for learning; even their

253

discomfort can motivate them to do something to change things. These reasons are important, but none of them really faces the issue of knowing that the client will talk about and experience the specific thoughts and feelings that she or he needs to.

The logic of the answer to the question is quite straightforward, and one student, when he heard it, said "That's it? That's too simple to be true."

1. *If there is an anxiety-based problem, there must be conflict.* If there is no conflict, then there is no problem, since the person will simply avoid the feared objects, situations, thoughts, and feelings.

2. *If there is conflict, there must be some motive to approach the feared thoughts, feelings, situations, and objects.* We won't know what those motives are in any one case, but we know they must be active, or the person would not be in conflict.

Thus, we have the picture of a person who is continually approaching and retreating from the things that cause his or her anxiety, getting as close as he or she can stand to get to the thoughts and feelings and then "backing off" through repression, self-defeating behavior and other kinds of avoidance behavior. Even the "well defended" person is continuously getting as close as he or she can stand to get before escaping through defenses—otherwise there would be no problem. The person vacillates, suffering, but doesn't advance enough to really face the source of pain before retreating.

The client will approach the elements of his or her conflicts. The therapist's job is to hear this attempt, which the client will be too frightened to articulate fully, and to put into words what the client was trying to say but couldn't quite say. If you are working with anxiety-based problems, you can trust your clients to try to talk about the things they need to talk about.

RELIEVING CONFLICTS—IN THEORY

Referring back to the principles of conflict and to the conflict diagram presented again as Figure 16-1, we can see that the way therapy relieves (mostly internal) conflicts is by lowering the fear of the feared thoughts and feelings. The client will vacillate in the "conflict region," trying to say difficult things and backing off in the face of the pain. The therapist hears the approach attempt (the leading

edge of what the client implies) and *prevents the retreat* by articulating the implied, slightly frightening thoughts and feelings. Now
the person is in the presence of mildly anxiety-arousing cues and
feels the discomfort, nothing bad happens, and some of the fear of
the cues (the thoughts and feelings) extinguishes. More accurately,
the person feels the discomfort, not only without something bad
happening, but also in the context of the therapist's acceptance of
the client as a worthwhile person. The strong therapy relationship
acts as a counterconditioning agent, taking the "curse" off feared
thoughts.

Step-by-Step Progress

Think of the "distance from the feared goal" dimension of Figure
16-1 as going from "partial experiencing of particular thoughts and
feelings" on the right to "accurate experiencing" on the left. The
person is constantly approaching accurate experiencing of the feared
thoughts and then backing off in fear when she or he reaches some
degree of completeness of the experience. When the therapist articulates the leading edge of the message, those thoughts become less
fear-arousing and easier to talk about because of extinction and the
counterconditioning effect of the therapist's acceptance. Because
the fear of the "goal" and related thoughts is now somewhat less,
the avoidance gradient will be lowered, and the "conflict region" is
closer to the goal. Thoughts that used to be too painful to think can
now be hinted at—implied—because the ones that the client could

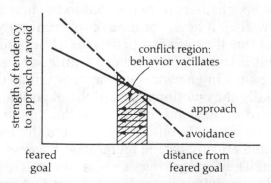

Figure 16-1 Diagram of approach-avoidance conflict showing the conflict area, in which behavior will vacillate between
approach and avoidance.

only imply before are now harmless. Step by step you approach more accurate, complete experiencing together. The client can now think more clearly, plan more wisely, and take more effective action.

Reinforcing the Client's Approach Responses

An incredibly important thing is also happening, in addition to the client's becoming clearer about specific issues. It is possible that another kind of therapist might cleverly guide the client to the correct feared thoughts and feelings, expose the person to them, and extinguish (and countercondition) the fears. But it is not just the "truth" that makes the client free; it is also the process of finding the truth that makes the client strong and independent.

In evocatively empathic therapy, the client makes an approach response (tries to experience painful things accurately), is held at the leading edge by the therapist, and feels some discomfort. Then the discomfort drops; the enormous power of anxiety reduction reinforces the last thing the client did—bravely approach painful experience. Thousands of times in therapy, the client goes through the experience of exploring, of thinking hard thoughts, of getting closer to feelings, of being a problem solver, and being rewarded for it. If the therapist engineers the facing of painful thoughts (expertly interprets, for example), it is the therapist's expertise and strength that lead to relief. Paradoxically, the client is being reinforced for depending on others.

RELIEVING CONFLICTS—IN PRACTICE

Since the first six chapters were devoted to the practice of therapy, we needn't dwell on it here. For the sake of continuity in this chapter, I'll just say that the therapist listens for the intended message—what the client is trying to say and can't quite say—and then articulates that message in an evocative way that brings the experience to life, especially the emotional part of the experience.

The beauty of understanding the term *the intended message* is that it gives you a handle on knowing where the leading edge is. Clients are automatically pacing themselves because of the dynamics of conflict. They are getting as close to the issues as they can stand to get by implying—intending for you to hear—as much as they can handle. *Your goal is to get as far ahead of the client as you can but have the client recognize what you say as part of what he or she meant.*

BREAKING OLD SCHEMES

We can also return to the language of information-processing theory to explain what happens when the client is held in the presence of his or her experiencing. Rice (1974) has used information-processing concepts to understand therapy without depending "on the concepts of unconscious motivation or defense mechanisms" (p. 293). Rice seems to be rejecting Freudian explanations that I would also reject, but her language is entirely compatible with my more learning-oriented talk. We seem to be describing similar processes at different levels of abstraction and from different perspectives. She says:

> The basic assumption is that for any person there are some classes of experience that have never been adequately processed, and for some people, there are many such classes. . . . [A] more or less enduring construction or set of constructions is formed, which filters one's experience and guides one's behavior whenever situations of that general class are encountered. . . . The problem for therapy, then, is to find a method by which the client can reprocess an important experience from such a problem class in a way that is relatively undistorted. It is this new, full, undistorted experience that is precisely what is needed to force reorganization of the old schemes. . . . If the client can fully explore his reactions to one such situation and become aware of the elements in a more accurate and balanced form, that is, can reprocess the situation, the effect will be to force reorganization of all the relevant schemes [pp. 293–294].

The only difference between this information-processing view and mine is that I would stress the role of anxiety in causing the distortions.

Therapy both permits and forces the breaking of old "schemes," giving the client the chance to reprocess or process more completely "schemes" (experiences) that normally would have been only glimpsed and prematurely abandoned.

THE EFFECTS OF THERAPY

I can briefly summarize the effects of therapy—in theory—by considering the three general characteristics of anxiety-based problems and the general goals for effective living discussed in Chapter 5. Keep in mind that these are just brief theoretical statements that assume you understand all the previous material.

Reducing Painful Emotions

If anxiety is the result of internal conflicts—fearing one's own motivated thoughts and feelings—then resolving the specific conflicts will relieve the anxiety. The client accurately faces the frightening thoughts and feelings, being more completely exposed to them so that the fear of them extinguishes and/or is counterconditioned. The client entered therapy saying "I feel awful and I don't know why." Therapy relieves the specific conflicts that led to these feelings.

Improving Problem Solving

The distortions and "neurotic stupidity" that plagued the client resulted from anxiety-based distortions about particular memories, feelings, and current thoughts. Therapy "makes the unconscious conscious" through step-by-step exposure of more and more complete experiencing of the client's thoughts and feelings. Now the client can think and act more wisely because he or she has more accurate information.

In addition, the client has become a better problem solver in general—beyond the solution of specific problems. He or she has been repeatedly reinforced for thinking and facing feelings and strongly seeking out experiences and solutions. The client no longer needs the therapist to solve new problems that will inevitably arise.

Reducing Maladaptive Behavior

Maladaptive behavior can be reflected in the inability to take effective action as well as in the self-defeating behaviors that often get called "symptoms." In the previous section I touched on the effective action that follows accurate self-knowledge. "Symptom" reduction follows from effective therapy because the anxiety that maintained the self-defeating behavior is reduced.

People do self-defeating things because they somehow lead to immediate anxiety reduction. The "symptoms" are by definition punishing, self-defeating behaviors (or they wouldn't be called "symptoms"), but they are preferable to the anxiety they help avoid. If the anxiety is reduced, the "symptoms" will no longer be reinforced and in nearly all cases will disappear because of the pain they cause naturally in the person's life.

Symptom Substitution

A sometimes unfriendly debate has been going on between psychoanalysts and behavior modifiers over the question of symptom substitution. Remove the symptom, say the behavior modifiers, and you have cured the neurosis. No, reply the analysts, the symptom is only an anxiety substitute, and if you remove the symptom, you only create a need for a new symptom, which you will get. My response is that both sides are partly correct, depending on the nature of a particular problem. I certainly reject the psychic-illness model, but a complex learning model using internal conflicts predicts that sometimes you will get symptom substitution if you take away a symptom directly.

In the instance of a directly conditioned fear, such as with the miner afraid of dark hallways, direct treatment of the fear symptom would settle the issue without symptom substitution. If the "symptom" is based on internal conflict, however, the answer is still "maybe" to whether the person will develop a new symptom. If we directly treat the conflicted teacher's fear of hallways, she will still be in intense conflict over her relationship with her parents and will find some way to deal with it, to reduce the anxiety. If the way she finds is somehow self-defeating we will say she has a new "symptom," but she might well be driven to talk with a friend and develop a relationship that helps her contain her anxiety—not a new symptom. Or she could do anything in between, such as throwing herself into graduate study to the exclusion of everything else and "succeeding" in a way that we would be hard put to judge as either self-defeating or adaptive.

Feeling Personal Worth

More positively, we can say how therapy contributes to high self-esteem; personal autonomy; open, full experiencing; and rewarding intimate relationships. Again, I will be using brief and too-mechanistic language, but my purpose is just to articulate theoretical connections. I am assuming that you will add the human complexity I intend from other chapters.

One of the most gratifying changes to hear in clients is when they say something like "I'm not sure why, but I just like myself better now" or "I guess I am a more selfish person than I would let myself know before, but that's OK, really. I mean, I'm OK as a person." Theoretically, what has happened is that the person came to therapy repelled by some of her own thoughts and feelings. What she *was* felt bad and unworthy. As therapy progresses, those thoughts and feelings, what she *is*, come to feel good, acceptable, and even worthy. She comes to feel personal worth.

Autonomy and Competence

I spoke earlier of improved problem solving that results from the client's doing the work in therapy. Beyond this, the client gains a sense of personal strength, a sense of control and independence that comes from facing a difficult challenge and winning—the "I did this myself" feeling.

Accurate Self-Experiencing

Also beyond "improved problem solving" that results from more complete information, the person has sought experiencing and become comfortable with it. He is not afraid to feel new feelings and seek new experiences and is congruent with himself.

Ability to Be Intimate

The effects of therapy listed previously can be understood as direct outcomes of evocatively empathic therapy; they follow directly from its nature. It is not so clear that this kind of conflict relief leads as directly to the ability to be in a close relationship, but this is one of the important goals of therapy. We can say, of course, that being in a good relationship helps the person feel comfortable and acceptable with another person. It is also likely that the client learns to be empathic from the therapist's example and that one of the important areas of understanding and action that the client will deal with in therapy is relationship issues. A consequence of this problem solving will be improvement of the client's relationships outside therapy. As with the chapter on relationship issues, though, the effects of therapy on the client's ability to be close are so complex that they are difficult to state succinctly.

THE CONSEQUENCES OF INEFFECTIVE THERAPY

The conflict-relief model predicts that both working "behind" the client and working "ahead of" the client's intended message will be ineffective.

Working Behind the Conflict Region

Being "behind" the client means giving largely "2" responses on Carkhuff's scale, in which the therapist tries to reflect understanding but either exactly restates what the client said or dampens the meaning and feeling of the client's remarks. The therapist might respond to a feelingful comment with cognitive talk *about* feelings or might try to draw some general principle about what the client said, moving the client away from current experiencing. This exemplifies the common and incorrect stereotype of the client-centered therapist who is supportive but passive. In theoretical terms, this kind of functioning should be totally ineffective. Since the therapist never articulates anything but the material that the client can already explicitly face, or even draws the client back from this, the anxiety cues would never be faced. The therapist would be participating in the avoidance of the feared experiences, working at the point of retreat rather than approach. Actually, this passive therapist probably would make some progress, but very slowly. Since clients often do explicitly verbalize conflict material, the therapist who responds only to explicit material will occasionally help the client face experiencing. Usually, however, progress will be painfully slow, the therapist and client may both perceive the therapist as inanely repetitive, and therapy will frequently be stuck on dead center.

The therapist's role is an *active* role. Doing therapy is hard work, not a passive listening. It is an active listening for the client's attempts to deal with conflictual material, or have I already said this somewhere before?

Working Ahead of the Conflict Region

Most therapists agree that passive reflection is an inappropriate approach to psychotherapy, but many will disagree when I say that working ahead of or out of the conflict region is also undesirable. I suspect that working behind the conflict region does its damage by frustrating the client and leading to failure experiences in therapy. I suspect that working out of the conflict region does its damage much more directly.

By using the conflict model, we could specify ways that a therapist could do some good by working ahead of the conflict region in ways that exposed clients to painful thoughts and feelings in the presence of a supportive therapist whose acceptance helped the person face those feelings. These benefits, although real, are won at a price—a price that need not be paid if the therapist is functioning maximally as evocatively empathic. In addition, there are risks growing out of therapist error about what thoughts and feelings need to be faced.

First, let's consider the therapist whose personal strength and great acceptance and reassurance help the client face thoughts and feelings that the therapist has directed the client toward, through suggestions, interpretations, and therapist-initiated confrontations. Such an approach might result in anxiety reduction and in the person's trying solutions the therapist has suggested, perhaps even breaking some vicious circles in the person's life. This directive approach, however, lacks the element of reinforcing the client's approach responses—of making the client strong and independent. In fact, I would argue quite strongly that although this approach might result in the solution of particular problems (assuming the therapist is very wise), it will reinforce dependency on outside help in the client. In the long run, this may be a far greater disservice than the solutions were a short-term help.

Another way that working ahead of the conflict region discourages independence and autonomy is by subtly punishing the client's own approach responses—attempts to think and face experiencing. In evocatively empathic therapy, the client is continually making approach responses, feeling mildly anxious, and then having the anxiety drop. If, after the client tries to take a step, the therapist arouses intense anxiety, the relief does not follow the client's attempt. It follows, when it comes, the therapist's expert guidance. Just as strength and autonomy come from thousands of small experiences of facing pain and then feeling better, dependency can be built by a powerful therapist.

In addition, changes in self-esteem occur in subtly different ways in these two different approaches to therapy. Low self-esteem is the result of being made anxious by one's own thoughts and feelings, and if the anxiety responses to those inner processes can be changed, an increase in self-esteem should result, regardless of the therapy approach used. An important difference, however, is that the empathy-oriented therapist responds to the thoughts and feelings *as emitted by and originating with the client*. It is quite possible that the *therapist* can elicit the thoughts and feelings and countercondition the fears aroused. If, however, the "curse is taken off" after the client emits the thoughts and feelings, it is he who is responsible for, and takes the emotional "credit" for, becoming a worthy person.

A further risk in working outside the conflict region is the arousal of intense anxiety that makes the client need defenses against the therapist and the therapy process. In learning terms, rather than the desired extinction, there will be higher-order conditioning of the therapist and therapy situation as anxiety cues. Not only is the therapist consistently being paired with powerful anxiety cues, she or he is seen as the source of these cues. The sometimes subtle effect that then escapes the therapist's notice is that therapy is slowed down as the client directly and indirectly engages in defensive avoidance. Do you remember the therapist who said "I don't have the patience to shape clients"? He believed that direct attacks were quicker, but I think this apparent quickness was an illusion—the same illusion that makes so many people use punishment with children and subordinates. It seems to work quickly because there is short-term compliance. This is an illusion because there is also long term resistance and defense.

Establishing the therapist as a source of threat, however subtle, sets the stage for a new conflict in which the client may fear therapy but be unable to leave it—because of the therapist's subtle pressures, society's pressures, and perhaps a desperate need for help. The therapist can create a conflict situation that itself calls for subtle and complicated kinds of defenses. The therapist's job is to take away the need for defenses in the therapy session. If the therapist creates a conflict situation, he or she is likely to meet therapeutic impasses, resistance, and perhaps most dangerously, flights into health. What better way to get rid of your therapist than to "get better" suddenly?

A dangerous consequence of flights into health is that they give aggressive therapists false feedback about the effectiveness of what they do. Many therapists insist that they do their interpreting and manipulating because they have seen them work. We all want to believe that we are effective, and it is difficult to face one's therapeutic failures. It is easier to remember the successes, and clients who "get well" quickly may be additionally reinforcing some destructive therapist behavior. As an aside, all of us therapists are vulnerable to selective perception of our effectiveness, and so each of us is obligated to know the research evidence, to be able to say why we do what we do, and to get frank feedback from another therapist who can observe our work.

One last consequence of working outside the conflict region— that is, from the therapist's frame of reference rather than the client's— is that the therapist is just going to be wrong a lot of the time about the best course of action or what the client is "really" feeling. The comments made so far have all assumed that the therapist was exactly correct in his or her interpretation or advice but helped the client see it too early. You and I are not that smart; people are too complex, and it is almost irrationally arrogant to think that one can tell another how to live and to experience. Even the most self-assured therapist would have to admit to *some* errors in judgment and interpretation. When the therapist does make the inevitable errors, he or she pays a price by making the client feel less understood, by punishing the client for approach responses, and by providing misleading and even dangerously wrong "answers" that the client may have trouble rejecting. Therapists can do damage.

CHAPTER
SEVENTEEN

Research Evidence

One of my professors in graduate school, after years of doing therapy research, told a group of us that if we ever wanted to do such research, we should have ourselves hospitalized until the urge passed. The problems are enormous in doing well-controlled research on such a complex process as psychotherapy, and it is easy to spend a lot of time with little or no payoff. Virtually all studies of actual therapy (as opposed to laboratory analogues to therapy) have some methodological weaknesses. Too few points were sampled; the therapists knew the purpose of the study; outcome ratings were not strictly independent of client perceptions; and so forth. We can't sit around waiting for perfectly controlled research, however. We have to use all possible sources of knowledge to offer honestly effective treatment and to improve treatment. Personal experience and the experience of others are certainly one such source of knowledge, but as the Yiddish proverb says "For example is no proof." It is sometimes said of the treatment of obesity that everything works and nothing works. There are patients who lose weight under virtually any program, but none of the programs is effective over large groups of people. There probably also are therapy clients who will benefit from nearly any kind of treatment, so that we constantly hear of marvelous new therapies (like the infamous tickling therapy of a few years ago) whose founders regale us with case histories of their successes.

Experience is valid but needs the corrective influence of research. Imperfect as our evidence is, we need to learn from it what we can. I think there is sufficient evidence to make several tentative conclusions that apply to the issues raised in this book. There are other valuable conclusions to be drawn, but I have selected ones that apply directly to us as therapists. For us the critical issue is whether we can honestly offer evocative empathy, acceptance and genuineness as the foundation of therapy.

An Overview of Findings

Six general conclusions seem justified by the evidence. Four of them bear directly on the skills I have been discussing, and I will therefore elaborate on them, referring you to more complete sources on the others so you can examine them if you wish.

1. There is a strong relation between levels of empathy, acceptance, and genuineness *as perceived by clients* and successful outcome.
2. There is a moderately good (or "only modest," depending on your perspective) relation between levels of empathy, acceptance, and genuineness *as perceived by trained judges rating recordings of therapy* and successful outcome.
3. Empathy can be taught through didactic/experiential programs, but evidence hasn't been gathered on whether changes in trainees lead directly to greater client benefit.
4. Some therapists clearly do damage.
5. Desensitization and operant procedures are effective with clearly definable problems, at least for short-term change (Bergin & Suinn, 1975; Smith & Glass, 1977; Gomes-Schwartz, et al., 1978).
6. Taken globally, psychotherapy is better than no treatment, but one school of treatment is not demonstrably superior to another when therapists are simply grouped by school (Meltzoff & Kornreich, 1970; Smith & Glass, 1977; Frank, 1979).

CLIENT PERCEPTIONS OF THE CORE CONDITIONS

There are three steps in empathic responding: the therapist must hear the message; the therapist must convey his or her understanding to the client; and the client must perceive the understanding. Barrett-Lennard (1981) points out that the process can break down at any of these steps and that the critical element is the third one. It is conceivable that a therapist might articulate an understanding without the client's perception of the message as accurate—for whatever reason—so that an observer would call the therapist empathic, but the expected impact on the client would not occur.

Thus, it is not surprising that the client's perceptions offer the strongest support for evocative-empathy-oriented therapy.

Gurman (1977) summarizes the results of 25 studies, 22 of which were of actual therapy conducted by therapists of different orientations—psychoanalytic, behavioral, client-centered, and eclectic. Of the 22 therapy studies, 21 showed a significant effect of client-perceived therapeutic "core conditions," and Gurman concludes that "there exists substantial, if not overwhelming, evidence in support of the hypothesized relationship between patient-perceived therapeutic conditions and outcome in individual psychotherapy and counseling" (p. 523).

The most commonly used instrument to measure client perceptions is Barrett-Lennard's Relationship Inventory (RI) (1962, 1978). Reliability and factor-analytic studies have shown that the RI yields repeatable measurements and that it does tap different factors independently, although the variables being measured do correlate with each other in practice. Empathy, level of regard (acceptance), unconditionality of regard, and congruence (genuineness) tap the core conditions. Barrett-Lennard added a "willingness to be known" variable, but it did not prove very useful. His dividing the regard factor into two concepts—overall level and unconditionality—has been supported as useful.

For our purposes, the RI also has some implications for training, and you might find it useful to obtain a copy (Barrett-Lennard, 1978) just to read the items that reflect the critical client perceptions—to see what you hope your clients will feel. Half the items are worded in a positive way and half in a negative, so that the empathy scale includes items like "He realizes what I mean even when I have difficulty in saying it" and "Sometimes she thinks that I feel a certain way, because that's the way she feels." The congruence scale includes "I feel that what she says nearly always expresses exactly what she is feeling and thinking as she says it" and "He wants me to think that he likes me or understands me more than he really does."

One understandable but distressing finding that Gurman (1977) reports is that there is "very little agreement" between clients' perceptions of their therapists and therapists' perceptions of themselves. This results from therapists' rating themselves consistently positively, so that there of course is little or no relation between successful outcome and what therapists, as a group, perceive themselves doing. That is scary.

RATERS' PERCEPTIONS OF THE CORE CONDITIONS

Although client perceptions are theoretically the most important measure of the core conditions, the bulk of research on them and of current controversy in the field has centered on data from trained judges using the rating scales developed by Truax and Carkhuff (1967) and others (Rogers, et al., 1967).

Rogers's pioneering work (Rogers & Dymond, 1954) is generally seen as the start of systematic research on psychotherapy, and his influence on theory, practice, and research has led to an enormous research literature. Earlier summaries of this literature (Truax & Carkhuff, 1967; Truax & Mitchell, 1971) were consistently enthusiastic about the findings from judgments of tape recordings of therapy and led many writers (including me [Martin, 1972], unfortunately) to uncritically accept the data as conclusive. It now appears that some of Truax's data "were presented somewhat selectively and did not convey the full findings that were available" (Gurman, 1977, p. 505).

It has also become clearer that there are many methodological problems with tape-based judgments that would make it very difficult to find even a strong phenomenon that might actually exist in therapy. For example, tape sampling takes only a few minutes of therapy, sometimes from among many hours, and this would inevitably reduce the validity of the measure. Tape ratings, client perceptions, and therapist perceptions do not correlate strongly with each other. Audiotape eliminates all the visual nonverbal cues. Sex of rater may interact with sex of therapist. There are some indications that the ratings may reflect some general dimension or "halo effect." The scales seem to measure therapeutic conditions as delivered by client-centered therapists more validly than therapists of other orientations even though the other therapists might well be perceived by clients as empathic, accepting, and genuine. (See Lambert, DeJulio, & Stein, 1978, for a critical discussion of these issues.)

Probably the most difficult methodological issue has been forcefully discussed by Mitchell, Bozarth, and Krauft (1977). In a great many of the published studies, therapists are compared as *higher* or *lower* on empathy, for example, rather than as high in absolute terms—that is, above the minimally facilitative level (3.0 on the rating scales discussed in Chapter 1). In many of the studies for which Mitchell et al. could reconstruct data, the "high empathy" therapists actually averaged less than the minimally facilitative level. Mitchell et al. conclude that the core-conditions hypothesis has not been tested adequately by these studies. It is clear that a study in which the best therapists averaged less than 3.0 on the rating scales would in no way be a test of evocative empathy.

That's the bad news. Although Mitchell, Bozarth, and Krauft say that the relation between outcome and rated core conditions is far more complicated than the early summaries implied, they also say "In some respects it is surprising that higher interpersonal skills levels were found to be related to positive outcomes as often as they were, given such problems as the low levels of most psychotherapists' functioning, marginally rigorous measurement criteria, the difficulties inherent in training raters, etc." (p. 486). They report some recent studies, some of which support the core-conditions hypothesis and some of which do not. Lambert et al. (1978) are generally critical of this literature (focusing mainly on tape-rating evidence) and say that "generally well designed and executed studies . . . present only modest evidence in favor of the hypothesis that such factors as accurate empathy, warmth and genuineness relate to measures of outcome" (p. 472). What they call "only modest" I would call "moderately good," but this difference obviously grows out of biases in judgment. In view of the difficulties with gathering valid data from tape ratings, that which does exist offers some support for the core conditions. And it is important to remember that, with the exception of behavioral methods, no body of evidence exists to support *any other* set of therapy skills.

CAN THE SKILLS BE TAUGHT?

Let's hope so. This whole book has been designed as a didactic and experiential training experience for you, although the experiential part will require you to implement the exercises and tape work that I have frequently recommended and to participate in practicum training. Truax and Carkhuff (1967) proposed a training procedure that included a therapeutic atmosphere in which the trainees received high facilitative conditions from supervisors; specific training on the skills, using the rating scales as a training device; and a therapy-like group experience for the trainees. Others (Ivey, 1974; Ivey & Authier, 1978) emphasize videotaped feedback to the trainee, along with specific didactic training on communication skills. The critical elements in these and other training programs seem to be the combined conceptual learning and actual practice, both in role playing and in seeing clients under supervision.

Mitchell et al. (1977) summarize research that suggests that at least empathy can be taught. Warmth and genuineness may be very important in therapy, but they depend enormously on personal factors that are difficult to describe, much less to teach. Several studies that Mitchell et al. cite suggest that beginning trainees function at low levels (around 1.5) on empathy but can reach an average minimally facilitative level (around 2.5–3.0) with as few as 6 hours of training but more typically up to 100 hours. One study (Myrick & Pare, 1971) reported that simply participating in group sensitivity training did not increase the level of trainees' skills or the therapy outcomes of their clients. Mitchell et al. report only "indirect evidence" that clients of trainees who improve their skill levels profit more from therapy than clients of others. Gantt, Billingsley, and Giordano (1980) reported that trainees increased their empathy level (as measured by a paper-and-pencil test requiring discrimination of empathic responses) and, over the course of a 6–14-month follow-up period, increased their scores to the level of experienced clinicians.

Generally, the evidence on skills training is quite hopeful, although it is still too sparse to be conclusive. Carkhuff and Berenson (1967, 1977), however, argue that traditional graduate training frequently has deleterious effects on therapeutic skill, and Truax and Mitchell (1971) argue that "there is no evidence that the usual traditional graduate training program has any positive value in producing therapists who are more helpful than non-professionals" (p. 337). Bergin and Solomon (1970) reported that empathic ability of graduate students had slightly negative correlations with the psychology subscale of the Graduate Record Examination and with verbal intelligence. I'm not saying I hope you're not smart, but these are remarkable findings. Of course, these findings are on students who were all smart enough to get into graduate school, so that the range of scores is small, and it seems likely to me that intelligence does bear some relation to therapeutic ability, if we consider the whole range of both measures. The point seems to be that cognitive, rational ability is only part of what makes a therapist therapeutic. Where have you heard this before?

FOR BETTER OR WORSE—SOME DO DAMAGE

Finally, I will end on a note that is both disturbing and indirectly confirmatory of the value of the therapeutic conditions. Bergin (1963, 1966) coined the term *deterioration effect* to refer to the finding that groups of clients had higher variability of adjustment after treatment than before and higher variability than various control groups. This suggested that simply looking at findings of average improvement was masking the fact that some clients were getting better in therapy and some were actually getting worse. Bergin's thinking received its first impetus from an observation of patients in the Wisconsin Project (Rogers et al., 1967) on therapy with schizophrenic problems. As a group, treated patients fared no better than nontreated patients. Some, however, had improved and some actually got worse; outcome was related to therapists' levels of empathy, acceptance, and genuineness. Subsequently, Bergin expanded his observations to a wide range of evidence and argued that many of the "negative effects" reported in the therapy literature resulted from lumping both positive and damaging therapy into group averages. Braucht (1970) criticized Bergin's position, but Bergin's response (1970) and a review by Lambert, Bergin, and Collins (1977) establish the deterioration effect as a frightening reality. Mays and Franks (1980; Franks & Mays, 1980) say that the "jury should still be out" on whether deterioration effects are the result of therapy, but Bergin (1980) responds that "the empirical case for therapist-induced deterioration is compelling" (p. 93) and that although the term jury isn't entirely appropriate, it is interesting that 90% of professionals surveyed (Strupp, Hadley, & Gomes-Schwartz, 1977) "agreed to the existence of the phenomenon" (Bergin, 1980, p. 98).

The critical issue is to determine what therapist variables cause client deterioration. Low levels of the core conditions certainly seem to be related but are not the whole answer. "Therapeutic encounters which are characterized by low levels [of empathy, warmth, and genuineness] can be expected to sustain a higher casualty rate" (Lambert, Bergin, & Collins, 1977, p. 464), but simply having low levels seems related to ineffectual rather than detrimental therapy. Important clues come from Yalom and Lieberman's (1971) study of "psychiatric casualties" in encounter groups. Of seven kinds of group leaders, the one that was most likely to do damage was the "aggressive stimulator," who was described as "intrusive, confrontive, challenging, caring, . . . self-revealing . . . charismatic, authoritarian, and as focusing on the individual" (Lambert et al., 1977, p. 471). A similar clue can be found in R. Mitchell's dissertation (1971, summarized in Mitchell et al., 1977). Mitchell was interested in immediacy, the tendency to focus on the therapist/client relationship. She divided the therapists in her study into four groups: high facilitative conditions and high immediacy; high facilitative conditions and low immediacy; low facilitative conditions and high immediacy; and low on both measures. None of her analyses predicted success very well, but group three—low empathy, warmth, and genuineness combined with a high tendency to focus on the therapist/client relationship—showed significant client deterioration over the course of treatment and was the only group to do so.

Mitchell et al. caution us not to make too much of one study but say that these findings have great intuitive appeal. I agree. Much of the damage that I think I have seen done by therapy has been related to inappropriate and conflicting messages through which some therapists trap clients in dependency conflicts while being insensitive to their experiences. Authoritarian intrusiveness combined with the failure to establish appropriate limits on the therapy relationship seems especially dangerous. This may be the same issue, but Lambert et al. (1977) also discuss therapist exploitation of the client—by therapists who "consciously or unconsciously utilize dependent individuals (in this case their clients) to satisfy the therapist's own personal needs" (p. 469).

I guess this is as good a way as any to finish this book—with a sharp reminder that therapy is a complex relationship process. Part of what makes therapy interesting and challenging and rewarding is that it is complex and personal. That also carries with it a big responsibility to be as skillful and as clear about yourself as a person as you can be.

BIBLIOGRAPHY

Alexander, F. *Fundamentals of psychoanalysis*. New York: Norton, 1948.

Allport, G. W. Defining healthy personality. In H. Chiang & A. Maslow (Eds.), *The healthy personality: Readings*. New York: Van Nostrand Reinhold, 1969.

American Psychiatric Association. *Diagnostic and statistical manual of mental disorders* (3rd ed.). Washington, D.C.: American Psychiatric Association, 1980.

American Psychological Association. Ethical principles of psychologists. *American Psychologist*, 1981, *36*, 633–638.

Bandura, A. *Principles of behavior modification*. New York: Holt, Rinehart & Winston, 1969.

Barrett-Lennard, G. T. Dimensions of therapist response as causal factors in therapeutic change. *Psychological Monographs*, 1962 (43, Whole No. 562).

Barrett-Lennard, G. T. *The Relationship Inventory: Later development and adaptations*. JSAS Catalog of Selected Documents in Psychology, 1978, *8*, 68. (Ms. No. 1732)

Barrett-Lennard, G. T. The empathy cycle: Refinement of a nuclear concept. *Journal of Counseling Psychology*, 1981, *28*, 91–100.

Beck, A. T., Ward, C. H., Mendelson, M., Mock, J. E., & Erbaugh, J. K. Reliability of psychiatric diagnoses: II. A study of consistency of clinical judgments and ratings. *American Journal of Psychiatry*, 1962, *119*, 351–357.

Bell, J. E. A theoretical position for family group therapy. *Family Process*, 1963, *2*, 1–14.

Berenson, B. G., & Mitchell, K. M. *Confrontation: For better or worse!* Amherst, Mass.: Human Resource Development Press, 1974.

Bergin, A. E. The effects of psychotherapy: Negative results revisited. *Journal of Counseling Psychology*, 1963, *10*, 244–250.

Bergin, A. E. Some implications of psychotherapy research for therapeutic practice. *Journal of Abnormal Psychology*, 1966, *71*, 235–246.

Bergin, A. E. The deterioration effect: A reply to Braucht. *Journal of Abnormal Psychology*, 1970, *75*, 300–302.

Bergin, A. E. Negative effects revisited: A reply. *Professional Psychology*, 1980, *11*, 93–100.

Bergin, A. E., & Solomon, S. Personality and performance correlates of empathic understanding in psychotherapy. In T. Tomlinson & J. Hart (Eds.), *New directions in client-centered therapy*. Boston: Houghton Mifflin, 1970.

Bergin, A. E., & Suinn, R. M. Individual psychotherapy and behavior therapy. *Annual review of psychology*, 1975, *26*, 509–556.

Beutler, L. E. Toward specific psychological therapies for specific conditions. *Journal of Consulting and Clinical Psychology*, 1979, *47*, 882–897.

Blum, G. S., & Barbour, J. S. Selective inattention to anxiety-linked stimuli. *Journal of Experimental Psychology: General*, 1979, *108*, 182–224.

Bourbonnais, Y. An innovative approach for training beginning counselors and a definition of good interviewer behavior. Unpublished dissertation, University of Regina, 1980.

273

Bibliography

Braucht, G. N. The deterioration effect: A reply to Bergin. *Journal of Consulting Psychology,* 1970, *75,* 293–299.

Broverman, D. M., Broverman, I., Clarkson, F. E., Rosenkrantz, P. S., & Vogel, S. Sex-role stereotypes and clinical judgments of mental health. *Journal of Consulting and Clinical Psychology,* 1970, *34,* 1–7.

Bruner, J. *On knowing: Essays for the left hand.* Cambridge, Mass.: Harvard University Press, 1962.

Butler, J. M., & Rice, L. N. Adience, self-actualization, and drive theory. In J. M. Wepman & R. W. Heine (Eds.), *Concepts of personality.* Chicago: Aldine, 1963.

Cameron, N. *Personality development and psychotherapy: A dynamic approach.* Boston: Houghton Mifflin, 1963.

Campbell, B. A., & Church, R. M. (Eds.). *Punishment and aversive behavior.* New York: Appleton-Century-Crofts, 1969.

Carkhuff, R. R. *Helping and human relations.* New York: Holt, Rinehart & Winston, 1969.

Carkhuff, R. R., & Berenson, B. G. *Beyond counseling and therapy.* New York: Holt, Rinehart & Winston, 1967.

Carkhuff, R. R., & Berenson, B. G. *Beyond counseling and therapy* (2nd ed.). New York: Holt, Rinehart & Winston, 1977.

Chesler, P. *Women and madness.* New York: Avon Books, 1972.

Cleckley, H. *The mask of sanity* (5th ed.). St. Louis: Mosby, 1976.

Cofer, C. N., & Appley, M. H. *Motivation: Theory and research.* New York: Wiley, 1964.

Corey, G. *Theory and practice of counseling and psychotherapy* (2nd ed.). Monterey, Calif.: Brooks/Cole, 1982.

Corteen, R. S., & Wood, B. Autonomic responses to shock-associated words in an unattended channel. *Journal of Experimental Psychology,* 1974, *94,* 308–318.

Crowne, D. P. *The experimental study of personality.* Hillsdale, N.J.: Erlbaum, 1979.

D'Alessio, G. R. The concurrent use of behavior modification and psychotherapy. *Psychotherapy: Theory, Research and Practice,* 1968, *5,* 154–159.

Diagnostic and statistical manual of mental disorders, third edition. Washington, D. C.: American Psychiatric Association, 1980.

Dixon, N. F. *Subliminal perception: The nature of a controversy.* London: McGraw-Hill, 1971.

Dollard, J., & Miller, N. E. *Personality and psychotherapy: An analysis in terms of learning, thinking and culture.* New York: McGraw-Hill, 1950.

Duncan, J. The locus of interference in the perception of simultaneous stimuli. *Psychological Review,* 1980, *87,* 272–300.

Egan, G. *The skilled helper* (2nd ed.). Monterey, Calif.: Brooks/Cole, 1982.

Ellis, A. *Reason and emotion in psychotherapy.* New York: Lyle Stuart, 1962.

Erdelyi, M. H. A new look at the new look: Perceptual defense and vigilance. *Psychological Review,* 1980, *81,* 1–25.

Eysenck, H. J. The conditioning model of neurosis. *Behavioral and Brain Sciences,* 1979, *2,* 155–166.

Eysenck, H. J., & Rachman, S. *The causes and cures of neurosis.* San Diego, Calif.: Robert H. Knapp, 1965.

Ford, D. G., & Urban, H. B. Psychotherapy. *Annual review of psychology.* 1967, *18,* 333–372.

Forgus, R., & Shulman, B. *Personality: A cognitive view.* Englewood Cliffs, N.J.: Prentice-Hall, 1979.

Forster, P. M., & Govier, E. Discrimination without awareness? *Quarterly Journal of Experimental Psychology,* 1978, *30,* 282–295.

Frank, J. D. The present status of outcome studies. *Journal of Consulting and Clinical Psychology,* 1979, *47,* 310–316.

Franks, C. M., & Mays, D. T. Negative effects revisited: A rejoinder. *Professional Psychology*, 1980, *11*, 101–105.

Fromm-Reichmann, F. *Principles of intensive psychotherapy*. Chicago: Phoenix Books, University of Chicago Press, 1950.

Gantt, S., Billingsley, D., & Giordano, J. A. Paraprofessional skill: Maintenance of empathic sensitivity after training. *Journal of Counseling Psychology*, 1980, *27*, 374–379.

Gendlin, E. T. *Experiencing and the creation of meaning*. New York: Free Press, 1962.

Gendlin, E. T. Focusing. *Psychotherapy: Theory, Research and Practice*, 1969, *6*, 4–15.

Gendlin, E. T. Client-centered and experiential psychotherapy. In D. A. Wexler & L. N. Rice (Eds.), *Innovations in client-centered therapy*. New York: Wiley, 1974.

Gendlin, E. T. *Focusing*. New York: Everest House, 1978.

Glucksberg, S., & King, L. J. Motivated forgetting mediated by implicit verbal chaining: A laboratory analog of repression. *Science*, 1967, *158*, 517–519.

Glucksberg, S., & Ornstein, P. A. Reply to Weiner and Higgins: Motivated forgetting is not attributable to a confounding original learning with retention. *Journal of Verbal Learning and Verbal Behavior*, 1969, *8*, 681–685.

Goldfried, M. R., & Davison, G. C. *Clinical behavior therapy*. New York: Holt, Rinehart & Winston, 1975.

Gomes-Schwartz, B., Hadley, S. W., & Strupp, H. H. Individual psychotherapy and behavior therapy. *Annual review of psychology*, 1978, *29*, 435–471.

Gordon, T. P. E.T. in action. New York: Wyden, 1976.

Greenson, R. R. Loving, hating and indifference towards the patient. *International Review of Psychoanalysis*, 1974, *1*, 259–266.

Grinspoon, L., Dwalt, J. R., & Shader, R. Psychotherapy and pharmacotherapy in chronic schizophrenia. *American Journal of Psychiatry*, 1968, *124*, 1645–1652.

Guerney, B. G. *Relationship enhancement*. San Francisco: Jossey-Bass, 1977.

Gur, R. C. & Sackeim, H. A. Self-deception: A concept in search of a phenomenon. *Journal of Personality and Social Psychology*, 1979, *37*, 147–169.

Gurman, A. S. The patient's perceptions of the therapeutic relationship. In A. S. Gurman & A. M. Razin (Eds.), *Effective psychotherapy: A handbook of research*. Oxford, England: Pergamon Press, 1977.

Hall, M. H. A conversation with Carl Rogers. *Psychology Today*, December, 1967, *(1)*, 18–21 & 62–66.

Hammond, D. C., Hepworth, D. H., & Smith, V. G. *Improving therapeutic communication*. San Francisco: Jossey-Bass, 1978.

Hebb, D. O. *A textbook of psychology* (3rd ed.). Philadelphia: Saunders, 1972.

Hefferline, R. F., & Keenan, B. Amplitude-induction gradient of a small scale (covert) operant. *Journal of Experimental Analysis of Behavior*, 1963, *6*, 307–315.

Helzer, J. E., Clayton, P. J., Pambakian, R., Reich, T., Woodruff, R. A., & Reveley, M. A. Reliability of psychiatric diagnosis: II. The test/retest reliability of diagnostic classification. *Archives of General Psychiatry*, 1977, *34*, 136–141.

Holmes, D. S. Investigations of repression: Differential recall of material experimentally or naturally associated with ego threat. *Psychological Bulletin*, 1974, *81*, 632–653.

Ivey, A. E. The clinician as teacher of interpersonal skills: Let's give away what we've got. *Clinical Psychologist*, 1974, *27*, 6–9.

Ivey, A. E., & Authier, J. *Microcounseling* (2nd ed.). Springfield, Ill.: Charles C Thomas, 1978.

Bibliography

Jacobs, D. Action and psychological explanation. Unpublished doctoral thesis, University of Chicago, 1981.

Jacobs, D. Empathy training. *Journal of Humanistic Psychology*, in press.

Karon, B. P., & Vanden Bos, G. R. The consequences of psychotherapy for schizophrenic patients. *Psychotherapy: Theory, Research and Practice*, 1972, 9, 111–120.

Kiesler, D. J. Some myths of psychotherapy research and the search for a paradigm. *Psychological Bulletin*, 1966, 65, 110–136.

Kiesler, D. J. A grid model for theory and research in the psychotherapies. In L. D. Eron & R. Callahan (Eds.), *The relation of theory to practice in psychotherapy*. Chicago: Aldine, 1969.

Klein, M. G., Dittmann, A. T., Parloff, M. B., & Gill, M. M. Behavior therapy: Observations and reflections. *Journal of Consulting and Clinical Psychology*, 1969, 33, 259–266.

Kramer, E. *A beginning manual for psychotherapists*. New York: Grune & Stratton, 1970.

Lambert, M. J., Bergin, A. E., & Collins, J. L. Therapist-induced deterioration in psychotherapy. In A. S. Gurman & A. M. Razin (Eds.), *Effective psychotherapy: A handbook of research*. Oxford, England: Pergamon Press, 1977.

Lambert, M. J., DeJulio, S. S., & Stein, D. M. Therapist interpersonal skills: Process, outcome, methodological considerations, and recommendations for future research. *Psychological Bulletin*, 1978, 85, 467–489.

Lazarus, R. S. Thoughts on the relations between emotion and cognition. *American Psychologist*, 1982, 37, 1019–1024.

Lichtenstein, E. *Psychotherapy approaches and applications*. Monterey, Calif.: Brooks/Cole, 1980.

London, P. *The modes and morals of psychotherapy*. New York: Holt, Rinehart & Winston, 1964.

Mahoney, M. J. Reflections on the cognitive-learning trend in psychotherapy. *American Psychologist*, 1977, 32, 5–13.

Malcolm, J. The impossible profession—II. *New Yorker*, 1980, 56 (40), 54–152.

Marmor, J. (Ed.). *Modern psychoanalysis*. New York: Basic Books, 1968.

Martin, D. G. *Introduction to psychotherapy*. Monterey, Calif.: Brooks/Cole, 1971.

Martin, D. G. *Learning based client centered therapy*. Monterey, Calif.: Brooks/Cole, 1972.

Martin, D. G. *Personality: Effective and ineffective*. Monterey, Calif.: Brooks/Cole, 1976.

Martin, D. G. Brain laterality and a learning model of repression and anxiety. Paper presented at the convention of the Canadian Psychological Association, Calgary, Alberta, June 1980.

Martin, D. G., Hawryluk, G. A., Berish, C., & Dushenko, T. Selective inhibition of aversive memories cued in the right hemisphere: A repression analog. Unpublished paper, University of Manitoba, 1981.

Martin, D. G., Hawryluk, G. A., & Guse, L. L. Experimental study of unconscious influences: Ultrasound as a stimulus. *Journal of Abnormal Psychology*, 1974, 83, 589–608.

Martin, D. G., Stambrook, M., Tataryn, D. J., & Beihl, H. O. Conditioning in an unattended ear: Testing an anxiety model. Unpublished paper, University of Manitoba, 1982.

Maslow, A. H. *Motivation and personality*. New York: Harper & Row, 1954.

Maslow, A. H. *The psychology of science: A reconnaissance*. New York: Harper & Row, 1966.

Masters, W. H., & Johnson, V. E. *Human sexual inadequacy.* Boston: Little, Brown, 1970.

Mathews, A. Fear-reduction research and clinical phobias. *Psychological Bulletin,* 1978, *85,* 390–404.

May, P. R. A., Tuma, A. H., Yale, C., Potepan, P., & Dixon, N. J. Schizophrenia—A follow-up study of results of treatment. *Archives of General Psychiatry,* 1976, *33,* 481–486.

Mays, D. T., & Franks, C. M. Getting worse: Psychotherapy or no treatment—The jury should still be out. *Professional Psychology,* 1980, *11,* 78–92.

McCauley, C., Parmelee, C. M., Sperber, R. D., & Carr, T. D. Early extraction of meaning from pictures and its relation to conscious identification. *Journal of Experimental Psychology: Human Perception and Performance,* 1980, *6,* 265–276.

McCullers, C. *The heart is a lonely hunter.* Boston: Houghton Mifflin, 1940.

Meltzoff, J., & Kornreich, M. *Research in psychotherapy.* New York: Atherton Press, 1970.

Menninger, K. *Theory of psychoanalytic technique.* New York: Harper & Row, 1958.

Menninger, K. *The vital balance: The life process in mental health and illness.* New York: Viking Press, 1963.

Messer, S. B., & Winokur, M. Some limits to the integration of psychoanalytic and behavior therapy. *American Psychologist,* 1980, *35,* 818–827.

Mineka, S. The role of fear in theories of avoidance learning, flooding, and extinction. *Psychological Bulletin,* 1979, *86,* 938–1010.

Mineka, S., & Kihlstrom, J. F. Unpredictable and uncontrollable events: A new perspective on experimental neurosis. *Journal of Abnormal Psychology,* 1978, *87,* 256–271.

Mitchell, K. M., Bozarth, J. D., & Krauft, C. C. A reappraisal of the therapeutic effectiveness of accurate empathy, non-possessive warmth, and genuineness. In A. S. Gurman & A. M. Razin (Eds.), *Effective psychotherapy: A handbook of research.* Oxford, England: Pergamon Press, 1977.

Mitchell, R. M. Relationship between therapist response to therapist-relevant client expressions and therapy process and therapy outcome. Doctoral dissertation, Michigan State University, 1971. *Dissertation Abstracts International,* 1971, *32,* 1853B (University Microfilms No. 71-23,216).

Mowrer, O. H. On the dual nature of learning—A reinterpretation of "conditioning" and "problem-solving." *Harvard Educational Review,* 1947, *17,* 102–148.

Myrick, R. D., & Pare, D. D. A study of the effects of group sensitivity training with student counselor-consultants. *Counselor Education and Supervision,* 1971, *11,* 90–96.

Naar, R. Client-centered and behavior therapies: Their peaceful co-existence—A case study. *Journal of Abnormal Psychology,* 1970, *76,* 155–160.

Ohman, A., & Ursin, H. On the sufficiency of a Pavlovian conditioning model for coping with the complexities of neurosis. *Behavioral and Brain Sciences,* 1979, *2,* 179–180.

Okun, B. F., & Rappaport, L. J. *Working with families: An introduction to family therapy.* Monterey, Calif.: Duxbury Press, 1980.

Ornstein, R. E. *The psychology of consciousness* (2nd ed.). New York: Harcourt Brace Jovanovich, 1977.

Ornston, P. S., Cicchetti, D. V., Levine, J., & Fierman, L. B. Some parameters of verbal behavior that reliably differentiate novice from experienced psychotherapists. *Journal of Abnormal Psychology,* 1968, *73,* 240–244.

Patterson, C. H. *Relationship counseling and psychotherapy.* New York: Harper & Row, 1974.

Bibliography

Paul, G. L. Strategy of outcome research in psychotherapy. *Journal of Consulting Psychology,* 1967, *31,* 109–118.

Peebles, M. J. Personal therapy and ability to display empathy, warmth and genuineness in psychotherapy. *Psychotherapy: Theory, Research and Practice,* 1980, *17,* 258–262.

Perls, F. S. Four lectures. In J. Fagan & I. L. Shepherd (Eds.), *Gestalt therapy now.* Palo Alto, Calif.: Science and Behavior Books, 1970.

Phillips, E. L. *Psychotherapy: A modern theory and practice.* Englewood Cliffs, N.J.: Prentice-Hall, 1956.

Phillips, J., Lockhart, J. & Moreland, J. Minimal encourages to talk. Unpublished manual. University of Massachusetts, Amherst, 1969.

Pierce, R. M., & Drasgow, J. Nondirective reflection vs. conflict attention: An empirical evaluation. *Journal of Clinical Psychology,* 1969, *25,* 341–342.

Posner, M. L., & Boies, S. J. Components of attention. *Psychological Review,* 1971, *78,* 391–408.

Rachman, S. T., & Teasdale, J. Aversion therapy: An appraisal. In C. M. Franks (Ed.), *Behavior therapy: Appraisal and status.* New York: McGraw-Hill, 1969.

Reich, W. *Character analysis.* New York: Noonday Press, 1949.

Reik, T. *Listening with the third ear.* New York: Noonday Press, 1948.

Rice, L. N. The evocative function of the therapist. In D. A. Wexler & L. N. Rice (Eds.), *Innovations in client-centered therapy.* New York: Wiley, 1974.

Rogers, C. R. *Counseling and psychotherapy.* Boston: Houghton Mifflin, 1942.

Rogers, C. R. *Client-centered therapy.* Boston: Houghton Mifflin, 1951.

Rogers, C. R. The necessary and sufficient conditions of therapeutic personality change. *Journal of Consulting Psychology,* 1957, *21,* 95–103.

Rogers, C. R. A theory of therapy, personality, and interpersonal relationships, as developed in the client-centered framework. In S. Koch (Ed.), *Psychology: A study of a science* (Vol. 3). New York: McGraw-Hill, 1959.

Rogers, C. R. *On becoming a person.* Boston: Houghton Mifflin, 1961.

Rogers, C. R., The interpersonal relationship: The core of guidance. *Harvard Educational Review,* 1962, *32,* 416–429.

Rogers, C. R. Empathic: An unappreciated way of being. *Counseling Psychologist,* 1975, *5,* 2–10.

Rogers, C. R. Client-centered psychotherapy. In H. I. Kaplan, B. J. Sadock, & A. M. Freedman (Eds.), *Comprehensive textbook of psychiatry* (Vol. 3). Baltimore: Williams & Wilkins, 1980.

Rogers, C. R., & Dymond, R. F. *Psychotherapy and personality change.* Chicago: University of Chicago Press, 1954.

Rogers, C. R., Gendlin, E. T., Kiesler, D. J., & Truax, C. B. *The therapeutic relationship and its impact: A study of psychotherapy with schizophrenics.* Madison: University of Wisconsin Press, 1967.

Rosenthal, D. Changes in some moral values following psychotherapy. *Journal of Consulting Psychology,* 1955, *19,* 431–436.

Rosenthal, R., & Rubin, D. B. Interpersonal expectancy effects: The first 345 studies. *Behavioral and Brain Sciences,* 1978, *1,* 377–387.

Sackeim, H. A., & Gur, R. C. Self-deception, self-confrontation and consciousness. In G. E. Schwartz & D. Shapiro (Eds.), *Consciousness and self-regulation: Advances in research* (Vol. 2). New York: Plenum Press, 1978.

Sanders, J. R. Complaints against psychologists adjudicated informally by APA's Committee on Scientific and Professional Ethics and Conduct. *American Psychologist,* 1979, *34,* 1139–1144.

Sanders, J. R., & Keith-Spiegel, P. Formal and informal adjudication of ethics complaints against psychologists. *American Psychologist,* 1980, *35,* 1096–1105.

Schubert, J. The therapeutic interview. Unpublished manuscript, University of Regina, 1977.

Seligman, M. E. P., & Johnston, J. C. A cognitive theory of avoidance learning. In F. J. Guigan & D. B. Lumsden, *Contemporary approaches to conditioning and learning.* Washington, D.C.: V. M. Winston and Sons, 1973.

Shevrin, H., & Dickman, S. The psychological unconscious: A necessary assumption for all psychological theory. *American Psychologist,* 1980, *35,* 421–434.

Shlien, J. M., Mosak, H. H., & Dreikurs, R. Effect of time limits: A comparison of two psychotherapies. *Journal of Counseling Psychology,* 1962, *9,* 31–34.

Singer, B. A., & Luborsky, L. B. Countertransference: The status of clinical versus quantitative research. In A. S. Gurman & A. M. Razin (Eds.), *Effective psychotherapy: A handbook of research.* New York: Pergamon Press, 1977.

Skinner, B. F. *Contingencies of reinforcement.* Englewood Cliffs, N.J.: Prentice-Hall, Inc., 1969.

Smith, M. L., & Glass, G. V. Meta-analysis of psychotherapy outcome studies. *American Psychologist,* 1977, *32,* 752–760.

Stambrook, M., & Martin, D. G. Brain laterality and the subliminal perception of facial expression. *International Journal of Neuroscience,* in press.

Stearns, B. C., Penner, L. A., & Kimmel, E. Sexism among psychotherapists: A case not yet proven. *Journal of Consulting and Clinical Psychology,* 1980, *48,* 548–550.

Stricker, G. Implication of research for psychotherapeutic treatment of women. *American Psychologist,* 1977, *32,* 14–22.

Strupp, H. H. A psychodynamicist looks at modern behavior therapy. *Psychotherapy: Theory, Research and Practice,* 1979, *16,* 124–131.

Strupp, H. H., & Bergin, A. E. Some empirical and conceptual bases for coordinated research in psychotherapy: A critical review of issues, trends, and evidence. *International Journal of Psychiatry,* 1969, *7,* 23–115.

Strupp, H. H., Hadley, S. W., & Gomes-Schwartz, B. *Psychotherapy for better or worse: The problem of negative effects.* New York: Jason Aronson, 1977.

Sullivan, H. S. *Schizophrenia as a human process.* New York: Norton, 1962.

Szasz, T. S. The myth of mental illness. *American Psychologist,* 1960, *15,* 113–118.

Temerlin, M. K. Diagnostic bias in community mental health. *Community Mental Health Journal,* 1970, *6,* 110–117.

Templeman, T. L., & Wollersheim, J. P. A cognitive-behavioral approach to the treatment of psychopathy. *Psychotherapy: Theory, Research and Practice,* 1979, *16,* 132–139.

Tesser, A., & Rosen, S. Similarity of objective fate as a determinant of the reluctance to transmit unpleasant information: the MUM effect. *Journal of Personality and Social Psychology,* 1972, *23,* 46–53.

Truax, C. B., & Carkhuff, R. R. *Toward effective counseling and psychotherapy.* Chicago: Aldine, 1967.

Truax, C. B., & Mitchell, K. M. Research on certain therapist interpersonal skills in relation to process and outcome. In A. E. Bergin & S. L. Garfield (Eds.), *Handbook of psychotherapy and behavior change.* New York: Wiley, 1971.

Von Wright, J. M., Anderson, K., & Stenman, U. Generalization of conditioned GSR's in dichotic listening. In Rabbit, P. and Dornic, S. (Eds.) *Attention and performance, Volume 5.* Oxford and Stockholm: Academic Press, 1975.

Walker, P. Binocular rivalry: Central or peripheral selective processes. *Psychological Bulletin,* 1978, *85,* 376–389.

Walters, G. C., & Grusec, J. E. *Punishment.* San Francisco: W. H. Freeman, 1977.

Weiner, B., & Higgins, J. A mediational paradigm for a study of motivated forgetting:

A critical analysis. *Journal of Verbal Learning and Verbal Behavior*, 1969, *8*, 677–680.

Welkowitz, J., Cohen, J., & Ortmeyer, D. Value system similarity: Investigation of patient-therapist dyads. *Journal of Consulting Psychology*, 1967, *31*, 48–55.

Whitely, B. E. Sex roles and psychotherapy: A current appraisal. *Psychological Bulletin*, 1979, *86*, 1309–1321.

Wilson, G. T., & O'Leary, K. D. *Principles of behavior therapy.* Englewood Cliffs, N.J.: Prentice-Hall, 1980.

Wolpe, J. *Psychotherapy by reciprocal inhibition.* Stanford, Calif.: Stanford University Press, 1958.

Wolpe, J. The Eysenck and the Wolpe theories of neurosis. *Behavioral and Brain Sciences*, 1979, *2*, 184–185.

Yalom, I. D. *The theory and practice of group psychotherapy* (2nd ed.). New York: Basic Books, 1975.

Yalom, I. D., & Lieberman, M. H. A study of encounter group casualties. *Journal of Abnormal Psychology*, 1971, *25*, 16–30.

Zajonc, R. B. Feeling and thinking: Preferences need no inferences. *American Psychologist*, 1980, *35*, 151–175.

Zajonc, R. B. A one-factor mind about mind and emotion. *American Psychologist*, 1981, *36*, 102–103.

NAME INDEX

Alexander, F., 53
Allport, G. W., 90
American Psychological Association, 111, 186, 195, 198
Anderson, K., 245
Appley, M. H., 227

Bandura, A., 181
Barbour, J. S., 245
Barrett–Lennard, G. T., 3, 13, 266, 267
Beck, A. T., 186
Beihl, H. O., 245
Bell, J. E., 216
Berenson, B. G., 12, 15, 63, 65, 67, 72, 99, 270
Bergin, A. E., 187, 215, 222, 223, 266, 270, 271
Berish, C., 243
Beutler, L. E., 187
Billingsly, D., 270
Blum, G. S., 245
Boies, S. J., 231, 244
Bourbonnais, Y., 36
Bozarth, J. D., 268, 269
Braucht, G. N., 271
Broverman, D. M., 117
Broverman, I., 117
Bruner, J., 56
Butler, J. M., 253

Cameron, N., 61
Campbell, B. A., 235
Carkhuff, R. R., 6, 12, 13, 15, 44, 63, 65, 66, 67, 72, 99, 268–270
Carr, T. D., 231, 245
Chesler, P., 117
Church, R. M., 235
Cicchetti, D. V., 29
Clarkson, F. E., 117
Clayton, P. J., 187
Cleckley, H., 190
Cofer, C. N., 227

Cohen, J., 116
Collins, J. L., 215, 271
Corey, G., 226
Corteen, B. S., 245
Coulson, W., 153, 244
Crowne, D. P., 239

D'Alessio, G. R., 181
Davison, G. C., 177
DeJulio, S. S., 268
Dickman, S., 230
Dittman, A. T., 179
Dixon, N. J., 188, 245
Dollard, J., 73, 236, 238, 246
Drasgow, J., 66
Dreikurs, R., 211
Duncan, J., 231, 245
Dushenko, T., 243
Dwalt, J. R., 188
Dymond, R. F., 268

Egan, G., 6, 52, 58, 72, 75, 181
Ellis, A., 53, 65, 69, 117, 231
Erbaugh, J. K., 186
Erdelyi, M. H., 245
Eyesenck, H. J., 229

Fierman, L. B., 30
Ford, D. G., 187
Forgus, R., 231
Forster, P. M., 245
Frank, J. D., 266
Franks, C. M., 266, 271
Freud, S., 85, 113, 117, 243
Fromm–Reichmann, F., 190

Gantt, S., 270
Gendlin, E. T., 12, 56, 57, 58, 120
Gill, M. M., 179
Giardano, J. A., 270
Glass, G. V., 266
Glucksberg, S., 243
Goldfried, M. R., 177

Gomez–Schwartz, B., 178, 266, 271
Gordon, T., 106
Govier, E., 245
Greenson, R. R., 98
Grinspoon, L., 188
Grusec, J. E., 236
Guerney, B. G., 120
Gur, R. C., 36, 245
Gurman, A. S., 3, 8, 12, 215, 267, 268
Guse, L. L., 245

Hadley, S. W., 178, 271
Hall, M. H., 10
Hammond, D. C., 6, 12, 41, 42, 48
Hawryluk, G., 243, 245
Hebb, D. C., 242
Hefferline, R. F., 245
Helzer, J. E., 187
Henderson, M., 169
Hepworth, D. H., 6, 12, 41, 42, 48
Higgins, J., 243
Holmes, D. S., 243

Ivey, A. E., 269

Jacobs, D., 120, 121
Johnson, V. E., 218, 219
Johnston, J. C., 231
Jung, C., 117

Karon, B. P., 188
Keenan, B., 245
Keith–Spiegel, P., 194
Kiesler, D. J., 12, 187
Kimmel, E., 117
King, L., 243
Klein, M. G., 179
Kornreich, M., 266
Kramer, E., 179
Krauft, C. C., 268, 269

Lambert, M. J., 222, 268, 269, 271,
    272
Lazarus, R. S., 231
Lee, R. E., 126
Levine, J., 30
Lewis, C., 172
Lichtenstein, E., 226
Lieberman, M. H., 215
Lockhart, J., 19
London, P., 74
Luborsky, L. B., 114, 115

Mahoney, M. J., 230, 231
Malcolm, J., 98
Marmor, J., 229
Martin, D. G., 60, 66, 90, 143, 181,
    224, 236, 243, 245, 268
Maslow, A. H., 90, 220, 226
Masters, W. H., 218, 219
Mathews, A., 178
May, P. R. A., 188
Mays, D. T., 271
McCauley, C., 231, 245
McCullers, C., 28
Meltzoff, J., 266
Mendelson, M., 186
Menninger, K., 7, 227
Messer, S. B., 53, 228
Miller, N. E., 73, 236, 237, 238, 246
Mitchell, K. M., 63, 268, 269, 270,
    271
Mock, J. E., 186
Moreland, J., 19
Mosak, H. H., 211
Myrick, R. D., 270

Naar, R., 181

Ohman, A., 238
Okun, B. F., 216
O'Leary, K. D., 177
Ornstein, R. E., 56, 243
Ornston, P. S., 29
Ortmeyer, D., 116

Pambakian, R., 187
Pare, D. D., 270
Parloff, M. B., 179
Parmelee, C. M., 231, 245
Patterson, C. H., 12, 52
Paul, G. L., 187
Peebles, M. J., 116
Penner, L. A., 117
Perls, F. S., 69
Phillips, E. L., 237
Phillips, J., 19
Pierce, R. M., 66
Posner, M. L., 231, 244
Potepan, P., 188

Rachman, S., 178, 229
Rappaport, L. J., 216
Reich, W., 65
Reik, T., 7, 24
Reveley, M. A., 187

Rice, L. N., 3, 7, 8, 45, 46, 56, 57, 245, 253, 257
Rogers, C. R., 9, 10, 90, 93, 94, 99, 226, 227, 243, 268, 271
Rosen, S., 58
Rosenkrantz, P. S., 117
Rosenthal, D., 116
Rosenthal, R., 117
Rubin, D. B., 117

Sackeim, H. A., 36, 245
Sanders, J. R., 194
Schubert, J., 36, 81
Seligman, M. F. P., 231
Shader, R., 188
Shevrin, H., 230
Shlien, J. M., 211
Shulman, B., 231
Singer, B. A., 114, 115
Skinner, B. F., 85, 245
Smith, V. G., 6, 12, 41, 42, 48, 266
Solomon, S., 270
Sperber, R. D., 231, 245
Stambrook, M., 122, 245
Stearnes, B. C., 117
Stein, D. M., 268
Stenman, V., 245
Strachan, J., 161
Stricker, G., 117
Strupp, H. H., 178, 181, 187, 223, 271
Suinn, R. M., 266
Sullivan, H. S., 190
Szasz, C. S., 233

Tataryn, D. J., 245
Teasdale, J., 178
Temerlin, M. K., 186
Templeman, T. L., 189
Tesser, A., 58
Truax, C. B., 12, 44, 66, 268, 269, 270
Tuma, A. H., 188

Urban, H. B., 187
Ursin, H., 238

Vanden Bos, G. R., 188
Vogel, S., 117
Von Wright, J. M., 245

Walker, P., 245
Walters, G. C., 236
Ward, C. H., 186
Weiner, B., 243
Welkowitz, J., 116
Wexler, D. A., 8, 57
Whitely, B. E., 117
Wilson, G. T., 177
Winokur, M., 53, 228
Wollersheim, J. P., 189
Wolpe, J., 229
Wood, B., 245
Woodruff, R. A., 187

Yale, C., 188
Yalom, I. D., 213, 215

Zajonc, R. B., 53, 69, 230, 245

SUBJECT
INDEX

Acceptance, as client's job, 78
Acceptance, communicating, 94 – 96
  explicit expression, 95
  in relationship, 93
Acknowledgment responses, 18
Acting out, as symptom, 249 – 250
Action, taking, 75 – 79
Additive responses, 6
Advanced accurate empathy, 6
Advice, client requests, 88 – 89
  giving, 62
Affection words, 49
"Aha" experience, 59
Ahead of conflict region, 261 – 264
Ambiguity, 137 – 141
Anger in therapy, 104 – 105
  provoke vs. evoke, 105
  therapist avoids, 115
Anger words, 49
Anti-social behavior, 189 – 190,
  249 – 250
Anxiety, and conflict, 236 – 241
  -based problems, 188, 233
  partially conscious cues, 244 – 245
  reduction as reinforcer, 241, 247
  in therapy, 256
Appointment setting, 202 – 203
Arguing with clients, 62
Assessment, bias in, 186 – 187
  purposes, 186 – 187
  within therapy, 191 – 192
  behavioral, 193
Attachment, 110 – 116
Attending, 18
Avoidance, vicious circle of, 251
Awareness, defining, 241 – 242
  learning without, 244 – 245
Awkwardness, initial, 34

Basic listening skills, 18
Behavior modification, 176 – 180
  combined with empathic therapy,
  176 – 180

Behavior Modification (continued)
  indications for use, 178 – 180
  methods, 177 – 178
Behavioral assessment, 193
Behavioral deficits, 178 – 179
Behind conflict region, 260 – 261
Big issue vs. last 12 words, 21,
  37 – 38
Bring it to life, 58 – 59

Case studies as inadequate, 265
Chicken, therapist as, 58 – 59
Client perceptions of core
  conditions, 3, 8, 13, 17, 266 – 267
Client's job, 72 – 78
Cognition, relation to emotion, 53,
  69, 230, 244 – 245
  as behavior, 231 – 232
  definition problem, 231 – 232
Cognitive theory, 230 – 232
Cognitive-learning theory, 16, 230
Combining approaches, 180
Communication, couple/family
  therapy, 217 – 218
Compassionate Friends, 169
Competence, ethics, 200
Concise and vivid responses, 46 – 47
Conclusions vs. experiences, 53 – 54
Concreteness, 44 – 45
Confidentiality, 97, 195, 198 – 200
Conflict, internal, 240 – 241
  philosophical, in approaches, 180
  principles, 236 – 241
  region, 238 – 239, 255
    working ahead, 261 – 264
    working behind, 260 – 261
  relief, practice, 256
  relief, theory, 254 – 256
  types, 237
Conflict attention, 66 – 67
Confrontation, 59 – 63
  abuses of, 59 – 60
  a different view, 66 – 67

Confrontation *(continued)*
  as direct attack, 66–67
  as part of empathy, 52–53
  as punishment based, 60
  self-', 52
  traditional meaning, 52
Confused words, 49
Connotativeness, 46
Consequences, ineffective therapy,
    260–264
  deterioration effect, 270–272
Consultation, need for:
  about confidentiality, 196
  judgment calls, 183
  on assessment, 188, 190
  on termination, 210
  therapist personal issues, 104, 114,
    201
Content of therapy, 82–86
  client returning to, 86
  as unpredictable, 83
Contradictions, dealing with, 61–62
Core conditions, client perceptions
    of, 3, 8, 13, 17, 266–267
  defined, 12
  raters' perceptions of, 268–269
  ratings of various groups, 15
Corrective emotional experience, 53
Cotherapy, 218
Coulson, Bill, observing, 153
  introductory comments, 153
  interview, 156
Countertransference, 114–116
  and termination, 210
Couple therapy, 216–220
  combined with individual, 219
  direction of process, 217
  goals, 218
  vs. individual, 219–220
Cure, defining, 91
Curse, taking it off, 47, 262

Deconditioning feared thoughts, 71
Defenses, taking away need for,
    65–66
Defensiveness, 63–68
Dependency, 110–116
  reinforcing in clients, 262
Detachment, as relationship
    weakener, 110
Deterioration effect, 270–272
Directive therapy, consequences,
    261–264

Directiveness, of process, 83, 87–89
Directly conditioned fears, 178
Disagreements, 107
Discomfort, therapist's, 100–101
Distortions, dealing with, 61–62
  by therapist, 114–116
  beginning therapist, 124
DSM III, 186

Eclecticism, 86, 180–181, 232
  schools fading, 233, 225
Effective person, definition, 90
Effects of therapy, 257–260
Emergencies, 182–183
  ethical issues, 195
Emotion, look for first, 20
  reducing painful, 258
  relation to cognition, 53, 69, 230,
    244–245
  tendency to avoid, 58–59
Empathic intent, 38, 40, 41
  vs. expertness, 63
Empathic guesses, 40
Empathic response leads, 42–43
Empathy, evocative, as not passive, 9,
    10
  confrontation in the spirit of,
    60–61
  levels of, 6
  rating scale, 12–30
  Rogers' definition, 9
  "too much" early, 6
  vs. interpretation, 6–8
  vs. sympathy, 8
Error, by therapist, 50–51
Ethics, client vs. therapist needs,
    194–195
  standards of professions, 194
  social needs, 195–196
Evocative empathy, defined, 3 (See
    also Empathy)
Evoke, defined, 32
  vs. provoke, 32, 104–105
Exercises, beginning, 120–121
Experiential focusing, 56–58
Expert, therapist as, on process, 62,
    85
Expertness, vs. empathic intent, 63
Exploration, as client's job, 73
  as mutual search, 143
Extinction, 55
  of fears of thoughts, 71, 255
  necessary to weaken fear, 53, 234

False understanding, 107
Family therapy, 216–220
  direction of process, 217
  goals, 218
  vs. individual, 219–220
Fear:
  as persistent, 234–235
  basic principles, 233–236
  complex, 234
  experiencing as necessary to
    weaken, 53, 234
  of internal processes, 55, 235
  weakening, 234
Fear words, 49
Feedback, need for:
  about confidentiality, 196
  judgment calls, 183
  on assessment, 188, 190
  on termination, 210
  therapist personal issues, 104, 114,
    201
Feelings, as fear cues, 235
  going for, 155
  looking for first, 20–21
Fees, 205–206
First person, as response format, 33,
  137
Five-phrase therapy, 43
Flight into health, 263
Focus and structure, 36–39
  vs. elaborate, 37, 46–47
Focusing, 56–58
Following vs. leading, 5
Formula response, 32, 77
  danger of overuse, 42
Frequency of responding, 39

Genuineness, 12, 99–101
  destructive, 99
Getting unstuck, 77
Glazed look, 153
Goals, as emerging, 90–91
  as values, 89
  couple/family therapy, 218
  general for therapy, 90
  setting, 89–91
Good intentions, assuming, 67–68
Group therapy, 213–216
  advantages and disadvantages, 215
  combined with individual,
    219–220
  curative factors, 213–217
  therapist role, 215–216

Growth group for trainees, 124
Guilt words, 49

Happy words, 49
Hard work required, 9–11
Hearing implicit message, 20–24
Henderson, Morgan, observing, 169
  introductory comments, 169
  interview, 170
Here and now, includes past, 23–24
Hierarchy emerges, 90–91
Humanism, 226–227
Humor, 143
Hurt words, 49
Hysteria, 249

I messages, 106
Identified patient, 216–217
Immediacy, 101–107
Impasse, breaking, 77
Independence as outcome, 11, 70,
  258, 260
Ineffective therapy, 260–264
  deterioration effect, 270–272
Information processing, 56, 230–232,
  245–246
Inhibition, basis of punishment,
  235–236
  basis of repression, 242–243
Initial interview, 206–208
Insight, 74
  as result of emotional change, 59
Intellectualizing, by therapist, 58–59
  as a defense, 64–65
Interpretation, 14
  timing of, 6–7
  vs. evocative empathy, 6–8
Interrupting the client, 88
Interventions, direct, 182
Intake interview, 191
Intended message, 3, 5, 6
Intimacy ability as outcome, 260
Introduction to client, 206
Involuntary clients, 198

Jargon, 109
Joy, facing it, 56
Joke, misunderstanding of Rogers, 10
Judgment and relationship, 92–93
Judgment calls, 182–183

Lead-in phrases, 41–43
Leading edge, 32
  identifying, 24–26, 256
Leading vs. following, 5
  how far?, 25–26
Learning principles, different
  applications, 177
Learning theory, 227–229
Learning without awareness,
  244–245
Lee, Bob, observing, 126
  discussion of session, 137
  basic attitude, 141–142
  client's reaction, 142–143
Legal testimony, 199
Limits, on relationship, 94, 110–113
  session length, 206
  on therapist's experience, 27
Listening skills, basic, 18
Little theories, 41, 83–84, 139

Maintenance response, 19
Martin, David, observing, 143
  introductory comments, 143
  interview, 144
Matching treatment to disorder,
  187–191
Maybe it's because game, 59
Minimal encourages to talk, 19
Minimally facilitative response, 13,
  20
Missing the client's message, 50–51
Mistrustful clients, 64
Modeling by therapist, 55
Money, 205–206
Moralizing, 109
Multiple-client formats, 212–220
  combined with individual, 219
MUM effect, 58
  beginning therapist, 124

Neurosis, general definition, 233
Neurotic/normal continuum, 233
Neurotic paradox, 246
Neurotic stupidity, 73, 246, 258
Nondirective, 83
Nonjudgmental, relationship as,
  92–93
Non-possessive warmth, 94
Non-sexist therapy, 118
Nonverbal communication, 22, 44
Notetaking, 204–205

Novice therapist, reflections by,
  122–125

Obsessive-compulsive symptoms,
  250–251
Opening the interview, 207, 208
Outcome of therapy, 257–260
Overdose, self-, by client, 32

Painting the picture, 32
Parents and confidentiality, 200
Particularity, 45
Passive therapy, consequences,
  260–261
Pause, the inevitable, 36
Perry Mason therapy, 80–81
Personal needs and theories, 27
Personal note on development of
  theory, 225
Personal therapy for therapist,
  115–116
Personal worth as outcome, 259–260
Phenomenology, 226
Phobia, 248–249
Physical setting, 203–204
Physical symptoms, 249
Poignancy, 29, 37, 56
Practice, as essential, 34–35
Preventing avoidance, 55
Privileged communication, 197
Prizing, 93–97
Problem/solving, by client, 69–91
  client independence, 11,70
  impaired, 246
  improving, 258
Problems in living, 233, 251–252
Process, directive in, 83, 87–89
  teaching, 208
Provoke vs. evoke, 32, 104–105
Psychiatric casualties, 271
Psychoanalysis, 229–230
Psychosis, assessment, 190–191
Punishment, as inhibition, 235–236

Questions, 79–82, 155
  beginning therapists ask more, 29
  disadvantages, 79
  empathic, 79–80
  genuine, reality, chatty,
    manipulative, 81–82

Subject Index

Rambling, by client, 37–38
Rapprochement, approaches, 181–182
Raters' perceptions, evidence, 13, 268–269
Reactions, first look for, 20–21
Real-time responding, 35
Reason, relation to emotion, 53, 69, 230, 244–245
Reassurance, 108
Reciprocal response, 19
Red flagging issues, 21, 38
Reinforcing thinking, 71–72, 256
Relationship as client, 216–217
  as nonjudgmental, 92–93
Relationship Inventory, 267
Realtionship weakeners, 107–109
Repetition of issues, 86
Repression, 241–246
  costs, 243–244
  learning view, 242–243
Research evidence, summary, 266
  need for, 265
Resistance, 63–68
Respect, 12, 93–97
Role conflicts, 196–198
Role playing, 121–122

Sad words, 48
Schemes, 56, 245–246
  breaking, 257
Schools of therapy, 223
Selective hearing, 26–29
  vs. manipulative, 28
Self-disclosure, 97–99
Self-actualization, criticisms of, 226–227
  substitute theory, 252–254
Self-confrontation, 52
  advantages, 63
Self-defeating habits, 180, 246–251
Self-esteem as outcome, 259–260
Self-fulfilling prophecies, 27, 116–117
Self-overdose by client, 26
Sex as relationship issue, 114, 116
Sex-roles and therapy, 117–118
Shadings of meaning, 48–50
Shaping toward experiencing, 54–55, 262–263
Silences, 29–30
Skillful tentativeness, 39–43

Sneaky interpretations, 28, 80
  as false empathic guesses, 41
Sociopathy, 249–250
Stages of therapy, 6, 72–78
Step by step progress, 47, 255–256
Strachan, Joan, observing, 161
  introductory comments, 161
  interview, 163
Strength words, 49
Structure and focus, 36–39
Subjectivity, 45–46
Successive approximations, 47, 54
  and immediacy, 103
  and suicide, 184
Supervision, 124
Suicide, 183–185
Summarizing responses, 38–39
Surprises in client content, 83
Sympathy vs. empathy, 8
Symptom, 233, 246–251
  as arbitrarily defined, 247–248
  relief, as outcome, 258
  substitution, 258–259
System, family and couple, 216

Tape rating evidence, 13, 268–269
Tape recording, 204–205
Tape work, 35–36, 122, 126
Teaching, as appropriate, 178–190
  the process, 87, 208
  the skills, evidence, 269–270
Tentativeness, skillful, 39–43
Termination, 208–211
Tests, 192
Theories, little, 83–84, 139
  personal, 27
  personality, 41, 85–86
Theory, functions, of 224
  key question, 224–225
  need for, 222–223
  preview of, 16
Therapist is not the solution, 110
Thinking, as behavior, 231–232
  reinforcing, 71–72, 256
  relation to emotion, 53, 69, 230, 244–245
Third ear, 7, 24–25
Thoughts as fear cues, 235
Time considerations, 205
Time-limited therapy, 211
Transference, 113–114
Trust, low, by client, 64

Trusting the client, 78, 96, 244−245, 252−254

Unconditional positive regard, 93−94
Unconscious influences, 230
Understanding, as client's job, 73−75
Uniformity myth, 187
Unique language, 43−50
Uniqueness of clients, 82

Values, and self-fulfilling prophecies, 116−117
  as goals, 89
Vocabulary, shadings of meaning, 48−50

Written exercises, 120−121

You are not the solution, 110